Ursula Anna Fischer Smith

PICKING TOMATOES
WHEN THE SKY WAS IN FLAMES

Growing up in Germany during World War II

Ursula Anna Fischer Smith

Picking Tomatoes When The Sky Was In Flames

ISBN: 978-1-935125-84-6
Library of Congress Control Number: 2010928672

Cover illustration by Ursula Anna Fischer Smith.
Photos from the author's personal collection.

To purchase additional copies of this book go to:
www.rp-author.com/uasmith

Robertson Publishing
59 N. Santa Cruz Avenue, Suite B
Los Gatos, California 95030 USA
(888) 354-5957 · www.RobertsonPublishing.com

To my parents
Gertrud and Anton Fischer

Acknowledgements

I would like to thank my writing group friends for their constructive critique and encouragement: Anne Darling, Norma Faulkner, Marti Henley, Vada Jo Hollingsworth, Ursula Meier, Rosemarie Niles and Annick Shinn.

My heartfelt appreciation goes to my brothers Alfred and Jürgen, and Aunts Hildegard and Grete for sharing their memories. Many thanks to Margot Brettschneider who allowed me to use Tante Martha's handwritten journal of her flight from the Russian army in East Prussia to the west. I thank my daughter Jasmin, and Catherine my daughter-in-law, for reading and editing the manuscript.

Thank you to granddaughter Brigid for feedback on the cover and Alicia Robertson for tips on the manuscript format.

My gratitude also goes to my fellow writers from Ann Thompson's Memoir Writing class for valuable lessons and helpful feedback. With a special thank you to Lonna Smith and Valerie Lee.

I particularly want to express my love and gratitude to my husband, Edward. If he hadn't kept my computer updated and edited my photos, this book might never have been completed.

Family	Born	Died
Father-Anton Fischer	08/03/1901	01/16/1977
Mother-Gertrud Fischer	01/03/1911	05/15/1995
Alfred	07/18/1934	09/06/2006
Jürgen	05/22/1936	
Ursula	01/24/1939	
Margarete	09/27/1949	
Edelgard	09/27/1949	
Mother's Family		
Opa-Ludwig Schmidtmann	01/13/1886	01/29/1963
Oma-Anna Schmidtmann	01/24/1890	11/19/1982
Gertrude	01/03/1911	05/08/1995
Änne	01/06/1919	01/01/1996
Kurt-husband	04/12/1919	10/06/2001
Manfred-son	09/01/1942	
Grete	01/07/1924	
Rolf-son	12/06/1943	
Ruth	06/17/1926	02/04/1945
Hildegard	12/01/1929	
Father's Family		
Sister, Kathel-Bavaria	08/19/1912	01/10/1993
Brother, Franz-Bavaria	__/__/__	05/1945
Oma's Family		
Brother, Otto-Berlin	06/18/1900	05/1945
Brother, Emil-East Prussia	10/16/1901	06/1945
Martha	11/30/1911	10/14/2002
Margot	01/18/1936	
Karl-Heinz	07/22/1937	
Ingrid-Christel	12/16/1944	02/10/1945

The World I Was Born Into

Germany 1939

My story began long before the day I was born. When I was an embryo, in the safety of my mother's womb, my world was peaceful. In the world outside, black clouds darkened the sky over Germany, preventing the angels from watching what was about to occur below. Oppression and intimidation within Germany had escalated. Individuals with opposing political views feared for their lives. In November 1938, organized destruction by Special Forces was ordered against innocent citizens of Jewish heritage—the infamous *Krystallnacht*.

This was the world I was born into on Tuesday, January 24, 1939 on Grandmother Anna Schmidtmann's birthday. My two older brothers called her Oma.

Five year old Alfred was happy to have a little sister. He wanted me to be named Ursula. Two year-old Jürgen was bothered by my arrival. He watched from afar as Mother nursed me. Then he crept close to us. "My Mamma," he said and slapped my face.

Oma, my maternal grandmother, was thrilled I was born on her forty-ninth birthday. My middle name became Anna in her honor.

My brothers were born at home, but Mother didn't want another homebirth. I came into the world in the City Hospital. We stayed there the customary ten days. My father worried about the long trip

1

home from the hospital and saved money so we could ride in a taxi instead of having to take a bus.

My family resided in the city of Essen, in the Ruhr Valley not far from the Dutch and Belgian borders. There was an acute shortage of housing. We lived in two upstairs rooms in Oma and Opa Schmidtmann's home.

My father and grandfather were fortunate to work in the coal mine as was every man living on our street. Germany was still suffering from the effects of the Great Depression that had begun more than ten years earlier. Men arrived from the farthest reaches of the country looking for work in the coal mines, speaking many different dialects. New arrivals, who could not find suitable living quarters, added their names to a waiting list. Many families lived in one room for a long time. My parents put their name on the list for bigger living quarters long before I was born.

My parents were grateful having two rooms, but now that we were a family of five, these had become cramped quarters. The combination kitchen-living room with white lace curtains on the window faced the street. In the bedroom, my parents and brothers shared the double bed, and I slept in a crib that was placed at the foot of the family bed. The stage was set for my life.

Wildstrasse, 1940

Chapter 1

The street where I grew up had history and character. It was named Wildstrasse after the wild horses, boars and deer that roamed the forest before the coal mines and houses were built. The Wildstrasse, at the northern edge of town, near the harbors of the Rhine-Herne Canal, was an important lifeline for the city of Essen. Cargo from the growing commerce of the area, passed along the street for distribution to all parts of Germany.

The history of the street was closely linked to the development of the coal mines. The mining company built the houses around 1920—forty years after the first coal mine began production. Huge areas of lush bush and mixed forest, once filled with game and songbirds, were cleared to make room for fifteen two-story, brick houses for the workers, five bigger, nicer houses for the foremen and one large home surrounded by lawns and big trees for the director.

We lived in the section built for the workers. Poplar trees lined the sidewalk. This portion became known as old Wildstrasse, because another section of houses was built later with a different design. Each house where the miners lived was for four families. Two families lived in the front facing the street and two in the back with a view of the coal mine. Each family had two bedrooms upstairs, and downstairs a living room and kitchen with a cold water faucet. The cellar was accessible from a door in the kitchen. Each family had a private entrance and a vegetable patch behind the back alley. Oma and Opa's home faced the street. Rent was affordable.

Attached to the main house, next to the stone steps leading to the front door, was the stall for small animals and next to it the outhouse that we called drop-closet. On the second story, above the animal stall was a little room accessible from the stairwell inside the main house and above the drop-closet, reachable only by ladder from the outside, was a small hayloft.

The character of the street was created by the diversity of the people who lived there. The families who moved into the Wildstrasse brought with them unique customs, habits, hobbies, songs and recipes.

Many came from East Prussia, the eastern-most state. There, the majority had been day laborers on large estates plowing fields, planting, harvesting and tending life stock. These workers were paid not with money but with farm products, room and board. Although they loved the soil they worked on and didn't want to leave the land, they couldn't resist the promises of recruiters from the coal mining company luring them away with train tickets, wages paid in cash and living quarters with a plot of land. They came in droves. They were God fearing, hard-working and eager to start a new life.

At the east end of the street was the single miners' home, where unmarried workers were offered room and board. They shared bedrooms and ate in a communal dining room.

Oma and Opa came from East Prussia and moved to the Wildstrasse when my mother was ten years old. Four more daughters were born there.

Years later, my father came seeking work in the Ruhr Valley. He left a little farming village in Bavaria, the southern-most state of Germany and found work in a coal mine. He rented a room in my grandparents' home after Mother had already left to live in a nearby town.

My parents met when Mother visited her family one weekend. They fell in love. Father showered her with love letters during her absence. She visited every other weekend, the only days she did not have to work.

ॐ

By the time I was born, the Wildstrasse had formed into a friendly neighborhood with heaps of children, who, unlike their parents, spoke the Westphalian dialect. The twenty-year-old red brick houses were soot stained and the poplar trees towered above the rooftops.

The baker delivered bread once a week and he knew exactly how many loaves each family needed. When the milkman came in his three-wheeled car, women carrying enameled cans chatted while waiting their turn to buy milk. In the middle of the week, the vegetable man rolled in with his horse drawn wagon loaded with produce, announcing his arrival by ringing a bell.

Children rushed to the street, congregating under the poplar trees, waiting for the vegetable man to throw them a piece of apple or a cherry, depending on the season. On Fridays, the fishmonger yelled out his selections with a tenor voice, "Smoked eel, fresh fish and herring from the North Sea."

These men knew everyone by name.

The children attended the nearby City Harbor School on the Kleinstrasse during the week. On Sundays the Catholics attended mass at church near the school and Protestants participated in services at the church two kilometers away in Bergeborbeck.

After school, boys tended to their homing pigeons or played ball in the field behind our gardens. The local soccer team used to practice there until it moved to the new stadium. Girls skipped rope, played with dolls or marbles in the courtyards between the houses.

A shepherd, followed by his flock of sheep, came through the street twice a year. Children and grownups watched them pass from the sidewalks.

ॐ

In September 1939, the German army invaded Poland—the war had began and the coal mines started around the clock production.

5

Father and Opa sometimes worked nightshift. A time of great uncertainty had begun.

In December my parents received notice that the apartment in the back of Oma and Opa's would soon be free. We moved in a few months later. One of the upstairs bedrooms had a view of our vegetable and flower garden, the field behind them, the smokestacks and wheel tower of the mine where Father worked. To the right were the tall coke furnaces that converted the coal into hard, porous pellets that could be used in steel foundries and to power trains.

The bedroom window became a window to my life. My brothers were happy they finally had their own bedroom and didn't mind sharing a bed. Mother enjoyed the new kitchen and the cellar. In the back part of the cellar we stored potatoes, canned goods, our sled and skates. The front part had a walled-off section for coal and a faucet for filling the wash tubs. Mother used a washboard to clean our garments until Father could buy a washing machine.

However, the excitement over our new home and our harmonious family life was soon disrupted. The Luftwaffe had attacked cities in England. Bombing attacks on Essen began in May of 1940. Life on the Wildstrasse changed.

In the Cellar, 1941

Chapter 2

The Ruhr Valley was known as the Industrial Breadbasket of Germany and during the war it became also known as Weapon Alley. Essen was nestled in the heart of it. The Krupp Steel Works were famous. Factories making weapons, tools, tank parts, munitions, and the coal mines were important for the military build-up. They were located in the north of the city and became primary targets during the war. From our home we could hear the anti-aircraft defense unit, the "FlaK", firing their cannons at bombers.

Although the industrial complex and mines were the targets, they were often missed and bombs exploded in the field behind our garden, in the vegetable patches and hit homes in our street.

A three stage alarm system had been established to warn citizens of air raids. Slow wailing sirens indicated the first stage. A more intense, louder wail meant bombers were coming our way. The acute third stage, a deafening, continuous shrill sound, meant the bombers were overhead. I learned their meaning quickly.

The peaceful life in the Wildstrasse had ended. Because the construction of our bomb shelter had not been completed yet, we went into our cellar during attacks. Although every house on our street had the same layout and was built with the same red bricks, our neighbors, my grandparents and my mother's three younger sisters—Grete, Ruth and Hildegard—came to our cellar during bombing attacks. Tante Änne worked in another city.

I remember one day clearly. Father worked underground in the mine. When I heard the first wailing, Mother immediately stopped what she was doing, grabbed two kitchen chairs and carried them into the cellar. I followed her. When she rushed back upstairs, I raced after her looking over my shoulder, fearful someone might grab me from behind.

Oma and Opa and our neighbor Frau Ehlert rushed in. They grabbed chairs Mother hadn't taken into the cellar yet. Tante Grete worked at Öttinger's grocery store and stayed there.

In the cellar the chairs were arranged in a circle. The women filled buckets with water, put them next to the chairs and draped a washcloth over each rim. The room was small and Opa opened the little cellar window under the ceiling for fresh air. When everyone was seated, we waited.

I watched a spider crawling up the whitewashed wall. Then I heard the droning of airplane motors and my stomach began to hurt.

Upstairs, the front door opened. Hurried footsteps clambered down the wooden stairs. Tante Ruth, Mother's fourteen year old sister, who loved sewing and never wanted to leave her sewing machine came in. Our neighbor, old Frau Mahr followed, clutching her purse under her arm. She sat next to Frau Ehlert. When her daughters Mia and Anneliese rushed in, the first bomb exploded. The girls sat on the bench against the wall.

"They're targeting the mine," Opa said.

"That's where Pappa is," I whispered.

Mother, who sat next to me, squeezed my hand. No one spoke. I stared at the window. We heard the FlaK shooting in the distance. The next explosion was closer and another, closer still. The ground shook. Upstairs, the windows rattled.

"That was close," someone said.

Soon dust billowed in through the open window. Everyone dipped a washcloth into a water bucket, wrung it dry and covered their nose. Mother placed one over mine.

My eyes remained glued to the window. Bombs exploded far and near.

A high pitched hiss pierced the air and a long projectile flew in through the window toward me. Not far from my chair, it changed course and landed on the floor near the open drain hole in front of Tante Ruth. She nudged it with her shoe. It disappeared in the drain and scuttled down the pipe. Tante Ruth grabbed a pail and poured water down it.

"A phosphor bomb!" Opa said. "We're lucky it didn't explode."

Frau Mahr's wrinkled face looked scared.

The explosions finally stopped. No one moved—we waited in silence until we heard the long wail of the sirens. Then I knew the attack was over. The grown-ups talked about how seriously we could have been burned had the firebomb exploded. My brothers and I looked at each other. They made faces but didn't say anything. They were the first to leave the cellar and raced outside searching for bomb craters, as they always did after an attack.

Mother said, "We were lucky this time." Her face relaxed and my stomach stopped aching.

The adults stood up and slowly left. That day, I didn't follow my brothers and stayed near Mother.

Another day, when bombs had exploded dangerously close to our house I followed my brothers outside after the attack. We ran down the garden path that separated Opa's vegetable and flower patches from ours.

A boy yelled, "Over here. This one drew groundwater."

My brothers and I climbed through a hole in the fence and I raced toward Ewald Lamm who stood on the mound of earth surrounding a crater in Frau Mahr's garden. My shoes sank into the loose dirt. I went down on my knees and clawed my way up to the rim. More boys arrived and soon several men joined us. We watched the crater slowly fill with muddy water. I wondered if the bomb was still in there.

"Look over there!" Rudi yelled. We looked to where he pointed. Shrapnel had hit the brick walls of our homes and pockmarked them with holes. The glass in several windows was broken.

From a distance, we heard men's voices. Everyone turned around. A group of men wearing helmets and carrying miner's lamps approached from the field behind us. Their eyes stood out like white pebbles from their soot covered faces. Their work clothes were covered with coal dust.

"Our mine shaft was hit. We walked underground to the other mine to get out. That's why we couldn't take a bath and change." one miner said. "Over there in the field is a much bigger crater."

The miners went home and we raced through the grass toward the old soccer field. My heart jumped when I saw Pappa walk toward us. I waved to him but rushed after the boys to the big crater. A few black-faced miners were on the dirt mound. The huge hole in the ground was filled to the rim with murky water.

"A duck pond!" I squealed and clapped my hands. The boys laughed.

"They're dropping bigger bombs," a miner said.

Back at the house, Mother leaned out the upstairs window and waved. I knew she was glad to see Father. She was always more anxious during an air raid when he was working in the mine. I ran after Father and pulled on his finger. He looked down and I pointed to our house. He waved and broke into a broad smile. His teeth stood out like alabaster.

"Let's go home," he said.

When we arrived in our front yard, the door to the animal stall was open. In the doorway, on the old wooden stool, was our aluminum tub. Mother came down the stone steps carrying a pot of hot water and a blue, checkered towel draped over her shoulder. She arranged the pig-bristle brush and a large piece of curd-soap in a dish next to the tub. Clean clothes hung from a peg on the wall.

Father turned to me and grinned. "She won't let me into the house like this."

He undressed to his waist and piled his shirt and undershirt on the floor. With powerful strokes he lathered his hands and scrubbed his nails with the brush. I watched him rub soap on the washcloth and clean his face, neck and chest. Black water streaked down his elbows making puddles on the brick floor.

From the kitchen wafted the fragrance of bean soup. I was hungry and went into the house. I climbed onto the sofa behind the kitchen table and waited for everyone else to come inside to eat. Father entered wearing clean clothes. His face was shiny clean and his damp, black curls fell over his forehead to his coal-rimmed eyes. I scooted over so he could sit next to me.

Wedding in the Potato Cellar, 1942

Chapter 3

My parents and grandparents belonged to a small church that held Sunday services in an unassuming cellar in a three-story brick building. The members called it *Kartoffelkellerkirche*, potato-cellar-church. The owner of a produce wholesale firm, who didn't use it as a warehouse anymore, offered it to the congregation free of charge.

A few years earlier my family left their old congregation with a heavy heart. They used to meet at the beautiful big church with a pipe organ and large choir. They left because the pastor openly flaunted his membership in the Nazi party. He even denounced from the pulpit, the story of creation from Genesis in the Bible. At Christmas, the children had to recite poems honoring the Führer.

Over time they appreciated and loved this small new congregation they had found. Oma and Opa attended services almost every Sunday. My parents participated when they could. I was too young for Sunday school. They alternated staying home with me.

Worshippers could not be seen from the street slipping through a door that led to the potato cellar. It was concealed in the inner courtyard of the three-story building that could only be reached by passing through a vaulted walkway. The horse-dealer, who closed his business in the courtyard years ago, left his sign above the entrance.

Opa thought that was why the Gestapo had not detected the church. Opa often chatted about the dedication the members of the church displayed. He usually visited us after Sunday dinner and smoked his pipe before taking a nap. While he and Father chatted, I looked at the colorful pictures in the *Struwwelpeter* book and also listened.

"Most men are miners," Opa said. "They converted the potato cellar into a sanctuary in their free time. They broke holes through the brick walls for windows, repaired the electrical wiring, installed lights and white-washed the walls. They acquired inexpensive, worn-out chairs from local pubs, built an altar and a simple cross from scraps of wood."

"That's real dedication," Father said.

Opa struck a match and lit his pipe. "The Schürmann family donated the harmonium," he said.

Father went into the pantry and came back with two shot glasses filled with schnapps. He gave one to Opa. "Prost!"

He said, "The women have donated white table cloths for the altar and brought fresh flowers from their garden for the service."

Mother ground coffee beans and stoked the coal stove. "It's nice to have a small mixed choir," she said.

The congregation belonged to the national Protestant Resistance Church, called the *Bekennende Kirche*. The founder, Martin Niemöller, had been working diligently to keep the church separate from Nazi influence. He had been arrested many times but always set free. He was finally imprisoned at the Dachau concentration camp near Munich.

~

Everyone talked about Tante Änne and Onkel Kurt's upcoming wedding but no one knew when it could take place. Tante Änne, the second oldest of the five Schmidtmann girls, lived in another town and promised to send a postcard as soon as she heard when the bridegroom would receive leave from the Army.

Since the increase in air attacks, Onkel Kurt had been re-assigned to an anti-aircraft FlaK unit in Berlin, and Tante Änne worried that he may not get any time off. She didn't want a stand-in-groom who would take the vows on behalf of her husband-to-be, as so many wartime brides had to do.

Oma watched for the postman from her kitchen window every day. She was excited when he delivered a telegram and waved it through the air showing it to Mother.

She read aloud, *"Good news, Kurt received weekend leave. I'm coming home."* Mother smiled. "We can start baking. I saved plenty of eggs and flour."

Oma nodded. "Opa will talk to the pastor on Sunday."

Several days later, Tante Änne arrived. The following day the women began baking in our home. Our kitchen had become a lively, happy place. From my seat on the sofa, I watched the women beat butter, sugar and eggs together for cakes, skin boiled potatoes, chop onions and whip oil with egg yolks to make mayonnaise. They chatted and laughed while they worked and made plans for the wedding day. When the first pound cake came out of the oven, the aroma of almond flavor and butter filled the kitchen.

Mother's youngest sister, twelve year old Hildegard, burst into the kitchen after school, "I want to help. I'm not going to the BDM meeting this afternoon."

"What is the BDM?" I asked.

"It's the Hitler youth group for girls." Mother said.

"What do you do there? Can I go?"

"No! You're too young," Mother said.

She looked at Tante Hildegard and pointed to a blue apron hanging on the hook on the wall. "Put my apron on and separate these eggs."

Tante Hildegard lined up two ceramic bowls on the table, cracked the eggs on the rim of a bowl and separated the yoke from the white.

Tante Ruth was fifteen years old. After graduating from eighth grade, she had her beautiful, long braids cut off before she started a three-year apprentice program with the seamstress Fräulein Hüttemann in Bergeborbeck. Tante Ruth helped with the preparation after she came home from work. Her shoulder-length, auburn hair made her look very grown up.

On the table two cakes cooled on racks—a vinegary smell from the potato salad made my mouth pucker.

"I'm getting tired," Oma said. "Let's pray we have no air raids tonight."

The next day, after a peaceful night, Tante Änne brought her dress to our house. "Ruth will hem it for me," she said.

After dinner, Tante Änne put on a pale blue dress with a row of countless buttons down the front.

Tante Ruth came in with a measuring tape dangling around her neck and a pincushion on her left wrist. She put scissors, thread and tailor's chalk on the table. Tante Ruth pointed to our little stool. "Stand on the wooden *Hocker*," she said.

The bride stepped on the stool and the seamstress marked a white line on the dress below the knees with the chalk.

She held several pins clenched between her teeth and used them to pin the fabric at the hemline. "Turn around," she mumbled. The pins bobbed up and down when she spoke. "When will the bridegroom get here?"

"I hope tomorrow morning. It's getting very difficult traveling by train because the marshalling yards and tracks around Berlin have been hit." Tante Änne sighed. "We haven't heard from Kurt's brother either. He's been re-assigned to the Russian front. He's supposed to be best man."

"You can get down now and take off the dress. I'd better start sewing if you want to wear it on Sunday." While Tante Ruth stitched, the sisters talked.

In the afternoon, Opa plucked two chickens in his front yard. Father hung the rabbit he had butchered by its legs on a peg at the wall in our animal stall. I watched him pull the fur off its body and clean out the insides. Later mother washed and seasoned the rabbit. She roasted it ahead for the wedding meal. Oma baked the chickens in her oven. She covered them and stored them overnight in the cellar.

Oma reminded everyone again to pray for a peaceful night.

The next day Uncle Kurt arrived. He looked handsome in his army uniform, cap and polished leather boots. I had never seen a soldier before and thought he must be very important. Tante Änne beamed all day.

After the last preparations for the wedding celebration were completed, we all ate the evening meal together in our house. The table was laden with potato, tomato and cucumber salads. Oma said the blessing. A platter with liverwurst, blood sausage, sliced tongue and wieners was handed around. My brothers and I ate at a small table under the kitchen window. Father poured beer for the men. Women and children drank sweetened peppermint tea.

After dinner, Oma started singing a hymn of thanks as was her habit on special occasions. Everyone joined in. The men's low baritone voices mingled with the sopranos. Then the women washed the dishes in the kitchen and the men went into the living room to smoke and drink a glass of schnapps.

My brothers carried the left-over food into the pantry and I sat on the chair next to the living room door. I watched the women wash and dry the dishes but it was the men's conversation that caught my attention.

"With the Americans entering the war and the expansion on the eastern front, how will this war end?" Father said.

"They have better bombers, bigger bombs and will be more accurate hitting the targets," Onkel Kurt said.

Opa blew rings with his cigar smoke into the air. It smelled good.

"Time for bed," Mother said. "We have to get up early in the morning."

My brothers and I scrambled upstairs. Cooking odors and cigar smoke wafted into our bedrooms.

On the morning of the wedding day, when I was already wearing my Sunday dress, Tante Grete came into our kitchen and said, "Ulla, let's go quickly into the garden and pick flowers for the bride and for the church."

I skipped beside her down the garden path. In Oma's flower patch, she cut white and red peonies and filled my outstretched arms with them.

"The white ones are for the bride's bouquet and the altar at the church and the red ones for the wedding tables."

When we returned to the courtyard, Onkel Kurt vigorously shook hands with his brother. I thought they looked alike. A duffel-bag lay on the ground.

"You made it just in time." Onkel Kurt beamed. "We're getting ready for church."

Opa appeared in the doorway wearing his good black suit and top hat, carrying a bottle of schnapps and glasses. "You men need some strengthening before we go to church." He handed a glass to each man and filled them. They raised the glasses and said, "*Zum Wohle.*"

Tante Grete rushed into Oma's house. I watched the men. Father joined them for a drink. He looked handsome in his white shirt, tie and Sunday suit.

One by one, the family gathered in the sun filled courtyard. The women looked nice in their short sleeved dresses and hats. Oma started the procession. As we walked toward Harbor Strasse under the poplar trees, windows opened and neighbors waved and smiled. Because I couldn't walk as fast as the rest, Father carried me.

Once we arrived at the Kartoffelkeller church, Tante Grete put the flowers into a vase and placed them on the altar. Sunrays streamed in through the windows under the ceiling and illuminated the wooden cross on the white-washed wall.

When the harmonium played a hymn, the pastor walked toward the altar. He motioned with his hand for the bride and groom to join him. The sermon was short. After the Lord's Prayer, everyone smiled and congratulated the newlyweds. They had rosy cheeks.

On the way home, the men stopped at the pub on Harbor Strasse for a beer, as they frequently did after church, and the women returned home to prepare the wedding meal at Oma's house. They sang songs while setting the table with an embroidered table cloth, fine china and a bouquet of flowers. As usual, the men arrived home from the pub talking and laughing, just in time to enjoy dinner with the family. Tante Ruth and Hildegard ate in the kitchen with my brothers and me. We ate chicken soup with tiny star noodles first. For the main course we had roasted chicken, rabbit, mashed potatoes with gravy and sweet and sour red cabbage.

In the afternoon, after everyone had a nap, we gathered again in Oma's house for coffee and the delicious cakes. Afterward, the women sipped peach liqueur from delicate stem glasses and told stories until I fell asleep.

Early the next morning everyone gathered at the corner of Oma's house and waved good-by to Oncle Kurt and his brother. Tante Änne accompanied them to the bus station. She left later that day.

As they shook hands Oma said, "Our prayers have been answered. We had no air attack."

Later that year, two Gestapo officers came to the church service and sat in the last row intimidating people with their presence.

"They've discovered us," Opa said.

Voice of America, 1942

Chapter 4

After our bomb shelter was completed we were advised not to stay in our cellars during air attacks anymore. Old Frau Mahr didn't trust the new shelter built near the mine shaft. She called it a flimsy burrow, dug under the mine's slagheap, and she preferred to go to the shelter on Harbor Strasse that had concrete walls. It was true, our shelter was under the slagheap. Everyone called it "Stollen" because from a distance, it looked like an oversized Christmas Stollen like Mother baked for the holidays.

Oma once said that Frau Mahr spends every night in the bomb shelter because she was afraid of the big bombs that were being dropped lately. I sometimes watched Frau Mahr leave from our upstairs bedroom window in the afternoons when I was supposed to be napping. She clutched her overnight emergency bags under her arms and hurried out of our courtyard.

Frau Mahr didn't like me. The problem began after Mother told me I was big enough now to use the drop-closet outside instead of the chamber pot in the bedroom during the day.

I protested. "Mamma! The hole in the drop-closet is too high and way too big for me."

Mother answered, "You have to hold on to the edge of the wood boards."

Once I went inside to check it out. The sitting console was high. On my tippy-toes, I lifted the lid and peeked through the hole. I was frightened and worried I would fall in.

When I had to go number two, and went to the drop-closet, I was surprised to see a little stepstool inside. Reluctantly I climbed onto the sitting console and slowly turned around. When I lowered my bottom over the hole, I lost my balance. My body collapsed like a broken stick and my bottom fell through the hole. Thank God my shoulders and legs kept me from falling in. I screamed and clung to the boards but no one came. I struggled until I eventually pulled my body up. After that ordeal, I was too scared to use the drop-closet again.

One day, I couldn't sleep again when I was supposed to nap. I went downstairs and snuck out of the house. I meandered down the back alley to look for my brothers and went as far as the last house. I needed to go number two but ignored it. When my stomach began to hurt, I ran back toward my home. At Frau Mahr's house, I was in trouble and quickly crouched behind her stone steps. Unfortunately, my bloomers got soiled. I took them off and left them there.

Frau Mahr must have found them because she stormed into our front yard waving a stick with my dirty bloomers at the end yelling, "Gertud, can't you control that child? That one jumped out of the devil's rucksack, I tell you." She threw the stick and bloomers on the ground and huffed away.

I couldn't understand why she was so upset.

Mother's face turned red. She wiggled her finger in front of my nose. "Ulla, if you do that again, you'll get a good whipping."

I was more scared of falling into to the honey-pit than getting a spanking. I searched for secret places behind bushes and sheds where no one would find my bloomers if they got a little soiled.

When Mother realized I had no more clean underwear, she made me take her to my hiding places. She put my bloomers in a pail and carried them home. She was so upset that she spanked me with a wooden spoon. Her face was red again when she grabbed me by my shoulder and dragged me to the drop-closet. "We're going to practice sitting on this hole until you've learned how to sit on it," she yelled.

Eventually, I caught on but continued to be anxious.

☙

Alfred was in third grade and Jürgen in first when the school was hit by bombs and burned down. The beautiful gymnasium was gutted. My brothers were upset because they couldn't go to school anymore but I liked having them around. I loved watching Alfred draw and sometimes Jürgen let me play with his blocks. Mother warned us not to stray far from home. It wasn't safe anymore.

Alfred often put our headset radio on. He'd sit looking into space and listen, and I always wondered what he could hear.

"Where did you get those?"

"Every family got a headset after the war started."

"What were you listening to?"

"Oh, just war news. Sometimes I think I hear the radio operator from the FlaK station behind the canal. He handed me the set and said, "Try it. This is the volume control knob. I wish we had a real radio," he said. "Maybe then I could get the Voice of America. The Amis are broadcasting in German."

"Who are the Amis?"

"The Americans—Dummkopf." He left.

The set was too big for my head and kept slipping. I held it in place with one hand and fiddled with the volume knob with the other. I was excited when I heard a man's voice. He talked about troop movement and weather conditions. It was boring. Disappointed, I took the headphones off and set them on the dresser.

We all surrounded Father when he brought a new radio home. He removed our breadbox from its place on the kitchen cabinet and put the radio there. It was made of shiny wood with brocade cloth and wooden control buttons in the front. Father plugged it in and turned it on. Everyone laughed when we heard music playing.

Father only listened to news. Mother liked music. Sometimes Opa joined Father and they listen to news together. They closed windows and doors before turning the radio on. Usually Opa stayed for a while afterwards and the men talked. Mother made coffee and I climbed on the chair next to the stove where it was warm.

Opa twirled the ends of his mustache. "It doesn't sound good. The Russian winter is costing our troops dearly on the eastern front."

I watched his Adam's apple jump up and down.

"The Allies run sorties with a thousand bombers and tons of heavy bombs on our cities. Köln is getting flattened," Father said. "They come our way with the bombs they didn't drop there. The Krupp's steel foundry was hit. "

I got scared when I heard those words and my hands began to shake. I knew that my father could not stop the bombs from hitting our house.

Sometimes, when the kitchen was quiet, I'd pull a chair in front of the kitchen cabinet, climb on it and turn the radio on. I loved listening to songs and hummed their melodies. Sometimes the Führer gave a speech. He yelled really loudly but I didn't understand what he was saying. When people cheered and chanted, "Sieg Heil!" I chanted with them.

Father always turned the radio off halfway through the Führer's speech. I was annoyed because I wanted to listen to the people chant.

"Pappa! Leave the radio on," I demanded. "I want to hear the happy people."

His face looked grim. "This is not for children," he said.

I was confused. The next day, the radio was on top of the cabinet where I couldn't reach it and the bread box was back in its old place.

My parents and grandparents listened to the radio regularly and talked about the news of the war afterwards.

"So far our FlaK has been successful in picking Tommy planes out of the sky." Opa said.

"That's why they've switched to night time attacks."Father said.

Mother lamented, "I can't let the children sleep in pajamas anymore."

She told my brothers and me to put our shoes at night near the bedpost so we could slip into them quickly when the sirens wailed. One evening when Father was working underground in the mine, an attack was announced. Mother, carrying me on her arm, hurried down Emscher Weg toward the shelter. It was dark. Alfred and Jürgen were ahead of us.

Mother stopped in the middle of the road. "Ulla, I can't carry you anymore. You're getting to heavy."

She put me down, took my hand and pulled me along. We made it to safety before the first bomb exploded.

One afternoon, Oma came into the kitchen and joined Mother at the table for a cup of coffee and streusel kuchen.

She looked at Mother. "You look tired."

"I can't sleep when Anton works night shift. I worry I can't get the children to the shelter in time. Jürgen is such a deep sleeper. I have trouble waking him when the sirens howl. Thank God, Alfred jumps out of bed right away but Ursula doesn't even wake up when I put her shoes on."

Oma said, "It's going to get worse with the Americans in the war. I worry about Ruth. She refuses to leave her sewing machine even for an air attack."

They looked worried, drank their coffee and ate cake in silence.

Brothers' Parting, 1943

Chapter 5

My brothers were buddies. They slept in the same bed, stormed outside to play together and used to walk to school side by side. On rainy days, when we couldn't go outside, they raced up and down our wooden stairs pretending they were airplanes. I chased after them with my arms spread like wings. That's when Mother would yell, "I can't stand this anymore. You better settle down, right now."

One evening after dinner Father said,"Children, stay at the table, Mother and I need to talk to you. You know how dangerous the air attacks have become."

The three of us nodded.

"All over Germany schools have been destroyed. The government has decided to evacuate children from the cities to the country where they will be safe from bombings and where they can attend school again."

Alfred and Jürgen sat up in their chairs and stared at Mother.

Clearing her throat, she said, "We have received permission for members of our family to stay with Tante Martha and Onkel Emil on the farm in East Prussia where Oma grew up." Mother unfolded a letter and continued. "The farmhouse is not big, but Tante Martha wrote in this letter that she has set up beds and a crib in a room downstairs. Tante Änne, baby Manfred, Tante Hildegard and Alfred will leave first."

"Do I have to go?" Alfred stuttered.

"We have no choice, the evacuation is mandatory. We are fortunate you can stay with family," Father said. "You'll have fun playing with cousins Margot and Heinz. They have horses and cows on the farm, fields were you can run and play and lakes were you can go fishing. You and Tante Hildegard will start school as soon as you get there."

"What about me?" Jürgen's eyes were huge.

"You'll go later. We're waiting for your papers." Mother said.

"When do we have to leave," Alfred asked.

"In a few days."

Mother brought a suitcase into the living room and filled it with Alfred's summer and winter clothes.

In March of 1943, Essen experienced huge bombardments on a momentous scale resulting in 80,000 civilians losing their homes, thousands being killed, and the total destruction of the city center. Several homes in our street were hit by bombs that missed the coal mines.

Train schedules were unreliable, because so many marshalling yards and tracks near major cities had been hit. But Mother, Tante Änne and Hildegard continued to pack the suitcases for the long journey to East Prussia. Opa expected the trip to take several days because he suspected that trains had to make a major detour around Berlin.

The night before they were to leave, Alfred took a bath in our aluminum tub in the middle of the kitchen floor. Mother made sandwiches and wrapped them in brown paper and packed hard boiled eggs for the trip. Alfred bit his lips nervously. His voice often cracked when he spoke. Jürgen didn't smile anymore.

The next morning, I woke from a commotion downstairs. Barefooted, I raced down the steps and burst into the kitchen. Alfred, dressed in his coat, cap and polished high top shoes, stood stiffly in the middle of the room next to his suit case. Mother helped him slip his leather backpack on. Jürgen stood close by Alfred.

"It's time to go." Father put his hat on, picked up the suit case and traveling bag. Mother opened the door. Cold air rushed in. The gray overcast skies hovered over the poplar trees.

I followed them into the courtyard. Oma's front door opened and Opa carried two suitcases down the stone steps. Tante Änne, with baby Manfred in one arm and a travel bag in the other, appeared behind him. Then Tante Hildegard jumped down the steps. Her blond braids whipped around her head. Oma followed. The women wore warm coats and colorful scarves on their heads.

Without saying a word, Opa placed the suitcases on his two-wheeled cart and proceeded toward the street. Everyone followed.

At the corner of Oma's house, teary eyed Mother kissed Alfred, "The thermos is in your travel bag. I filled it with sweet peppermint tea."

Alfred nodded.

Mother, Oma, Jürgen and I watched the travelers proceed toward Harbor Strasse.

"Is Pappa going to Prussia too?" I asked.

"No, he's just taking Alfred to the Bergeborbeck station to help put his suitcase on the train."

I peered up at Mother. Her face looked flushed and her cheeks were wet. I leaned my head against her side. "When is Alfred coming back?"

"I don't know. It depends on the war."

When the travelers reached the end of our street, they stopped, turned and waved. Oma and Mother waved with their white handkerchiefs. Then the travelers disappeared.

"I don't have my brother no more." Jürgen sobbed.

Mother patted his shoulder and said, "You'll see him soon. Let's have some breakfast."

Trip to East Prussia, 1943

Chapter 6

Since Alfred left for East Prussia our home became too quiet. His chair was empty at meal times and I missed hearing him chase Jürgen through the house, bursting into laughter when he caught up with him.

What made it worse was that my kindergarten where I went every morning had been hit and lay in rubble. I missed singing with boys and girls and playing with wonderful toys I didn't have at home.

Jürgen and I had to stay in the house because of the air attacks during the day and at night. My mood lifted when Mother shared news from Alfred with us. He and Tante Hildegard had started school and had fun playing with cousins. Margot was a grade below Alfred and Heinz was in first grade.

Finally Jürgen's evacuation papers arrived and Mother began preparing his clothes for an extended stay. She also packed a suit case with my clothes and her garments. We were going to visit for a little while. The night before we had to leave we repeated the same ritual as before Alfred left. Mother made sandwiches, boiled eggs for our trip and heated water for our baths. I was too excited to eat my favorite chicken vegetable soup that night because this was to be my first train ride.

Father always fed the animals after we had eaten dinner. When he came back into the kitchen he said, "The grey rabbit had five young today."

"At least we won't starve," Mother said.

After she finished packing, Father closed the suitcases and lined them up against the wall.

Mother said, "It's time for you two to go to bed. We're leaving before dawn in the morning. Ulla, you can sleep with Jürgen tonight."

Father said, "Because it takes days to travel to East Prussia, you're going to stay overnight with Oma's brother Otto and Tante Emmy in Berlin."

"I haven't seen them for a long time," Mother said.

Father picked up the newspaper and sat on the sofa. "I polished your shoes and placed them at the foot of the bed."

Jürgen and I said, "Gute Nacht," and clambered upstairs. Mother came up later and tucked us in. Jürgen fell asleep before I did, and I listened to my parents' voices downstairs for a long time.

It seemed like I had just fallen asleep when someone shook my shoulders. "It's time to get up," Mother whispered.

Half asleep, I got dressed, tied my high top shoes and went down to the kitchen. The radio was on. Father listened to the news and slurped his coffee. My brother and I washed our faces with cold water from the kitchen faucet and shared a towel hanging on a peg on the wall.

We ate slices of rye bread with liverwurst and drank warm milk sweetened with honey.

"Papa, are you going with us?" I asked.

"No, I have to work but I'll take you to the Altenessen train station.

"Why are we leaving form the Altenessen station?"

"Because the tracks around Duisburg have been hit and trains can't get to the Bergeborbeck station."

Mother handed us our jackets. "We better go," she said reaching for her hat on the hook behind the door.

Father picked up both suitcases, Mother carried traveling bags and Jürgen slipped his leather school satchels over his shoulders. While Mother locked the door, Oma and Opa came out of their house to say, "Auf Wiedersehen und Gute Reise."

While we walked along Vogelheimer Strasse, the sky turned light. The train was already at the platform when we arrived. Travelers rushed past us carrying boxes and suit cases. The train had many cars. Steam rose from the locomotive and water poured from a huge faucet into a funnel on top of the engine compartment. Father rushed along the train, searching for the car that had a sign with Berlin written on it. We boarded and found a compartment that had three empty seats. Father greeted the people already seated and lifted our suitcases into the overhead nets.

"Keep an eye on your things; the train will get crowded." He hugged Mother, kissed us on the forehead and left the train.

Through the open window Mother talked with him on the platform until an attendant called, "All aboard!"

Jürgen and I went to the window. The attendant blew a whistle and waved a sign. The train jerked and pulled away. Father tipped his cap. "You mind your Mother. " We waved until we left the station and couldn't see him anymore.

Jürgen and I found our seats and sat down. Mother was on the bench across from us between a lady at the window who was sound asleep and a young woman who snuggled close to a soldier in uniform. I sat between Jürgen and an old woman dressed in black who clutched her purse with both hands. At the window next to Jürgen sat a friendly lady with a feather in her hat. She greeted us with a smile.

The wheels screeched over the metal tracks. I looked out the window and saw soot-stained buildings and trees swoosh by.

It seemed not much time had passed when we stopped at another station. The lady who had been sleeping left and Jürgen claimed the window seat. I scooted into his spot next to the lady with the feather in her hat. A pipe-smoking old man came and sat next to me. The train chugged along through cities with tall buildings and wide streets. I saw bomb-damaged factories and apartment houses. At the edge of town I saw coal mines, smoke stacks and mounds of black coal next to them. We rumbled across iron-railed bridges over rivers and canals.

When we left the industrial Ruhr region, we passed through pastures and villages with white houses, red roofs and flowers blooming in window boxes. Then the train came to a screeching halt. The soldier jumped up, opened the window and leaned out as far as he could.

"What's going on?" asked the man with the pipe.

"It looks like the tracks ahead have been bombed. I see a big crater."

"That means we're going back to the last station and find a different route to Berlin," the man said.

I pulled on Mother's sleeve. "What are we going to do?"

"We'll have to wait. It'll take longer to get to Berlin."

The soldier and the man opened the compartment door and stepped out. I climbed on the bench next to Jürgen and looked out. The smoke from the engine floated overhead and filled my nostrils with acrid, soot filled air.

Men hurried toward the crater. The conductor and engineer leaned out the window of the locomotive pointing to other craters nearby. A crowd gathered where the tracks were hit. We're stuck I thought and I sat down feeling grumpy. The old woman dressed in black hadn't moved. She leaned her head against the back wall. Her sunken eyes were closed and her bony hands still clutched the handbag on her lap. Was she dead? While I laid my head on my school pack I watched her wrinkled face.

I woke when Jürgen said, "We're moving."

It took a while for me to realize that we were in a train. "Are we going back home?"

Everyone snickered.

"No. We're returning to the station where we stopped last," the soldier said smiling. "We'll have to wait there until the train can be rerouted. We'll be alright."

The lady with the feather in her hat pulled the little tray up that was attached to the wall under the window. It made a little table. She looked at me. "I bet you're hungry. Would you like a slice of kuchen?"

I peered at Mother.

"Go ahead." she said.

The lady took a package from her bag and opened it. She gave Jürgen and me a slice of streusel kuchen. It smelled good.

"Danke schön," we said together.

Later, everyone in our compartment and people in the aisles started eating. The old man emptied his pipe in the ashtray mounted at the wall. He put it in his coat pocket and put his rucksack on his lap. He pulled out a bottle of beer, a hunk of brown bread and smoked bacon. He covered his rucksack with a checkered dish towel and used it as a tray for his food. With a pocket knife he sliced a piece of bacon and put it in his mouth.

Even the old woman chewed on an apple and a hunk of cheese. We ate our sandwiches. Mother poured sweetened peppermint tea from the thermos and said. "You two, share it."

"Where're you headed soldier?" asked the pipe smoker.

"I'm returning to my regiment in Berlin."

"How are things there?"

"Air attacks day and at night. Countless people are homeless, neighborhoods are in rubble and civilians are fleeing the city."

My stomach started to ache.

"My God," said the nice lady wearing the hat. "My husband is stationed at the eastern front." Soon everyone chewed on something and joined in the conversation. While the adults talked, I looked out the window and recognized the smokestacks I had seen earlier. We must be close to the station we left this morning. The train slowed, moved onto a track outside the station and pulled next to passenger train filled with travelers. Children waved.

Outside, an attendant yelled into a bullhorn, "Everyone, stay inside."

We opened our window.

"Where are you heading?" a man from the other train asked.

"To Berlin!" Someone shouted from our side.

"We're coming from Hamburg and traveling south."

People yelled back and forth between the trains. The orange sun hung low in the sky when we finally pulled out. Jürgen and I took turns sitting at the window. The nice lady removed her hat, placed it in the net above and leaned her head against the wall.

In the dark we made another stop. Many soldiers in uniform and school aged children boarded. Every compartment was crowded. In the aisles children were sitting on boxes and adult had no place to sit. The soldier in our compartment gave his seat to a woman holding a toddler in her arm. Mother pulled me on her lap to make room for an elderly woman.

As we chugged through fields and forests, I watched the stars in the clear, pitch black sky. The overhead lights cast a yellowish glow over the faces of the travelers. I leaned against Mother and fell asleep.

The sudden stopping of the train woke me. It was dark in our compartment. I heard motors humming in the distance. My chest tensed and I felt scared. Jürgen scooted closer. Mother put her arms around us. We huddled together and waited in the dark. No one spoke. The planes came closer. The motors sounded as if they were directly above us. I was afraid to breathe. Mother's hand dug into my shoulder.

"They're passing," someone said.

"Gott sei Dank!" Mother let go of my shoulder. When we couldn't hear the bombers any more, the yellow overhead lights came on and the wheels began to roll. After that, I slept fitfully for the rest of the night. The hours passed slowly. When the sun was high in the sky, we stopped at a small station.

An attendant on the platforms shouted through a bullhorn, "One hour lay-over, you can get out."

People streamed from the train. We debarked too.

A friendly lady pointed to the hall and said, "We're serving hot soup inside."

We queued in at the end of a long line. When we were finally inside, a friendly relief worker directed us to a table. We picked up bowls and utensils and shuffled to another table where women served soup from big pots.

"It's split pea. Hold your bowl straight."

We went to a table against the far wall and sat next to strangers. Mothers tended to small children and old men talked about the war. Boys done eating chased others outside. I stayed near Mother. A lady served the grown-ups a hot beverage in enamel mugs and sweetened rosehip tea to the children.

Before I finished drinking my tea, the attendant came into the hall with his bullhorn. "The train leaves in ten minutes."

Mother got up right away and whispered, "Let's get back so we won't lose our seat."

When we reached our compartment, two strangers were sitting where the soldier and his girlfriend used to sit. We got our old seats back. People streamed back into the train. The soldier and his girl came in, looked at the strangers but didn't say anything. They had to stand. Mother pulled me onto her lap to free a seat. It was an uncomfortable journey. We traveled through the night. I woke every time I slipped off of mother's lap.

In the morning, Mother said, "We're getting close to Berlin. Gather your things."

I stretched and buttoned my jacket. Jürgen yawned and rubbed his eyes. "I got up, opened the compartment door and stepped into the aisle.

"Stay close by," Mother said.

The aisle was not as crowded anymore. People must have left during the night. I scooted next to a handsome soldier at the window. He had the bluest eyes and the friendliest smile I had ever seen.

As we approached the outskirts of Berlin, the train slowed. We passed rows and rows of houses in rubble. Debris had spilled onto the sidewalks. I could look into apartments where people once lived. A bed frame hung halfway through the ceiling of the apartment below. Pictures and mirrors hung crooked on the walls. Smoke-stained lace curtains flapped in the wind. I felt guilty looking into someone's home uninvited.

People rummaged through debris inside the ruins. A bent-over old man pushed a two-wheeled cart loaded with bricks—dogs nosed through rubble. A lump formed in my throat and I wished I was at home.

In the distance, I saw several locomotives without cars parked on the tracks. Our engine crawled toward the gigantic arched roofs of the Berlin station.

Behind me, Mother pulled our suitcases from the overhead net and put them on the bench and on the floor.

Then the handsome soldier rushed away without saying good-bye. I hurried after him. I followed him through several cars. He stopped inside a freight car filled with boxes, yanked the heavy sliding door open and grabbed a handle on the wall. Cool air hit my face. I stepped behind him. He didn't notice me. The train slowed. I saw the first people on the platforms.

The soldier eyed every person we passed on the platform. His face lit up when he saw a beautiful woman and waved. She waved back and started running alongside the slow moving train, holding on to her hat. He leaned out and shouted a name. She flashed a broad smile.

Suddenly the soldier jumped out of the moving train onto the platform. He landed on his feet, turned on his heel and steadied himself in front of the beautiful woman. They hugged and kissed.

That looked like fun. My heart raced. In a split second, I jumped like he did. My body flew through the air, pigtails whipping against my face. When my feet hit the ground, I stubbed my toes and fell onto my hands and knees with such force that my chin hit the platform and my body skidded across the cement. Pain pierced my body.

Voices shouted, "A child jumped from the train."

Did they mean me? I turned around, surprised how fast the cars sped by and saw my mother's horrified face get smaller as the train pulled into the shadows of the station.

I tried to sit up. My knees and hands were stiff and bloody. My chin ached. People came running toward me. One woman pushed through the crowd and advanced faster than the others. It was Mother. Is she going to whip me in front of all these people?

"What were you thinking?" she yelled kneeling next to me. "Let me see you."

"I jumped like the soldier did." I stammered.

"Why?"

"Can I help?" a man asked.

"Nein, danke—someone is meeting us." Mother retorted red faced. She turned back to me. "Can you stand up?"

Several travelers gathered around us. My knees smarted. I couldn't straighten them. They hurt too much. Mother pulled me up. I could feel blood trickling down my shins. Two women bent down offering white handkerchiefs.

Mother blushed and looked embarrassed. "Danke," she said.

She folded the handkerchiefs, used them like bandages around my knees and wiped the blood from my hands. When she touched my chin, a scream slipped from my lips. With her hands firm on my shoulders, she turned me around and checked me over.

"She'll be all right—the scrapes will heal." Mother said to the onlookers.

She's not going to spank me I thought and wiped my runny nose on my sleeve.

One by one the people walked away. Mother picked me up and carried me into the station. I rested my head on her shoulder and whimpered.

Jürgen guarded our suitcases and traveling bags. His huge brown eyes rested on my face. As usual, he didn't say a word. We took our bags into the big hall. It was crowded. People stood in long lines at several ticket windows. There were duffel bags on the floor. Soldier gathered in small groups, smoked and laughed. Some leaned on crutches others had bandages around their heads and arms. I stared at one soldier passing by who had only one leg.

I pulled on Mother's sleeve. "What happened to him?"

"He was injured in the war and had his leg amputated."

The pant leg was folded up where his leg was cut off and tucked under his jacket. It looked odd.

A policeman rushed toward us. Mother laughed when she saw him. "You got here safely, "he said.

They shook hands vigorously, smiled and said a few words. Then Mother turned around. "This is Onkel Otto."

He shook hands with Jürgen and stroked my head. "Guten Tag, I'm glad you are here. Let's go. Tante Emmy is waiting for you."

We picked up our bags and went through the tall doors. Outside a multitude of streetcars loaded with people stopped and rode away. When people left, others climbed on board.

My first ride in an electric street car was exciting. I sat on Mother's lap and watched in awe the tall, apartment houses on both sides of the broad street. Streetcars coming toward us looked like they were going to crash into ours. We got off in front of a three-story apartment house.

"Here we are." Onkel Otto said.

We put our bags on the ground. On the wall of the house, next to the door were rows of nameplates with black buttons next to them.

"Ulla, would you like to push this one?"

I pushed and heard a ringing sound inside. A window opened above. "Ach! You're here," a woman shouted.

I strained my neck and saw a lady wave. A buzzer rang and Onkel Otto opened the door.

"How come you could open the door without a key?" I asked.

"We have an electric buzzer in our apartment that unlocks the door when we press it. I bet you have never seen that before have you?"

I shook my head. I liked him.

We carried our traveling bags up to the third floor. A door opened and Tante Emmy wearing a white apron rushed toward us. She picked me up and carried me inside. The room smelled of coffee and cake. She put me on a chair.

"Ach du Lieber, what happened to you?"

"She was a very foolish girl," Mother said.

"Let me look at your hurt." She pulled the stained handkerchief off my knees and it started bleeding again. "We'll clean out your wounds and put some salve on it. Then it won't hurt much anymore."

It was an exhausting ordeal of crying and doctoring until finally the salve eased my pain.

Jürgen looked out the window. "We're really high."

The table was set with gold-rimmed dishes, platters with cake and chocolate swirls, and a crystal dish filled with whipped cream.

"Are you hungry?" Onkel Otto asked. "Jürgen, come and sit next to me."

Tante Emmy poured coffee for the adults and sweetened ersatz coffee with milk for Jürgen and me. But I couldn't eat.

We remained at the table. The adults shared news of the family. "We saw the bomb damage when we drove into Berlin but Essen is getting pummeled as well.' Mother said.

Jürgen looked at a book. I noticed a bowl filled with bright red cherries on a cabinet against the wall. They looked plump and juicy and made my mouth water.

"Where did you get the cherries?" I asked.

"At the market," Tante Emmy said but didn't offer a single one.

"They must be sweet." No one paid attention to me.

I scooted my chair away from the table so I could see the cherries better. I had never tasted big ones like that before. I stood on the chair and leaned over its back to get a whiff of the enticing fruit. Suddenly the chair tipped back and I crashed to the floor.

"What are you doing now?" Mother yelled. Chairs scraped over the floor.

Onkel picked me up and touched my forehead. "It's just a bump. You'll be as good as new in the morning."

I could tell Mother was angry. I didn't cry. She looked embarrassed but she didn't spank me. "You're going to bed right now."

To the Farm, 1943

Chapter 7

We left Berlin early the next morning. Onkel Otto, dressed in his police uniform, accompanied us to the station. The platforms were crowded with soldiers.

"They're heading for the eastern front." Onkel said. "All the trains going east will be packed."

He helped us into our compartment, put one suitcase in the overhead net and the other against the wall at the window. Mother thanked him for his and Tante Emmy's hospitality.

He said. "Aufwiedersehn, it's time to go to work. Please give my heartfelt greetings to my baby brother and his family."

He shook hands with all three of us and left. Our compartment was filled with mothers, children and soldiers. More people squeezed in even though they had to stand. Jürgen sat on the suitcase, and I on Mother's lap.

"When are we going to get there?" I asked.

"We're probably half-way there but it won't take as long as getting here because there're fewer stops," Mother said.

After we left the populated area of the big city, we traveled through pasture and small villages. I saw blue lakes shimmering in the distance and green forests behind them.

When we finally arrived in the country station with the sign Osterode, I was anxious to leave the confined space of the train and happy to step onto the platform to stretch my legs. It was a sunny outside. The mild breeze felt good on my face. As soon as we put our traveling bags down, a woman with a tanned face rushed toward us. Her colorful summer dress swayed with each step.

"Here you are." She shook Mother's hand and said, "I'm so glad you made it through."

"And you must be Ursula and Jürgen." She smelled of fresh cut hay and warm milk.

"Where's Alfred?" Jürgen asked.

"He's in school, but he'll be home when we get there. He missed you, too."

"The horses are in the front—let's load your luggage on the wagon."

Mother said, "Anton sent boxes with winter clothes for the boys before we left. I'd like to check if they arrived."

Only a few people were in the station—I looked around, but saw no soldiers. We lugged our suitcases through the door to the front of the station. It was quiet outside. There were no cars, buses or street cars like in Berlin. Under a tree, two horses, tethered to a fence post, were eating oats from canvas bags that hung around their necks.

Tante Martha said, "Let's put your bags in the back of the wagon."

As we got closer to the horses they stopped feeding, lifted their heads and looked at us.

"They won't hurt you." Tante Martha said stroking one horse's mane. "This is old Hans. He's almost blind, but he's a good work horse." She turned to the other one and patted his gray tresses. "This is Baldur. He's young and strong. Come closer so he'll get to know you."

I held onto Jürgen's sleeve and inched closer to Tante Martha.

"They're so big," I said. "And they smell."

"They're sweating a little. When we get home, you can rub them down."

Baldur's huge belly was round and slick. He looked down at me. I looked up into his wet nostrils. My brother and I rubbed his belly cautiously.

"You'll get used to him. Let's load your bags in the back.

It was already filled with crates, boxes and wicker baskets. "I've been shopping." Tante Martha said. "I don't come to town often."

Mother returned. "Our packages haven't arrived."

"We'll check on them in a few days. The war is taking its toll. Nothing arrives on time anymore," Tante Martha said. "You two can sit on the stack of empty potato sacks in the back."

My brother and I jumped in and Tante Martha closed the tail-gate. The women climbed onto the driver's bench in front. Tante Martha unwound the leather reins from its post and clicked her tongue. Hans and Baldur pulled the wagon around and trotted away from the station.

Jürgen and I looked at each other and giggled with delight, excited over our first ride in a horse-drawn wagon.

When we turned onto the tree-lined country road, the horses fell into a steady trot. The steel-rimmed wagon wheels crunched over the gravel. Mother and Tante Martha talked the entire way. Fields of grain swayed in the wind on both sides of the road. A farmer guided a team of brown oxen as they ploughed a field. We passed two men on foot on the side of the road carrying long handled scythes over their shoulders.

I stood up and peered at the horses. With every step their big, rounded rumps swayed and their heads bobbed up and down. Every once in a while they swished their long tails.

Jürgen had stretched out on the potato sacks. I lay down next to him. We watched fluffy clouds move overhead against the blue sky. The gentle afternoon sun warmed my face.

I woke when Tante Martha said, "Whoa!" The wagon slowed and stopped. Jürgen and I sat up. We had arrived in the farm yard in front of a brick farm house. Alfred came running through the front door, climbed on to the wagon wheel and grinned at us. Jürgen scrambled to his feet and rushed next to our brother. They stood close with foreheads touching. Then a blond-haired boy and a girl, with tanned faces came out of the house. The children in the city looked pale compared to them.

Tante Martha and Mother climbed down.

Mother rushed to the side of the wagon where Alfred still stood on the wheel and said, "Let me look at you. You've grown so tall." Alfred jumped down and leaned against Mother's chest.

Tante Martha looked at the children. "Karl-Heinz, and Margot, come and greet our visitors."

They came running, looked up at us and said, "Guten Tag."

"And there comes Onkel Emil."

A man, wearing rubber boots and work clothes, stepped out of the barn. He wiped his hands while he hurried toward us.

I remembered when back home Oma talked about Onkel Emil's childhood pneumonia and the complications he had. That's why he was released from service in the *Wehrmacht* before the war. He was too ill to be a soldier.

He shook Mother's hand, "It's good to see you."

Mother said, "I'm surprised you're here. I expected you to be in Poland, managing the big Estate."

"I'm on leave and have to go back soon."

Mother nodded. "I'm happy to see you."

He came around the wagon and opened the tailgate. "You two will sleep well tonight."

"This is a welcome change for all of us," Mother said. "At home, they haven't slept in pajamas for a long time."

"Here you can because bombers don't come this way."

Across the barn yard, cackling chickens scratched in the dirt. Jürgen and I jumped from the wagon and Onkel Emil climbed in, "Let's unload."

Mother looked toward the house. "Where are my sisters?"

At that moment, Tante Änne with baby Manfred in her arm and Tante Hildegard came out of the house and rushed toward us. We hadn't seen them since they left Essen a few months ago. Their faces were tanned. Tante Hildegard's hair seemed more golden. One-year-old Manfred had grown and looked chubby. The sisters were happy to see each other. They laughed and chatted and kissed the baby.

For the evening meal, everyone gathered around the long table in the kitchen. The children sat on the wooden bench against the wall and the adults on chairs. Tante Martha stood at the built-in stove in the corner. I had never seen a stove made of forest-green, glazed tiles. Tante filled dinner plates with boiled potatoes, meat, gravy and cooked fresh vegetables. Tante Hildegard carried them to the table. The aroma of roasted meat made my mouth water.

"What a feast!" Mother said.

When everyone had a dish of steaming food, Tante Martha joined us. "Let's give thanks for our blessings and for the safe arrival of our family." We folded our hands and bowed our heads.

After dinner, the big kids and Onkel Emil went outside and Mother gave me a bath in a wooden, round tub in the kitchen. After rubbing my body with a towel, she slipped a nightgown over my head and shoulders. It felt soft and airy around my body.

"We won't have to run to the bomb shelter tonight," she said.

I felt safe and sleepy.

Tante Martha said, "The beds in the attic are ready for you and Ursula."

While my aunts washed dishes, Mother and I climbed upstairs. Two beds stood against the wall under the eaves. Mother tucked me in. "I'll leave the door open a bit." She went downstairs. I relaxed as I listened to the women talk and laugh in the kitchen. Then I heard them sing, "Land der grünen Wälder." The song I heard them sing at home sometimes. I remembered almost all the words.

When I woke the next morning, Mother's bed was empty. Through the open window, a gentle breeze caressed my face, but I heard no sounds from the kitchen, only a dog barking in the distance. In the morning light I saw sacks of grain leaning against the opposite wall, an old chest and shelves filled with tins and containers. The attic looked like our little room, half-way up the stairwell at home, where we stored feed grain, winter clothes and books.

Barefoot I descended the wooden steps. Cool air drifted under my nightgown. Where was everybody? I hurried through the kitchen into the entrance and climbed on the little bench under the open window. When I straightened up I bumped into the face of a brown cow. Warm air from her nostrils washed over my face. She opened her mouth and mooed. I screamed and gripped the back of the bench. I wanted to jump down, but my legs wouldn't stop stomping. My screams echoed through the house. Mother and Tante Martha came running across the barnyard.

Mother grabbed me and held me tight. Tante Martha laughed heartily, "This is Liesel. She won't harm you—she comes to this window every morning to greet us. Why don't you say guten Morgen to her?"

I shook my head. Tante Martha stroked the brown face and said, "Guten Morgen Liesel, this is Ursula, Alfred's little sister. She'll be visiting for a while."

My body stopped shaking a little. "You talk to her?"

"All the time—she's like a member of the family." The cow turned around and paraded toward the barn, swinging her tail.

"Let's have some breakfast. That'll calm you," Mother said. "You'll enjoy the fresh baked bread with churned butter and homemade strawberry jam."

"Where is everybody?" I asked.

"The big kids are in school. Jürgen was registered this morning. You slept in for a long time," Mother said.

"When you finish eating, put the clothes on I laid out for you. I'm going to help Tante Martha in the vegetable patch."

After breakfast, I put on my dress, pinafore, and high-top shoes, and went out into the barnyard. The women were busy in the garden. I wondered what was in the big barn across the yard. When I stepped inside, I was awed at how gigantic it was. After my eyes got accustomed to the darkness, I saw straw and hay strewn on the dirt floor. In the middle stood the big threshing machine, and on the walls hung farming tools.

I skipped to the far side and climbed the ladder to the loft. Bales of hay were stacked against the far wall. Rakes, pitchforks and shovels leaned against the wood partition. I looked down on the threshing machine and wondered how it worked.

I heard faint squeaks, stood still and listened. There it was again, soft squeals and rustling near a stack of hay under the window. On tiptoes I inched toward the sound. The noise came from within the pile of hay. With care I removed an armful and shuddered at the sight of tiny, squirming, pink, hairless, mice. I dropped the hay and ran to the ladder. I hoped mother mouse wasn't going to chase after me. Frantically I clambered down and jumped from the third rung to the ground. My apron caught on something; the weight of my airborne body tore the yoke. I yanked the caught fabric, ripped the material and fled from the barn.

"Did you see a ghost?" Onkel Emil asked pushing a wheelbarrow filled with potatoes.

Breathless I blurted, "I saw mice."

Onkel Emil laughed.

I ran into the house. Tante Änne looked up from peeling potatoes. "Come and sit next to me."

On the Farm, 1943

Chapter 8

I loved visiting the farm. I only wished Father could be there—then our family would be together again. During the day, while the adults worked in the fields, the garden, or tended animals and the big kids were in school, I ventured outside and explored the surroundings.

Sounds in the country were different from the noise in the city. Here, birds chirped, cows mooed and dogs barked. At home the wheels of the mineshaft clanked, coal trucks rumbled down Emscher Way, aircraft motors threatened and bombs exploded.

On Saturday, I enjoyed watching the women bake kuchen and bread. They let the yeast dough rise in huge ceramic bowls on the bench next to the tile stove until it doubled—rye dough for bread and wheat for kuchen. While they shaped the rye into oval loaves and put them on big metal baking sheets, they chatted, laughed and hummed melodies.

They rolled the wheat dough into flat sheets, put them on cookie sheets and topped them with apple slices, sour cherries and butter streusel. Tante Martha made a poppy seed filling, spread it across a flat piece of wheat dough and rolled it up into a log. They worked all day. The oven was so big, several sheets could bake at the same time. Tante Martha used a long stick to push the baking sheet to the back. The cakes were done first. Soon the mouth-watering aroma from the oven permeated the house.

On Sunday morning the family went to church. Everyone gathered in the kitchen wearing their good clothes. Mother put a white pinafore over my dress. The boys with clean faces and neatly combed hair scooted behind the table onto the bench saying, "We're starved."

Tante Martha and Margot's dresses were made from the same fabric—they looked nice. Onkel Emil wore a suit and Tante Hildegard a beautiful white dress. Mother's hair, as always, was parted in the middle and made into a bun at the nape.

We ate soft boiled eggs served in egg cups and slices of stuten, a braided white bread with raisins—a special treat. We only had rye bread at home.

"Ursel, stay here with Tante Änne this morning. Help her prepare Sunday dinner," Mother said.

"Why can't I go?"

"It's too far. The church is in Kraplau, the village we drove by when we came from the train station."

After breakfast, everyone went outside, mounted bicycles and left the barn yard one by one. Karl-Heinz sat on the cross bar of his father's bike and Margot on the rear rack of her mother's. I had never seen my mother ride a bicycle. It wobbled when she turned on to the country road. The women's dresses flared out as they pumped the bicycle pedals—a barking dog raced after them.

Tante Änne went back into the house. "After I put Manfred down for a nap and then I'll start preparing the midday meal. You can help me."

I stayed outside and watched until the cyclists faded into the horizon. Then I heard the droning of war planes from a distance—I was frightened. Tante Änne came back outside and said, "Ulla! Don't worry—they're German planes flying to the Russian front."

I liked being in the fresh air and crossed the yard to an old wagon with a broken axel that was parked at the side of the barn. I climbed on to the driver's seat. Chickens fluttered out of the wagon and startled me.

From my high-perched seat I surveyed the area. Pink foxglove, blue delphiniums and white phlox bloomed along the fence in the garden. They seemed taller than those at home. When Pappa and I strolled through our garden, he'd name every flower, bush and tree.

Across the country road, I saw another farm house. A man carrying a basket filled with eggs came out of the chicken coop and walked into the house. As I sat still, enjoying the warm sunshine, I heard chickens cackle and wings flutter behind me. They landed in the wagon and scratched in the straw. A screeching rooster flew across the farmyard. He landed near me, flapping his wings. I thought he was going to attack me. Panicked, I clambered down the bench, missed a step and caught my white pinafore on a wooden post. I searched with my dangling feet for a place to stand on and was relieved when I found a spoke of the wagon wheel. I pulled hard to free my apron. Unfortunately, the fabric ripped, I slipped from the wheel and fell to the ground. Gravel dug into my hands and my bottom.

As I got up, I kept my eyes on the menacing rooster. His silhouette against the bright sky was frightening. I got up and straightened my apron. The material stuck to my hands. To my horror they were covered with wagon grease and I had smeared it all over the front of my white Sunday apron. Maybe Tante Änne could fix it before Mama came back from church. Bawling, I ran into the house.

"Ulla, this apron can't be repaired. It's torn in too many places and the grease will never come out."

"Please don't tell Mamma," I pleaded as I rushed upstairs to the attic and hid the apron under my bed. Reluctantly, I returned to the kitchen.

Tante Änne said, "Scrub your hands and help me set the table in the gute stube. We don't use it very often."

She opened the door to the gute stube, a big room that I had not been in before. In the middle stood a long table surrounded by chairs, a china cabinet on one side and a sideboard on the other with a bouquet of burgundy peonies in a porcelain vase.

"This room is beautiful," I whispered.

"We use it only on special occasions. Did you know that Oma Schmidtmann and her brothers and sisters grew up on this farm?"

"Ja, Mamma told me."

"When your mamma and I were little, we used to come here so Oma and Opa could help with the harvest."

"Did Oma have many brothers and sisters?"

"There were eleven of them, but only seven are still alive. The oldest brother was killed in the first war and three others died when they were young during a tuberculosis epidemic around the turn of the century."

"I know that Onkel Emil had tuberculosis, "I said.

"That's right." She spread an embroidered tablecloth over the table. "Hold the cloth at the other end so I can straighten it." From the china cabinet she brought stacks of plates and soup bowls and arranged them in straight rows on the table.

"Ulla, place knives on the right, forks on the left, and soup spoons at the head of the dinner plates. Can you remember that?"

I nodded.

"I have to baste the chickens and start the potato dumplings."

Through the open door the aroma of roasting chicken wafted into the gute stube. All of a sudden, I was hungry. While Tante Änne was busy in the kitchen, I set the silverware just like I was supposed to and admired the unusual wood pattern of the china cabinet.

Later I heard voices through the open window and looked outside. The boys peddled into the yard and took their bicycles to the barn. Behind me, I heard Manfred babbling in the bedroom. When the adults returned, the kitchen was filled with laughter and conversation. Onkel Emil changed into work clothes and went outside. The women covered their good dresses with aprons and helped prepare the meal. Tante Martha fried wild mushrooms in butter. My mouth watered.

We ate a light chicken soup first. Then the aunts carried platters heaped with golden brown chicken, bowls filled with carrots and peas in cream sauce, sprinkled with chopped parsley, and round dumplings to the table. They added gravy boats filled to the rim and tender butter-leaf lettuce, mixed with oil and vinegar dressing and chopped green onions. Dumplings topped with gravy and wild mushrooms were my favorite.

After we finished the delicious meal, the women washed dishes and sang, "Land der dunklen Wälder," Land of the dark forests. I was sent upstairs to take a nap, but couldn't settle down because the torn apron under the bed was on my mind. Even the grown-ups took a Sunday afternoon nap.

I woke when I heard voices through the open attic window. I must have slept for a long time. When I went downstairs, I smelled coffee in the kitchen but saw no one. Voices drifted in from outside. I went into the back yard. The grown-ups sat at the long wooden table at the back of the house drinking coffee and eating slices of cake baked the day before. The neighbor I had seen earlier at the farm across the country road and a woman in a colorful summer dress were visiting and engaged in conversation.

"Ulla, come and have a slice of kuchen."

"Can I have some poppy seed cake?" It was delicious.

Later in the evening when I stepped into the front yard, I heard pinging sounds coming from the cow barn. When I peeked in through the barn door, I saw Onkel Emil sitting on a three-legged stool close to Liesel's bulging flank. The pinging came from the quick and even streams of milk hitting against the side of the tin pail wedged between Onkel Emil's knees. Liesel turned her head toward me and blinked with her big lashes. Anna, the other cow, stopped her chewing and looked at me with hay hanging from her mouth.

Suddenly a warm fluid hit my cheeks. I jumped backwards. Onkel Emil laughed. He aimed the cow's nipple at me. Wherever I moved, the stream of warm liquid hit my face.

"Milk, right from the source." He laughed with delight. He got up and put the bucket filled with milk against the wall next to the open barn door.

I relaxed and laughed, too.

"Ulla, bring me the empty pail and try milking. Liesel will not mind."

"I don't know how."

"Sit on the edge of the stool. I'll be right behind you. Put your right hand around this tit in front—your left around this one and squeeze. Don't pull on the udder, she doesn't like it. I'll hold on to her tail."

Warmth emanated from the cow's belly. I liked the way she smelled, but I felt nervous.

"Squeeze!" he said.

The nipple felt solid. I squeezed but no milk came out.

"Try again."

I squeezed harder. A few white drops came out.

"Again! Pull your fingers into a tight fist as hard as you can," Onkel Emil said.

I tried that—a short stream of milk squirted into the pail ending in a trickle. I tried again. The flow became stronger, but not enough to hit the side of the pail and make a ping. Soon my hands ached.

"Don't pull on the udder."

Swoosh; Liesel's tail hit my head. "That hurts!" I gasped and jumped up ramming my head into the cow's belly. Onkel Emil grabbed the pail.

"At least you can tell your friends in the city that you've milked a cow," he said.

Swelling with pride, with my face and neck sticky from dried milk, I skipped into the house to tell my mother.

The next morning, I was upset when Tante Änne told me that my mother had left with Onkel Emil, for the train station in Osterode.

"Why did they leave without me?" I bellowed.

"They'll be back. They're picking up the boxes with the boys' winter clothing."

Tante Änne put Manfred into a stroller and went outside.

Alone in the quiet house, I panicked, convinced that my mother went home without me. Brokenhearted I lay down on the bench behind the kitchen table and sobbed.

Tante Martha rushed in, "What's the matter—I can hear you all the way in the garden."

"Mamma left without me."

"No!" she said patting my shoulder. "You're shaking. Don't cry. Your mamma will come back; she just went to the train station to pick up packages with your brothers' clothes."

"She's been gone for a long time," I whimpered.

"What matter with little one?" Irene the Russian woman asked.

"My mamma left without me," I moaned.

"She'll come back, I know. Here! Take good, red apple."

I turned around, wiped my nose with the corner of my apron and took the apple. It was so big it filled the hollow of my hand.

"They'll return before the midday meal," Tante Martha said.

That calmed me a little. After the grown-ups returned to do chores, I wiped the tears away and went outside to the country road and looked to where the road emerged from the forest. After a while I leaned against the fence and bit into the apple. It was juicy and sweet. When the sun felt like it burnt the top of my head, I saw shadows emerge from the forest.

I climbed on to the cross bar of the fence and strained my neck for a better view. The heads of two horses bobbed up and down in slow motion. Excited I put one foot on top of the fence post and stood up. The sole of my shoe slipped—I lost my balance and fell. My dress and apron got caught on a stake and I heard a tear. My feet dangled above the ground. I yanked on my clothes and tore a hole in the fabric but I was still attached to the stake. Again, I pulled, this time harder and my dress and apron ripped loose. I looked down the road. The horses and wagon were closer and I recognized my mother. I ran toward her waving and yelling, "You've come back."

Onkel Emil pulled on the reigns. "Whoa!" The wagon slowed and stopped.

Mother reached down to pull me up. "You're bleeding. Your clothes are shreds. What did you do this time?" She looked very upset.

"I thought you left without me."

Her face softened. "I wouldn't leave without you. We only picked up our packages from the station and did some shopping in town. How in the world did you rip your last apron?"

"I fell off the fence."

"I found the apron you threw under your bed." She did not look happy.

When we arrived at the house, Eugene, the French war prisoner who worked on the farm, greeted us in the yard and unloaded the wagon.

After supper, Tante Martha filled a tub in the kitchen with water for my bath. "We want you to be clean for your trip home tomorrow," she said.

After the evening meal Tante Martha and Mother sat in the kitchen fixing my torn dress and apron. Everyone else was outside doing evening chores. I sat on the bench behind the kitchen table nibbling on a baked apple.

"Alfred looks so good." Mother said. "At home, his anxiety attacks increased with every bombing attack. We finally took him to a doctor. He has angina pectoris. Anton worried he might not survive the war."

"When he first arrived, he wouldn't go outside. Now we can't keep him in."

"When did Eugene and Irene start working here?"Mother asked.

"A while ago. Without them, I wouldn't be able to manage the farm. It doesn't make sense that Emil has to go to Poland and manage a big Estate there. He doesn't want to go back. The Polish farm workers resent being told what to do by an uninvited foreigner."

"That's understandable." Mother said.

"It's impossible to hire workers here. All our able men have been drafted."

"Aren't you afraid of having the war prisoners here? Do they speak German?"

"No, I'm not afraid of them. Eugene speaks some German. He's a fine horse man and takes good care of all our animals. After work he sometimes plays ball with the children in the yard."

"How about Irene?"

"She's from Russia and was forced into a labor camp. Nazi soldiers mandated her to give up her little child, but she couldn't let go. They shot her."

"Oh my God!" Mother clasped a hand over her mouth.

These words scared me, but I stayed on the bench.

"Irene is a good worker too and is sweet with the children. It's against the law to have Irene and Eugene eat with us at the dinner table. We are subject to unannounced inspections at any time. Violating the rules would result in severe consequences. We could lose the farm."

Mother looked concerned. "Where do they sleep?"

"They go back to the prison camp at night."

"How do you handle it all?" Mother asked. "You have no idea how grateful I am that Alfred and Jürgen can stay with you instead of having to stay with strangers."

"Es geht. Everyone has been assigned chores. That helps." Tante Martha said.

The boys came into the kitchen, Alfred carried a bucket filled with milk and Tante Hildegard carried a basket overflowing with eggs. Margot held a bowl of red raspberries.

"It's time to wash up, tomorrow there's school." Tante Martha said.

Going Home, 1943

Chapter 9

Mother and I dressed in our traveling clothes and carried our suitcase and bags downstairs. Tante Hildegard—cousins Margot and Karl-Heinz—and my brothers Alfred and Jürgen were ready for school even though it was early.

Jürgen looked like he was going to cry, so did Mother. Her eyes were red. Onkel Emil brought his duffle bag into the kitchen.

"I'm leaving with you, but I'm traveling in the opposite direction back to Poland," he said.

While we ate breakfast Mother looked at my brothers. "You two mind Tante Martha and don't get into trouble." Then she turned toward me. "It's time to go."

I was sad to leave without Alfred and Jürgen but felt excited to see my father soon.

Onkel Emil got up first. "Ulla! Come, Liesel wants to say good bye."

I rushed into the entry. The big head of the brown cow peaked through the window. I climbed on the bench, no longer afraid to stroke her.

"Auf Wiedersehen Liesel, I have to go back to Essen and see my pappa."

Heavy hearted I strolled into the farmyard where Hans and Baldur waited, hitched to the wagon, ready to go.

Onkel Emil lifted me onto the driver's bench. "You can sit in the front today."

Everyone came outside and gathered in front of the house. Mother shook hands with everybody and muttered a few words. Alfred and Jürgen stood close as if they didn't want to be separated again. Mama climbed up onto the driver's seat. I sat between her and Tante Martha. Onkel Emil climbed into the back.

When the wagon pulled out of the yard, the group followed us to the road. I looked back. Everyone waved. Tante Änne with Manfred on her arm wiped her eyes with a handkerchief. A refreshing breeze pushed my bangs from my face and cooled my damp cheeks.

"I hope your train ride will not have many detours," Onkel Emil said.

"I do too," Mother replied.

While they talked I watched two men in the field cutting hay. They swung their scythes over the grass in unison from right to left with even strokes and at the same time moved forward in step as if marching to the beat of a song.

At the station in Osterode one train was already there. We said good bye to Onkel Emil. His train left first. Tante Martha cried. An approaching locomotive blew its horn.

"That must be ours," Mother said. We shook hands with Tante Martha and said, "Aufwiedersehn."

Mother and I boarded the train. It was crowded and had no compartments, only rows of wooden benches. We found two empty seats. Mother swung our suitcase into the overhead net and opened the window. I cuddled up next to her. Tante Martha was on the platform.

Mother said, "Please write to us and let us know how the boys are doing. I'm concerned about Jürgen. He didn't want to leave home."

Tante Martha nodded and waited until the train pulled out of the station.

During the ride to Berlin, Mother looked out the window and didn't talk much. Once we pulled into the gigantic Berlin station, we transferred to a train that headed to the Ruhr Valley.

"Why aren't we staying with Onkel Otto and Tante Emmy in Berlin?

"Pappa is waiting for us. We've been gone for a long time."

Even though this train had many more cars it was more crowded than the one we just left. Every seat in our compartment was filled. When a person left, someone else took their place right away. Several men smoked cigarettes—the air was stuffy. After two tiring days on the train, we finally arrived in Essen.

"This isn't the station we left from," I said.

"No, this is the main station in Essen, the Hauptbahnhof"

"Will Pappa pick us up?"

"No. He doesn't know we're here. We'll take the street car to the swim hall in Altenessen and walk from there. If we're lucky, we might be able to catch the bus to the Stadthafen."

I had never been downtown before. Outside the Hauptbahnhof, across from the aisle where we waited for the street car, most tall buildings had been hit by bombs and lay in rubble. The street was covered with debris. It scared me.

"I hope we don't get an alarm on our way home," I said looking up at Mother.

She patted my hair. "Maybe we'll be lucky."

I was glad when a street car pulled in front of our aisle. A man helped us with our suitcase all the way to our seat. I sat with my back to the front across from Mother. We passed street after street with bombed buildings. When we finally reached the swim hall and got out of the street car, a bus was stopped at the corner of Vogelheimer Strasse.

Mother said, "Let's hurry so we can catch it—it's going in our direction."

She ran ahead. I followed her, pulling the rucksack along. She raced to the front of the bus and yelled, "Komm schnell."

When I got there, the driver said, "You have to get off at the Wiehagen Strasse—the bus will be out of service there."

Mother paid him and as soon as we sat down, the bus rumbled along Vogelheimer Strasse under the familiar big trees. I knew we were close to home. On the corner of Wiehagen Strasse we had to get out and walk. When we reached the curve in the street where its name changed to Wildstrasse we stopped in front of my bombed out kindergarten. Mother put the suitcase and bags down and rubbed her shoulders and neck. Then we continued down our street.

Half-way down old Wildstrasse, in the shade of the poplar trees, I saw a person but couldn't tell who it was.

"Mamma, look! Is that Pappa at the corner of Oma's house?" My heart beat faster.

"I think it is."

We hurried along. I waved.

Then the shadow stepped away from the corner of the house and came running toward us. He scooped me up and hugged Mamma. She cried. He took the suitcase from her and we walked home together.

When we arrived in our courtyard, Oma and Opa came out of their house and followed us into ours.

Mother unpacked the suitcase. She put wurst, butter, cheese, jars of wild blueberry jam, two tins of goose lard and Tanta Martha's good rye bread on the table. She talked all the time and separated out what was for Oma.

"We'll eat well for a few days," Father said. "The shelves at the grocery store don't have much on them these days."

Mother talked about the bomb damage we saw downtown. Father served Opa a glass of schnapps.

"We've had brutal attacks while you were gone."

Mother said, "Ulla, you can sleep in your brother's bed."

That night, I slept in my day clothes again.

Spring Soup, 1943

Chapter 10

We slept through the night without being woken by an alarm. In the morning Mother and I were the only once home. Father was at work. The house was empty and quiet. I missed my brothers.

Mother said, "Let's surprise Pappa today with his favorite Frühlingssuppe. You can help me pick the vegetables."

"Why do you call it Frühlingssuppe?"

"I make it only once a year in late spring or early summer with the first tender carrots, peas and string beans."

"Why don't you make it more often?

"Because we want the vegetables to grow to their full size—when we harvest them then, I make vegetable soup."

Mother wouldn't let me play outside.

"It's too dangerous. We have too many air attacks," she said.

I was happy to accompany her to the garden and pick vegetables for the soup. She showed me which carrots were big enough to pull.

"You remove the soil with your finger like this. If the orange top is about the size of a five penny coin, you can pull it."

When we had enough carrots we went to where the peas were growing. Mother reached for one. "You can pick them when the pod is swollen like this."

We also picked tender beans, green onion, leaves from the maggie bush and parsley for flavor.

Back in the kitchen, she made chicken stock first. It simmered at the back of the stove while she cleaned and chopped the vegetables. I helped remove the peas from the pods and put them in a bowl. Soon our kitchen smelled like the one on the farm.

Usually Oma and Opa ate with Tante Grete and Ruth at their house. I was happy they joined us for our midday meal. While we ate Mother talked about our trip to the farm.

Days later we received the first letters from Tante Martha. Jürgen was very quiet and was homesick even though he didn't talk about it. He clings to Alfred and sits very close to him on the bench when they do homework. Alfred was doing well in school and likes his teacher. They both did their chores willingly.

Oma, who watched for the mailman every day, always knew when we received a letter and came over to hear the news from the boys and shared news she had received from Tante Änne and Hildegard.

One day Mother turned white when she read a letter from the farm. Oma came in as Mother reached for her handkerchief.

"Was ist los?"

"Alfred had an accident." Mother wiped her eyes and nose.

"He got his hand caught in the chaff-cutter. Tante Martha was not there. Änne wrapped it in towels, hitched the horses and rushed to the hospital in Osterode. When they arrived at the hospital, the horses wouldn't stop and raced past it for miles. They finally stopped in the next village. Änne realized she had forgotten to put the bridal bit into the horse's mouth."

Oma held her handkerchief over her mouth. "How is he?"

"He's still in the hospital. He had lost a lot of blood. The doctors are hoping that they won't have to amputate his middle finger."

"That is very serious."

"Ja, it's bad. He has a severe infection."

"Oh my!"

I had a lump in my throat and watched the women cry.

Green Tomatoes, 1943

Chapter 11

Wash day was my least favorite day because my mother spent the entire day in the cellar and Father worked many hours in the mine. I had no one to play with and felt lonely. What made it worse, Mother wouldn't let me play outside anymore.

"Our sky is in flames day and night," she said.

The night before washday, she soaked the whites in soap suds in one big aluminum tub and Father's work clothes in another. On Monday morning, she started early boiling the whites and scrubbing the work clothes on our washboard before she put them into the washing machine.

By the time I got up, the heavy soap laden air had permeated every room in the house. Mother had left a slice of rye and some sausage on a little wooden sandwich board for me and a mug filled with milk. I didn't like eating breakfast alone.

The air raids during the day came faster at us and more often. That was the reason why Mother didn't spread whites on the lawn with the special grass anymore for the sun to bleach. We were not allowed to step on it, so grass wouldn't bend and keep the clothes away from the dirty ground.

I was surprised when she came into the kitchen carrying the wicker basket filled with wet clothes.

"Ach, Ulla, you're up. It's such a beautiful day and there's no soot in the air. I'll take a chance on hanging the clothes on the line. They'll dry quickly—there is a little breeze."

After breakfast, I skipped into our garden. The sun warmed my face. In the vegetable patch, I noticed how tall our tomato plants had grown. Father had planted three rows in the spring, more than he usually did because food was getting scarce in the stores. The tomato plants were taller than I, and their vines were loaded with big green tomatoes. Each fruit had a shiny white star where the sun's rays hit the plump, round part.

Delighted by their magic, I walked between the rows and touched the shiny stars. Then I plucked one fruit and smelled it. I hadn't smelled a green tomato before. It felt firm and smooth. Then I pulled another and another.

I took the corners of my apron and made a pouch so I could fill it with plump, round bulbs Mother would be so surprised when I gave them to her. I went from plant to plant and filled my apron. I went to the house and piled the tomatoes on the kitchen table. Then I rushed back and filled my apron again. When I left the tomato patch and stepped into the garden path I bumped into Mother who was returning from hanging the wash.

"Mamma! Look! I picked these shining stars for you."

She looked at my apron. Her eyes narrowed. "Ursula, what have you done? These tomatoes aren't ripe," she shouted. She grabbed the apron straps at my shoulders and pulled me all the way into the kitchen. I held tightly on to the pouch so I wouldn't drop any of the green fruit.

"Why did you do that?" she slapped my hands so hard that my apron slipped from my fingers and the round fruit tumbled to the floor. "Now we have no tomatoes to eat and none to can for the winter," she screamed. Red blotches appeared on her face. Her anger horrified me.

She grabbed my arm, pinned me over her thigh and spanked my bare bottom with a wooden spoon yelling, "What am I going to tell your father?"

I hollered and squirmed under her fury, promising never to do that again. When she finally released me, I scurried upstairs, holding my sore bottom with both hands. I hid under the bedcovers and sobbed. I didn't go down for dinner that night.

The next day when I went downstairs, the tomatoes were gone. I didn't see them anywhere and I didn't ask.

Mother was ironing shirts on a folded cotton blanket covered with a piece of unbleached muslin on the kitchen table. She had no ironing board. She heated the heavy iron on the stove top but never looked at me.

I climbed on the sofa behind the kitchen table and ate my butterbrot, careful not to drop any crumbs that could irritate Mother. I glanced at her face. She still seemed angry with me.

Potato Pancakes, 1943

Chapter 12

I was very quiet all morning, afraid to ignite Mother's fury again. I looked at the pictures of the Struwwelpeter book and practiced drawing like Alfred used to do.

There was a knock on the door, and Oma walked in. Mother wiped her forehead. She had been ironing for hours. Stacks of folded clothes were on the living room table.

Mother looked at me and said. "Oma is making potato pancakes for us today."

Everyone in our family considered a meal of potato pancakes a special treat, but we haven't had them for a while because they required so much time to prepare.

"Ulla, go into the back cellar and bring us a pail full of potatoes."

"Why me?"

"Because your brothers aren't here."

I had never gone into the back part of the cellar by myself. It was too dark and scary. When we used to go down there during bombing attacks, I always made sure the door to the back part was closed.

Sometimes on wash days I'd go down when I was bored because Mother was there. But I never stayed long. Now I had to get the potatoes? Mother kept the pail on the top step of the stairs that led down. But I didn't take it with me. It would be too heavy for me to carry up the stairs filled with spuds. Cautiously, I descended down the creaking wooden steps so I could hear if something moved down there. Alfred always had warned me not to let the boogieman catch me.

On the wall above the last step was the light switch. I reached it by standing on tiptoes. The cellar smelled musty. A tiny shadow scurried along the opposite wall. A tail disappeared in a hole in the mortar between the bricks. I shuddered.

I inched toward the door to the back part and pushed against it. The hinges squeaked. The daylight streaming in through the metal grid at the window under the ceiling made strange shadows on the floor. I could barely breathe.

Slowly, I moved toward the potato chute. I made a pouch out of my apron and filled it with spuds. I scurried out of the cellar, up the wooden steps and dumped them into the bucket. I looked over my shoulder to see if anyone had followed me. The light in the cellar was still on. I ignored it and cleaned the dirt off my apron. I went into the kitchen and dropped the pail at Oma's feet.

She picked it up and filled it with water. It turned muddy right away. Oma scrubbed the potatoes with a brush, rinsed and peeled them and put them in clean water. While Mother ironed, Oma peeled the potatoes.

"We are so fortunate to have a garden." she said. "The vegetable man isn't coming around anymore."

Oma had an odd way of grating the potatoes. She sat on our little wooden stool wedged a ceramic bowl between her thighs and pushed it against the leg of the kitchen table.

"Why do you sit like that?" I asked.

"It's easier this way. On the table the bowl always dances away from me."

When Oma finished grating, she put a square piece of white cloth over a colander and poured the mush into it. She picked up the ends of the cloth and squeezed pinkish liquid from the potato mush.

When she was done, the mush looked like a ball. She put it in a bowl, added eggs, salt, and flour and stirred it with a wooden spoon until it was smooth and creamy.

Mother stopped ironing and cleared the table. She went into the cellar and emerged with the cast-iron frying pan and a tub of lard.

"You left the light on in the cellar," she scolded. "Electricity is expensive."

She put the frying pan on the stove and added a chunk of lard. When it sizzled, she dipped a spoon into the dough and made four mounds in the skillet. With the back of the serving spoon, she made the dough into flat pancakes.

"They have to be thin and crispy," she said.

Oma set the table with plates and silverware then fetched a pot of sugar-beet syrup from the pantry. "We'll be done before Anton and Opa come home from the mine," she said.

The pancakes sizzled. They smelled delicious and my stomach began to rumble. Mother arranged them tower fashion on a plate and kept them warm at the back of the stove. I climbed on the chair next to her and snitched a pancake from the pile when she wasn't looking.

Mother declared, "We made enough for today and tomorrow." She then put the plate on the table.

As she sat down, the sirens wailed. "Schon wieder?" Mother said annoyed.

"Are we going to endure attacks every day now?" Oma said as she rushed out of the house. "I have to get my things."

Mother covered the pancakes with a dishtowel, grabbed our coats and her bag. We took the short cut through our garden path and ran through the field toward the entrance near the horse stable. Oma was behind us. We rushed to our assigned seats inside the shelter. It was filled with elderly people, women and small children. The first bomb exploded and the ground shook. I snuggled closer to Mother. A deafening explosion above our heads made the lights flicker and the rafters creak. I jumped on Mother's lap. My hands trembled.

"I'm glad Alfred is spared these attacks," Mother said. "He wouldn't survive this."

Oma nodded. "I hope our men are safe."

I was glad to hear the release sirens. People got up and shuffled toward the exit.

When we arrived home, our kitchen window was shattered. Glass splinters were everywhere—on the floor, on the table, chairs and sofa. The dishtowel over the tower of potato pancakes was covered with glass splinters. Mother removed the towel. Pancakes stuck to it. She lifted several from the stack and examined them.

"We can't eat these," she said looking up, "They are full of glass."

Waiting for News, 1943

Chapter 13

Mother kept the front door open a crack every morning so she could hear the mailman's approaching footsteps. The autumn air chilled our house and leaves from the poplar trees whirled into our entrance way. I knew Mother worried about my brother Alfred. We had not heard if his injured finger had to be amputated.

Sometimes I saw her cry while scrubbing the floor or stirring the soup pot on the stove.

Finally, our friendly postman came to our house. He pulled an envelope from his leather pouch and gave it to Mother. "Guten Morgen Frau Fischer, I know you've been waiting for this. It took a long time getting here."

She said, "Danke," and rushed back into the kitchen.

I scooted under the kitchen table and climbed on the sofa. She sat on the chair between sofa and stove, tore the envelope open and read. Her lips mouthed the words.

Oma came in and tiptoed to the chair at the other side of the stove. Mother didn't move. Oma gazed at her face.

Finally Mother looked up and clutched the letter to her chest. "He didn't lose his finger, but he'll never be able to bend it."

Oma lifted her eyes to the ceiling, "Gott sei Dank," she whispered.

"Mamma, is Alfred still in the hospital?"

"No, he's back home on the farm, but he is still in a lot of pain."

❧

Air raids became even more dangerous. Hundreds of bombers were used by the Allies in every attack and thousands of bigger and more destructive bombs were dropped on our city. Tenth of thousands of families became homeless. Many were relocated. Others were taken in by families who had not lost their homes.

Sirens pierced the air day and night and we spent more time in the shelter. Sometimes our shelter was hit five or six times. The wooden rafters creaked and moaned so much that I worried they would collapse and the bombs would crash through the ceiling. My body trembled uncontrollably. Even if I sat on my fingers, they didn't stop shaking.

The old men sitting near us counted the hits aloud. They even guessed which factories had been hit. During one attack, an old man said, "That one was aimed at the ammunitions plant."

Bombs didn't seem to scare Tante Ruth. Oma worried about her because she still didn't want to leave her sewing machine during an attack. Even her boss Fräulein Hüttemann had to remind her to go to a shelter when she was at work.

Our windows were broken so often that mother left them partially open during an attack so they wouldn't break from the air pressure of a bomb exploding nearby or shatter from flying shrapnel. Often we found shrapnel burrowed in our wooden floor planks after an attack.

I was surprised to hear that our neighbor Frau Hempel gave birth to twins. They were born early. The mother was too weak to go to the shelter. During an evening attack, her sister insisted on taking the babies in a wicker basket to safety. The next morning we learned they were killed running through the field behind our gardens. Their bodies could not be found. Days later our cat brought a finger into our front yard and left it on the ground. Mother wrapped it in her handkerchief.

After that, I refused to go to bed for fear I wouldn't make it the shelter on time. I begged to sleep with my parents in their bed again.

It got worse when both coal mines were hit when Father and Opa were at work. They didn't come home after their shift that day. At dusk Mother paced between our kitchen and the corner of Oma's house. I also went to the corner to watch for them. Several women up and down the street were in front of their houses all looking in the same direction from which they expected the miners to come.

I picked up yellow poplar leaves that had fallen to the ground into a little bouquet. Then I heard the women stir and murmur. When I looked in the direction from which I expected Father and Opa to come, I saw shapes move.

Someone said, "It's them."

I started running toward them then realized Mother was in the house. I ran back into front yard and yelled, "They're coming!"

I hurried back to the sidewalk and ran toward the group of men wearing safety helmets and carrying miner's lamps. Mother passed me. She ran faster than I. The men all looked alike with their faces covered in coal dust. When they saw us run toward them, they broke into broad smiles. Their white teeth and eyes stood out in the dim evening light.

When I reached Father, I gave him the bouquet of yellow poplar leaves. He took them and smiled.

"We're lucky to get out, "he said. "So many mines were hit. We went to four before we found one with a working wheel tower that could bring us above ground."

Mother said, "I'll fill the tub with warm water so you can wash up."

I skipped next to them all the way home.

Wedding in Bavaria, 1943

Chapter 14

One morning, the mailman delivered two letters. "This one is from the boys and this one from Bavaria," he said. "I hope it's all good news."

"It's from Tante Martha." Mother smiled and went inside. She went to her favorite chair and opened the envelope. I curled up in my usual corner on the sofa and watched her face. I could tell whether the news was good or bad. When she pulled a handkerchief from her apron pocket I knew it was not good.

"What's wrong, Mamma?"

"It's Jürgen. He did exactly what his older brother had done and stuck his finger in the chaff-cutter. This boy has to mimic everything his older brother does."

"Is he in the hospital?"

"No, his injuries weren't as severe as Alfred's, but he is in a lot of pain. Tante Martha said he'll be alright."

She took a deep breath and waited for a while before opening the letter from Bavaria. While she read her face looked happy.

"What is it?" I wanted to know.

"Pappa's younger brother Franz is coming home on a short leave from the Army to get married."

When Father came home from work, she gave him the letter. "Franz wants me to be best man. I'll see if I can get time off."

He looked at me. "Ulla, we're going on a trip. You probably don't remember my sister Kathel. The village where she lives has not been bombed. I grew up in the house where she lives now."

"When are we going?"

"In two weeks."

"Is it far?"

"Bavaria is in the south of Germany. The little village is surrounded by forest and fields. It's near the Czechoslovakian border."

"Does Tante Kathel live on a farm?"

"No. The house is in the village. But she does have two cows, a pig, chickens, geese and fields."

Then Mother told him about Jürgen's accident and said, "You must visit the boys for Christmas this year and have a good talk with them. They're getting into too much trouble."

Father looked concerned and nodded.

A few days later, my parents and I left for Bavaria. This trip, like the one we made earlier in the year to East Prussia, took days because many tracks were bombed and our train had to be rerouted through different cities several times.

When we finally arrived in the little country station in Poesing, we were the only passengers who disembarked. The sun shone brightly and the sky was blue as far as I could see. Father smiled when he saw Tante Kathel standing on the platform. Her curly dark hair looked like his.

She walked toward us. "Grüss Gott Toni."

Father's eyes sparkled. "Grüss Gott Kathy. You got our postcard."

They shook hands. He looked up to the sky and breathed in deeply. "I love this fresh country air."

The women laughed and shook hands. "And this must be little Ursula. You were just a baby when I saw you last." She stroked my hair. "You must be tired from the long trip. Let's take your bags to the front of the station where Pongratz is waiting with his horse and wagon. He had business in town and will give us a ride home."

71

She looked at me and said, "Pongratz and your father went to school together. He lives across the street."

The men slapped each other on the shoulder and shook hands. "I hear the war is raging where you live." Herr Pongratz said.

"It's getting worse. Everyone is exhausted—no one is getting any sleep."

"You'll be able to relax here," he said.

The women sat in the front next on Herr Pongratz on the driver's bench. Father lifted me into the back and joined me there. I sat on a folded tarp. The horses pulled on to a narrow dirt road toward a village. Every house was painted white and had red geraniums blooming in planter boxes at every window. We traveled up and down hills past wheat fields and through the forest.

I heard bells ringing.

Father turned around. "See the church on the hill?"

A white church tower glistened in the sun.

"Tante Kathel's house is between the trees on the hill below the church."

The horses labored up the hill and stopped in front of a light yellow house with small windows, white curtains and red geraniums in wooden boxes. Attached to the house was a brown, wooden barn.

Father lifted me out of the wagon and pointed to the house. "This is where I grew up. The house is almost one hundred years old." He pointed to the barn. "The animals live in there."

Above the roof, on the hill behind the house was the church.

"I like the glittery tower," I said.

"That's an onion dome. Most churches in Bavaria are built with one." Father said. "Hundreds of years ago, nomadic horseman from Mongolia invaded these parts. It is said that they insisted our church towers were built with a rounded domes on top."

Inside the house the wonderful aroma of something baking made me hungry. "When are we going to eat?" I asked.

"Soon, the Dampfnudeln are almost finished." Tante Kathel walked to the wood stove and opened the heavy oven door. She pulled an iron pan forward and lifted its lid. The pan was filled with plump, yeast dumplings simmering in sweet milk. She tapped their golden-brown tops. "They're done." She lifted the pot and carried it to the table.

A dog, spread out under a chair, lifted his head and went back to sleep. Father carried our suitcases upstairs while Tante Kathel set the table and filled each bowl with Dampfnudeln. They swirled around in the hot milk. With a dab of plum compote, they tasted delicious.

"When is Franz coming home?" Father asked.

"He's already here, staying with the bride's family. The Army gave him only a few days leave. He'll be shipped out to the Eastern front on Monday."

"So soon?" Father lowered his head. He looked sad. "No time for a honeymoon during war time, I guess."

"That's true, but Franz feels lucky to get a few days of leave." Tante Kathel said.

While brother and sister talked, I struggled with Mother who wanted to pull my dress over my head. "How can I put my day clothes back on when the bombers come during the night?"

The adults laughed. "Ursula, we have no air raids," Tante Kathel said. I looked at my parents. They nodded.

"Remember when we were on the farm in East Prussia? You slept in your night gown there too, because there were no air attacks," Mother said.

I remembered. After a while Father carried me upstairs and laid me on an old, creaky bed. "This is where I slept when I was a boy."

The church bells rang. Father counted aloud. "It's eight o'clock. The bells will clang once for every hour through the night. Think of something nice every time you hear them." He tucked me in and patted my head. "Schlaf schön." I listened to his footsteps descending down the wooden steps.

On the wedding day morning Mother laid out my red, hand-knit dress, white voile pinafore, knee socks and polished high-top shoes. She had bartered potatoes for the red yarn for my dress and a neighbor lady knitted it for me in a scalloped shell pattern.

"That is a beautiful dress," Tante Kathel said.

I enjoyed wearing it. While the adults got ready for the wedding, I skipped outside into the back yard. "Don't get dirty." Mother warned.

The sun felt warm. In the back of the house, foul smelling, liquid manure flowed in a shallow ditch across the yard from the animal barn to a pit on the other side. I jumped over the ditch and looked into the barn where the cows were feeding on hay. They looked at me and never stopped chewing. The pig grunted in the back. This barn was much smaller than the one on the farm in East Prussia, and it smelled terrible inside.

I left in a hurry and meandered up the hill where a flock of white geese foraged in the grass under an apple tree. They sounded like chatterboxes, busy gobbling up worms they pulled out of the ground. Enchanted, I approached the hill. The geese ignored me. I couldn't take my eyes off them and stepped closer. The gander looked up, stretched his neck toward me and hissed. I stopped. When he returned pecking at the ground, I inched closer.

Suddenly, the gander lifted his head, hissed and took a few steps toward me. I jumped back. He lowered his long neck almost to the ground, opened his beak, flailing his red tongue. He advanced toward me. Startled, I backed up, afraid to turn around and run. The rest of the geese looked up and followed the gander, making a racket. I retreated faster—they gained on me. My foot got caught in the urine-trench—I pulled it out—liquid manure filled my shoe. I stepped back and lost my balance at the edge of the urine pit and fell in.

Panicked, I bellowed out a blood-curdling scream, never taking my eyes off the advancing horde. My parents and Tante Kathel appeared in the doorway. Tante Kathel grabbed a broom and rushed toward the geese, yelling, "Get back!"

The gaggle retreated reluctantly hissing.

Father's strong hands grabbed my arms and pulled me out of the pit. The awful smelling yellow fluid dripped from my drenched, hand-knitted dress. It felt heavy.

"Why do you always get into trouble when we go somewhere?" Mother yelled. "Look at you! I can't take you into the house—I'll have to clean you outside."

Tante Kathel, in her good dress, rushed into the house and returned with a tub. She filled it with cold water. Father, in his best suit, removed my white voile pinafore, red dress, shoes, knee socks, and underwear. He dropped them onto the ground. I felt awful and tried to hold back the tears.

Mother scrubbed my body with curd soap and a pig-bristle brush. "I don't want to hear a peep out of you," she hissed. Her strokes felt like a spanking. If I dared to complain, I knew she would let me have it. "We'll have to hurry or we'll be late for the wedding," she said.

Even after I had clean clothes on, I could smell the manure. We walked along the country road to the village where Tante Fannie lived. In front of the beautiful church, with a shiny onion dome, several people had gathered and smiled at our approaching group.

Father hugged his brother. They looked a lot alike. Onkel Franz looked handsome in his army uniform. Tante Fannie, wearing a short-sleeved dress with a tiny flower design held a bouquet of wildflowers. She broke into a big smile when she saw us.

"Everyone is here," someone said.

Mother took my hand. We followed the wedding procession into the church. Beautiful organ music captivated me and made my spirit soar.

Christmas, 1943

Chapter 15

When we returned home from Bavaria, it was harvest time. In the kitchen, canning jars bubbled in boiling water. Mother had picked vegetables to can for winter. Oma and Mother sat on low wooden stools in our entrance way pulling threads from green beans. They dropped the beans in a bucket on the floor. Then they removed peas from their pods and put them into a ceramic bowl. Later they cleaned carrots and prepared kohlrabi.

I didn't like canning days, because everyone was so busy.

"Ulla, move out of the way, we have to get this batch done before bombers arrive," Mother said. 'Sit on the sofa and look at a book."

"When are Alfred and Jürgen coming home?"

"I don't know," Mother said. "Aren't you happy they can go to school?"

"I wish I could go to school."

In the evening, jars filled with beans, carrots, peas and kohlrabi stood bottom up on the table. "Why do you put them upside down?" I asked.

"It helps seal them tight without air getting into the jars."

When the canning season was over, the potatoes and rutabagas were harvested and stored in the back cellar.

Temperatures dropped. The first snow flurries announced winter.

One Advent Sunday at dusk when we had just finished our evening meal, Oma came into our kitchen carrying a blue eyed doll wearing a light blue dress with a lace color. Could this doll be for me? My heart beat faster, but Oma didn't give it to me. The doll was bigger than a baby. When Oma laid her on the sofa, her eyes closed. She was the most beautiful doll I had ever seen.

"Anton, when you visit the boys for Christmas on the farm, would you have room in your suit case for Hildegard's doll? Even though she's fourteen, I want to surprise her with it."

"This is Tante Hildegard's doll?" My voice quivered. I fought back tears.

Everyone turned and looked at me. Father patted my head. "I'm sorry Ursel. Tante Hildegard has had this doll for a long time and misses her. She hasn't seen her since she left home to live on the farm with Tante Martha and Onkel Emil."

He turned to Oma. "I can take it."

"Why are you going to visit Alfred and Jürgen alone?" I complained.

"They are so far from home and deserve to celebrate Christmas with one parent."

"Why can't we all go?"

"Someone needs to stay home, guard our house and feed the little pig and the chickens."

A few days later, we said goodbye to Father. We didn't accompany him to the train station. While he was gone, Mother let me sleep in his bed.

One cold winter evening Oma, Opa and Tante Ruth came to visit dressed in their Sunday clothes. Tante Ruth was wearing another nice dress she had made. Her shoulder length brown hair framed her beautiful face.

"Why are you wearing your good clothes?" I asked.

Tante Ruth smiled at me. "Because it's Christmas Eve."

I looked at Mother. She looked like she was going to cry. "It doesn't feel like Christmas without a tree, and Anton and the boys so far away."

"Our families are split apart this year," Oma said. "I'm sure they'll have a festive Christmas. Martha does that so well."

We gathered around our kitchen table. Mother lit the four partially burned red candles on the green Advents wreath. She placed two plates filled with cookies, walnuts and apples in the middle of the table. The small plate had a pair of wool stockings on it. She pushed it toward me. "This is for you." Because my mother looked so sad, I felt sad too.

Then, with a cracking voice Oma started to sing Silent Night. Opa's baritone chimed in. His handlebar mustache moved up and down with every word. When Tante Ruth and Mother joined in, my heart beat with joy.

Buying Liverwurst, 1944

Chapter 16

Father returned from visiting my brothers for Christmas in East Prussia after New Year's. Every evening he and Mother talked about his trip to the farm and how the boys were doing. I loved listening.

Onkel Emil had cut a beautiful Tannenbaum in the forest for the holidays and Tante Martha had roasted a goose for Christmas dinner. Jürgen was lucky, his finger healed but Alfred was still in pain.

"He can't bend his middle finger." Father said.

Mother's lips quivered. She reached for her handkerchief.

I enjoyed eating the juicy apples, the butter made from sweet-cream and Tante Martha's home-baked bread Father brought back from the farm.

Mother said, "The weather was cold here while you were gone. People have slipped on the icy roads running to the bomb shelter. Many have sprained an ankle."

We ate breakfast together on the days when Father didn't work in the mine. One calm morning after we finished eating, the sun broke through the clouds and Father said, "Ulla, put your coat on. I want to show you something."

"Where are we going?"

"Just come with me."

Mother buttoned my coat and I followed Father outside. Cool wind whipped around the corner of our house and stung my cheeks. In the garden, the sun warmed me. Patches of snow remained on the empty flower beds. The ground looked barren and dull. I skipped behind Father until he stopped in front of a raised bed. He bent down and asked me to come closer.

"See this?" He pointed to a tiny green tip barely visible in the ground. "These are crocus. They'll bloom later. But look at this." With his forefinger, he gently pushed the cracked top soil away. Two green spikes sprung forth. Then two delicate white petals opened up. "These are Schneeglöckchen announcing Spring." Father looked at me. His eyes sparkled. "Snowdrops bloom just for a short while. When the petals open, they'll look like tiny, white bells. In a few days the whole bed will be covered with white blossoms, even though there is still snow on the ground."

"They are beautiful. Can I pick them for Mamma?"

"I thought you might like them. Wait until all of them are in bloom then you can give her a bouquet. Let's go back inside now— it's cold out here."

As we walked back to the house, the sun hid behind the grey clouds and the wind picked up. "I like Spring," I said.

When the planting season arrived, Father couldn't buy the vegetable seeds and planting potatoes he needed. "I'll have to cut the potatoes into pieces and hope they'll grow. This year, it looks like we'll have to tighten our belts."

∂

For months our butcher on Harbor Street hadn't been able to offer the meat and sausages allotted on our rationing cards. Mother sometimes cut a piece of her meat and put it on Father's plate.

She looked at me. "Pappa has to work so hard, he needs extra calories."

Toward the end of summer, Mother called me into the kitchen one day and said, "Oma told me that Herr Wollbeck is selling fresh liverwurst today. Because your brothers aren't here, and I have to cook dinner for Pappa, I want you to go to the butcher shop and buy a quarter pound of liverwurst."

She hung a shopping bag on my arm and showed me a mustard colored rationing card. "Give it to Frau Wollbeck—she'll cut off this corner. Don't forget to bring it back. We need it to buy groceries — you understand?"

"I'll take good care of it." I felt very grown up and excited to get out of the house.

Mother knelt in front of me, looked straight into my eyes and said, "If you hear the sirens, you must come straight to our bomb shelter. Don't go to the bunker on Harbor Strasse that is close to the butcher shop."

"Why not?" I asked.

"That's how families can get separated."

She took my hand and walked with me to the corner of Oma's house. "Don't dawdle."

Sunshine warmed my head as I skipped along the sidewalk under the poplar trees toward Harbor Strasse. The butcher shop was half way down the hill in a two-story brick house. I hurried up the stone steps to the front door and noticed that the shop windows were empty. They used to be filled with fresh cut roasts, chickens, smoked hams, bacon, sausages and pots of lard.

In the store the black and white ceramic tiles on the floor and the white tiles on the walls looked scrubbed and shiny. It smelled of smoked sausages and ham. I noticed that the glass display case was also empty. I saw no meat or sausages anywhere. The shop looked so bare.

Frau Wollbeck, the butcher's wife, was surprised to see me and said, "Guten Tag, Ursula. Can I help you?'

"Ja, Mamma wants a quarter pound of liverwurst."

"You're lucky. We have some left." She went through the swinging white door into the back room, returning quickly holding a ring of liverwurst.

My heart beat faster.

With a long knife she cut off a chunk and placed it on the scale. The black arm of the scale quivered and settled on the 125-gram mark. Frau Wollbeck wrapped the wurst in brown butcher paper and placed it in my shopping bag.

I jumped when the sirens wailed.

"An attack!" she said.

She cut a square off the corner from the rationing card. I gave her money from my billfold.

"Ursula, go to our shelter—it's just up the street."

I nodded but ignored her warning. I scrambled down the stairs jumping over two steps at a time and ran back up the hill on Harbor Strasse. The shopping bag sometimes got tangled between my legs. When I turned into the Wildstrasse, I heard the second alarm. The bombers were coming. I ran faster. When I reached Emscherweg the path to our shelter, I heard the droning of the engines. I sprinted, gasping for air. The third alarm shrieked. I knew the bombers must be above. Wheezing and out of breath, I ran even faster. I heard my own voice whimper, "Please, God, protect me."

My eyes searched the sky. I saw the planes. There were lots of them. All glistening in the sun and gliding through the air in formation. Cigar shaped projectiles fell from their bellies. Spellbound I stopped and watched them glide toward Earth. The roaring of the planes reminded me of the danger. My feet took off toward the bunker.

Seconds after I dashed through the entrance, the first bomb hit. The ground shook. I bit my tongue and tasted blood.

Where was Mother? I ran toward our and our neighbors assigned seats barely noticing the old men, women and children sitting in rows on chairs and benches along the shelter's walls. The second bomb exploded in front of the entrance blocking it with debris, locking us in. My ears plugged. Several more exploded, one after the other. Some hit the shelter.

An old man counted, "Three—four—five—six. We've never had that many hits."

"The shelter held up," someone said.

I pushed on. The light bulbs flickered, swaying back and forth on their short cords. Loose gravel dribbled from above. The pilings moaned. Out of breath, I stopped behind our neighbor, Frau Ehlert. My body trembled—I realized that I had made it into the shelter just in time. The women stood in a circle. I couldn't move. My feet felt like they were bolted to the ground.

I heard mother's quivering voice. "I've sent Ursula to the butcher shop. She hasn't returned."

I opened my mouth to let her know that I was right behind Frau Ehlert, but no words came out. I heard my teeth rattle. I tried to call Mother, but my voice box wouldn't work.

The neighbor ladies shifted position and Frau Ehlert moved. The ceiling light shone on my face and Mother noticed me. Her lips parted into a crying smile. Her red-rimmed eyes filled with tears. She stepped into the circle and pulled me toward her. It felt good. All the women turned around and looked at me. Then I remembered the shopping bag and gave it to Mother. She looked inside.

"She brought me liverwurst."

Everyone smiled.

My Skin is Too Tight, 1944

Chapter 17

Although Mother often said that we lived in dangerous times and that I must stay near the house, I went outside sometimes when she made beds upstairs without telling her. I skipped along under the poplar trees and waved to the men who gathered in small groups on the sidewalk talking. I smiled at the old men who relaxed on benches in front of their houses.

Lately the men looked over their shoulders and whispered when I came near. In the shelter the old men, too, talked quietly as if they didn't want anyone else to hear.

When Father turned the radio off in the middle of the newscast and said, "Lies! All lies," I wondered what was going on.

One day when I saw several men talking in front of Ehlert's house, I went around the corner where they couldn't see me and listened.

One man said, "The Allies have landed in Normandy and their infantry is pushing inland. Before you know it, they'll be here."

Frightened, I ran home, burst into our kitchen and jumped on my mother's lap. "Ulla! Watch out! I'm holding a darning needle."

I didn't say anything but I couldn't sit still either and jumped off her lap. One foot landed in the mending basket spilling the clothes on the floor.

Mother grabbed my arm and said, "Stand still! Why are you so jumpy?"

"The Allies are coming." I blurted.

"Where did you hear that?"

"The men on the corner are talking about them."

Mother frowned. "We don't know if that is true, do we?"

"What are we going to do if they come here?"

"I don't know. For now, fetch me some potatoes so I can prepare dinner for Pappa."

After Father came home, we ate our midday meal but only he had meat on his plate.

"This is the last of the bacon," Mother said.

Father nodded. "I'll have to chance a trip to Bavaria and see if the farmers can spare some sausages and meat. I'll talk with my foreman about getting time off."

"Take Ursula with you. She's been jumpy and needs a break from this war."

Mother looked at me and said, "Remember, when we went to the wedding last year and stayed with Tante Kathel?"

"I'm scared bombs will hit the train."

"Trains are hard to hit. They move too fast." Father pulled on my braids and smiled. "Eat!"

That relaxed me a little and I took a bite of fried potatoes. They were crispy and the salad tasted vinegary, just the way I liked it.

Summer was coming to an end and Mother worried about my brothers. I heard my parents and grandparents discuss Russian troop movement on the Eastern Front. Mother looked worried because the farm where my brothers were was not far from the Polish border and we had not received a letter for a while. When Father and I left for Bavaria, we had not received any news.

Mother's eyes looked sad when she said good-bye to us. "I wonder if you can get through Köln and Frankfurt." She hugged Father. "Come back safe, you two, and you be good for Pappa."

I nodded.

Father stroked her cheek. "Aufwiedersehn."

He picked up the two suitcases. Mother followed us to the corner of Oma's house and waved until we turned south on Harbor Strasse.

We hurried. I had trouble keeping up. When we heard a train whistle, we started jogging. Out of breath we arrived at the station as the train pulled in. We rushed into the lobby, bought our tickets, hastened through the gate to the aisle and climbed into the car heading for Nürnberg. As we chugged along, everyone in our compartment gazed out of the window and looked horrified as we passed the unbelievable destruction from the war. We saw rows of houses in rubble, more than on earlier trips.

Father broke the eerie silence. "We're not far from Köln. I wonder if the Dome Bridge over the Rhine River was hit."

An old man said, "I haven't heard that but the north spire of the catherdral got hit but it didn't collapse. The entire city is in ruins."

"Oh, my goodness," a lady said.

Father opened the window and craned his neck. I see the twin spires, they're both standing tall—I also see the arches of the bridge. He stepped away from the window to let others look out.

The train slowed as we crossed the river. The Dome's spires were very close and reached so high into the sky that I could not see where they ended.

One man said, "I think they are the tallest man made spires in the world."

We continued south along the Rhine River and were rerouted several times. On the outskirts of Frankfurt, the train slowed and stopped on a track outside the station. We were parked there for a long time. Everyone unpacked their sandwiches. While we ate, the men talked about the assassination attempt on Adolph Hitler earlier in the year.

"They're hanging everyone involved."

Father didn't say anything. The conversation frightened me.

When we arrived in the city of Nürnberg we left the train and rushed to another aisle to catch the train going to the Bavarian Forest. Every platform was crowded. Soldiers and civilians rushed by us carrying suitcases, bags and cardboard boxes.

We boarded a train that had only a few cars behind an old locomotive. Father found a seat and put one of our suitcases next to the bench in the aisle because there was no room for it in the over-head net. I sat on his lap.

I was glad when the train started moving. On the bench across sat old men with weathered faces, women wearing colorful head-scarves with red-cheeked children on their laps. They didn't talk much. We traveled through fields and villages with whitewashed houses. Some of them had angels with wings and St. Christopher carrying a child painted on one wall.

Eventually, the monotone rhythm of the wheels lulled me to sleep. I slept fitfully because I kept sliding off Father's lap. I was uncomfortable and always heard the chugging of the train in the background.

Father said, "You're getting too heavy," and lifted me onto the suitcase. The compartment smelled of sweat and damp clothes. It was difficult to sleep sitting up on the suitcase. Father pulled me back up when I slipped off. I was tired and miserable and wished I could stretch out in my bed at home. Exhausted, I leaned against Father and held on to his arm.

I woke when the brakes squealed and the train slowed. Tall trees moved by the windows on both sides. The full moon hung low in the sky. The train stopped. I looked out the window and saw the engineer walking toward us.

"Verdunklung!" he shouted.

Everyone pulled the window shades down. The lights dimmed in-side—then went out. In the dark, someone said, "Air raid." Terrified, I scooted closer to Father. My stomach tightened. "Can we go to a shel-ter?"

"There are none in the forest. We have to wait it out."

I heard the familiar hum of approaching airplanes. My skin started to tingle. I had difficulty breathing.

"Pappa, I'm scared."

"Pray," he said.

No prayer came to me.

"Pappa, are the bombs going to fall on us?"

"No, they're heading for the city."

"Are the children in the city praying, too?"

He didn't answer. I worried that God might hear the prayers of the children from the city first. Would he protect me too? I knew the pilots could see the train from the sky in the moon light.

I began to shake. My skin pulled so tight over my body that I gasped for air. Whimpering, I squirmed trying to stay on the suitcase. Suddenly my skin split open as if it had a zipper. I stepped out of it and frantically ran out among the trees. Moon light flooded the forest. Oh God! I can't hide here—I can't get away from the bombs. If I keep running, I might not get back into my skin. The train could leave without me and my body would be lost in the forest forever.

Petrified I stopped and retraced my steps, jumped back on the train and into my skin. It closed around me with a sound like suction. I was whole again.

The planes passed above. When we couldn't hear the droning of the motors anymore, the train lurched forward and our journey continued.

Exhausted, we finally stopped in Pösing. I recognized the station we had arrived at when we came for the wedding. But no one was there to greet us.

Days of Rest, 1944

Chapter 18

We waited for a while on the bench outside the station in the morning sunshine. "Tante Kathel must not have gotten our postcard. We'll have to walk to Stamsried," Father said.

"How far is it?"

"Five kilometers."

After the train left, it was so quiet, I heard the leaves rustle in the trees.

Father got up and stretched. "We'd better go. I was hoping a farmer with horse and wagon might come along and give us a ride."

He put his knapsack on and picked up the suitcases. We walked side by side on the path along the tracks and through the village with whitewashed houses. The geraniums were still blooming in the flower boxes at the windows. Through open barn doors, I saw cows swoosh flies away with their tails, and enjoyed the smell of dry straw and wood-burning smoke from kitchen stoves.

Father said, "Thank God, the war has not reached this quiet farm community."

We passed women carrying wicker baskets, strolling toward the bakery. We climbed up the steep country road and left the village behind. Church bells rang for morning prayers.

Golden wheat fields were on one side of the road and green pastures on the other. In the distance, the rolling hills were covered with thick, green fir trees. Blue cornflowers and red poppies swayed in the wind on the side of the road.

"How much farther do we have to go?"

"We have a stretch ahead of us."

"I wish Mamma had come with us."

"She's guarding our home."

We continued in silence. "My feet hurt," I complained.

Ahead of us, a horse drawn wagon turned onto the country road. Father waved and shouted, "Can you give us a ride?"

The farmer stopped and waved for us to come. I recognized Herr Pongratz, father's school friend, who had picked us up from the station when we came for the wedding.

"Grüss Gott Toni," he said. They shook hands. "Hop in!"

I climbed into the wagon and sat between our suitcases on a stack of empty sacks. Father sat on the driver's bench next to Herr Pongratz. Happy for the ride, I leaned back watching puffy clouds drift above.

I woke when we stopped in front of Tante Kathel's house. She came out, waving and shouting, "You've come. Griiss dee Toni." She helped unload our suitcase.

Father thanked his friend. He tipped his hat, took the reins and clicked his tongue. The horses pulled the wagon across the street into his barnyard.

At that moment the postman delivered the postcard we had sent announcing our visit. Tante Kathel read it out loud. Everyone laughed. Inside, the house smelled of wood smoke.

After my nap, when I went into the kitchen, Tante Kathel filled a stoneware urn with fresh, sweat cream. "I'm making butter." She pinned the urn under the hollow of her arm, and reached for a whisk made of thin branches. While whipping the cream with even strokes, she walked back and forth in the kitchen talking to Father who relaxed on the bench under the window smoking his pipe.

I watched her with fascination.

"Why aren't you using the churn to make butter?" Father asked.

"Butter just doesn't taste as good. The fresh cut birch branches give it a special flavor."

I asked, "How long do you have to beat it like that?"

"I stop when the cream has separated from the buttermilk and it can be made into a ball. I'll show you when it's ready. Is she ever going to get done? Finally Tante Kathel put the urn on the table fished out white lumps, formed them into a ball and put them in a bowl filled with cold water. "Now I'll massage it like this to remove the buttermilk still trapped inside air bubbles."

"Why do you do that?"

"Buttermilk splatters in the frying pan," she said.

"I can't see any."

"I'll show you." She took the butterball out of the water and squeezed it with both hands. I heard a pop and an opaque liquid oozed out. She split the lump in half and stored them in a cabinet with wire-mesh doors in the pantry.

"I better start mixing the bread dough so you have bread to take home. Toni, would you go to the baker and ask him if he has room in his oven tomorrow. Ulla, go along. A little walk will be good for you."

Tante Kathel will you make dampfnudeln for dinner tonight?"

"It'll be a surprise."

Father and I walked up the hill to the village square. We stopped in front of the baker's window. It displayed loaves of big, round bread, breakfast buns and sweet rolls. My mouth watered. We went inside. The baker's wife looked up.

"Grüss Gott, Toni—and is this your little one?"

"This is Ursula, she's the youngest. The boys have been evacuated."

"Where are they?"

"With Gertrud's Tante and Onkel on their farm in East Prussia."

"Oh, my!" she said covering her mouth with her hand.

"Kathy would like to bake bread tomorrow. Do you have room in your oven?"

The lady looked at a list hanging on a peg on the wall. "I can do it in the afternoon when everyone else's bread is done."

We left the bakery, walked to the fountain in town square and sat on a bench. "Why doesn't Tante Kathel bake the bread in her oven?"

"The farmer's bread has to bake a long time at an even temperature. Her wood stove can't do that. Years ago a big clay oven used to stand here where all farmers baked their bread."

"An oven outside?"

"That was before big iron baking ovens were made."

That evening we had dampfnudeln steamed in milk with melted butter and cinnamon for dinner and home-made plum compote for dessert.

After the sun had set and it turned dark, the entire sky filled with thousands of twinkling stars. They seemed so close. Where we lived, emission from the coal mines covered the entire Ruhr Valley with a blanket of soot and smoke. Tante Kathel turned the light on and closed the wooden shutters on the windows.

"Now I can't see the stars anymore," I complained.

"We have black-out instructions like you have in the city."

"Mamma said that you have no air attacks here."

"We've had none so far. It's just a precaution so our houses can't be seen from the air."

Father said, "Come over here and sit next to me on the bench. Have I ever told you the story of the Knights of the Bavarian Forest?"

"No."

"Let me tell you." He winked at me and pulled me closer.

"In the evening, when it's dark, the good Knight who lives in the Kiirnburg in the hills behind the village mounts his white steed and swoops down from his fortress. He circles over the farms in the area and flies from houses to house in the village to make sure everyone's safe and children are tucked into their beds."

"Does he steal children?"

"No, no! He is a good Knight."

"But across the river lives another Knight. He and his men ride on black stallions. They pillage and plunder the farmers and villagers."

"Does he steal children?"

"He can't, because the good Knight protects his people. His soldiers ride strong and fast horses. They win all the battles."

"You've never told me a story before."

"Because it's so difficult in war time." He stood up and said, "It's time to go to bed." He unbuttoned the back of my dress.

"You can't take my dress off. What if there is an air attack?"

"Remember, the bombers don't come here."

He carried me upstairs to bed, stroked my cheek and said, "We're safe here. Sleep well."

I listened for the Knight's clashing swords and started when the church bells struck.

When I woke the next morning, the sun had raised high in the sky. I jumped out of bed, put a clean dress and apron on and rushed downstairs. Tante Kathel stood at the kitchen table and kneaded the bread dough. The table was covered with flour. Stacked on the bench were several round, shallow baskets.

"Ursula, I made you a butterbrot with farmer's bread and smoked ham. It's on the plate over here and a mug of fresh milk."

I climbed on the bench and watched Tante Kathel.

"Hmm, the smoked ham is delicious. Where is Pappa?"

"You can have more after I'm done. Your Pappa is visiting Herr Kraus across the street."

Then she divided the big lump of dough into four even pieces and put one in each basket."

"Why are you putting the dough in baskets?"

"That's how bread is prepared in these parts. Your grandmother already used these baskets; they are woven in a special pattern. It will leave an imprint on the bread."

"Why?"

"Every family has a different weave so the baker can tell our bread apart."

She placed the baskets on a big metal sheet and covered them with blue and white checkered towels.

"Now they have to rise again. This afternoon, we'll take them to the baker."

"Won't the baskets burn?"

"The baker will tip the basket upside down with the pattern side up and bake the bread on a big sheet in his huge oven.

In the afternoon, Tante Kathel hoisted the metal sheet with the breadbaskets filled with risen loaves onto her shoulder.

"Open the door for me."

We walked up the hill. The church bells announced the time. I looked up to the church tower with the copper onion dome. We crossed the town square to the baker's shop.

The baker said, "Griiss Gott Kathy—I've been waiting for you."

"Griiss Gott. These loaves are for Toni."

He took the pan with the baskets from Tante Kathel and carried it into the back room. We followed him. He opened the huge oven door and pulled a big metal sheet out. Then he turned our baskets over. The bread tumbled onto the sheet. He arranged the loaves just so with a long stick and stacked the empty baskets on a bench next to him.

"Come back later. We'll be closed—just ring the bell," he said.

Tante Kathel picked up grandmother's baskets and walked out. I skipped along behind her on the narrow, downhill sidewalk along the brick wall of the churchyard all the way home. I looked at the weave of the baskets before they were stored away.

At dusk, Father brought the bread home from the baker on the same metal pan we used in the morning. He put it on the sideboard in the kitchen. I looked at the loaves. Each had the coiled design from the baskets on top. That evening, Tante Kathel filled one of our suitcases with apples, dried mushrooms, fresh baked farmers bread, liverwurst and blood sausages.

"This bacon is from Pongratz. He brought it over this afternoon," she said.

At dawn the next morning another farmer from the village who was heading for his fields gave us a ride to the train station in Pösing. I liked the sound of the wagon wheels grinding on the gravel. A screeching crow fluttered out of a tree along the road disturbing the morning stillness.

But when I thought of the upcoming train ride back to the Ruhr Valley where air attacks could happen any day, my stomach fluttered. I worried that bombers would force the train to stop again. Will they drop bombs on us this time?

The trip back home took over two days. When we stopped late at a train station because the tracks ahead had been destroyed, the soup kitchen was already closed. I was not dressed for the cool night air and didn't sleep much. Early the next morning, miserable and tired, we boarded the train again and continued the last leg of our journey back to Essen.

When Father and I finally turned the corner into the Wildstrasse, I felt like running home. When we got closer to our house, a figure hurried toward us.

"Mamma is coming to greet us," Father said.

Homecoming, 1944

Chapter 19

News was spreading that the Russian army was marching west and had taken 350,000 German soldiers prisoner. Soon they would be in East Prussia. Mother worried about my brothers. Her eyes were swollen—she looked like she had a headache all the time.

The long-awaited letter finally arrived. Tante Änne was bringing the boys west.

"When will they get here?"

"Their travel orders are to go to Obersdorf, a village in southern Germany. They'll stay there on a farm."

"That's not fair. Why can't they come home?"

"They have no choice. They have to go where their traveling passes tell them to go."

She stroked my hair, sat on a chair and pulled me onto her lap. Her body trembled. She hugged me tightly and sobbed. I didn't know what to do and was very still. When she finally relaxed I said, "I wish the war was over."

"I wish for that too," she whispered.

Tante Hildegard left the farm earlier in the year after she graduated from eighth grade and began serving her Pflichtjahr, a social service requirement for young girls to work for one year. Oma was glad that Tante Hildegard was closer to home. She was assigned to a large family who lived in a big house where she cooked, cleaned, washed clothes and cared for four children while their mother worked in a munitions factory.

"Will Tante Martha, Onkel Emil, Heinz and Margot also have to leave the farm now that the Russians are coming?"

"Tante Martha is going to have a baby in December and Onkel Emil was drafted into the army again along with the horse Baldur."

"Who will help Tante Martha on the farm?"

"Remember Eugène, the French war prisoner who played games with you when we visited the farm last year, and Irene, the Russian woman who helped in the house?"

I nodded.

"They'll bring in the potatoes, sugar beets and harvest the grain. Tante Martha is grateful they are good people and hard workers."

"Eugène and Irene were nice. Maybe they don't have to sleep in the prison camp at night anymore."

Mother stroked my shoulders. "Go and play now so I can start cooking."

Not long after Father came home we ate our midday meal. After we finished eating, he turned the radio on. I recognized the voice of the Führer.

He shouted, "Sieg fürs Vaterland."

Father shook his head, turned the radio off and went outside to feed the chickens. Everyone waited anxiously to hear from Tante Änne and my brothers.

"Traveling with a two-year-old wasn't easy." Mother said. "But Alfred and Jürgen are old enough to take care of their own luggage."

After many days, the mailman gave Oma a postcard. "This is what you've been waiting for," he said.

Mother rushed into the courtyard to where Oma was. She read. *"Arrived in Obersdorf. All are safe. Don't know when we can come home."*

Oma looked to the sky, "Thank you, Lord."

Mother just smiled. In the afternoon, Father took a pen and ink from the little compartment in the kitchen cabinet, sat at the table and wrote a note to Tante Änne. "Ulla, let's go and mail this letter," he said. "I also have to go to the mining office."

I welcomed getting out. It was lonely in the house without my brothers. When the letter was mailed and Father finished talking to the man in the mining office, we strolled home. In our street several houses had been hit and lay in rubble.

No children played in the courtyards. No women walked home with shopping nets filled with groceries as they used to. On the opposite sidewalk a tall man with blond curls came toward us. Father didn't seem to notice him and walked on looking down.

I raised my arm and yelled, "Heil Hitler!"

Father yanked on my arm.

"That hurts!"

"Children don't have to do that." He sounded angry.

The young man stretched out his arm and shouted, "Heil Hitler."

Father raised his hand a little and mumbled in response.

I loved the way adults paid attention to me when I hailed the Führer and didn't understand why Father didn't like it. We hurried home. He didn't say another word. As I went into our front yard, Father walked on toward the shed behind our house with the empty rabbit hutch.

I don't remember how many days passed when we received a postcard from Tante Änne with the news. *"We're coming home."*

Oma, Opa and my parents took turns watching for them from the corner of Oma's house. We didn't know from which direction they'd come. That depended on which train station was operational. If they arrived at the station in Berge Borbeck, they'd come from the west, and if they arrived in Altenessen, they'd come from the east. When the grownups were busy, they asked me to stand watch. I loved doing that because I wanted to be first to great my brothers. Just thinking about them coming home made my heart beat faster. I could feel it thump all the way in my neck.

Days went by. I saw no sign of them. Keeping my post at the corner was getting harder. My legs hurt and my neck felt stiff from looking up and down our street. Sometimes when I saw people in the distance come toward me, I'd get excited and was disappointed when it wasn't them.

One afternoon I noticed a group of tall and short people burdened with suitcases coming from the east. I watched them intently. When they came closer, I recognized Tante Änne with Manfred on her arm.

I started running toward them then remembered that I had to tell Mother first. Racing back to the house I yelled, "Mamma, they're coming. Komm schnell, they're here."

I turned around and ran up the street to greet them. Mother passed me and reached them before I did. They dropped their suitcases and rushed toward us. We hugged and laughed and hugged again. Jürgen walked around smiling for days. He never wanted to leave home again.

My brothers had grown since we saw them last year on the farm. Alfred was ten years old and had celebrated two birthdays away from home, and Jürgen was eight. Our house filled with laughter and noise again.

That evening Mother said, "Ulla, set the dinner table for five tonight."

I had to give up my brothers' bed and sleep with my parents again. I liked having my own chamber pot. Now I had to use the one in my parent's room again. Until it started to freeze, they used the drop-closet but I didn't have to go outside.

Even though the boys were home, I often looked out their window to watch our neighbors walk home from the mine and the trucks loaded with coal rumble down Emscher Weg.

The weather changed and temperatures plunged. When it started to snow, even though it was cold, I would still look out the window and occupied myself with catching snowflakes. One evening at the window, I heard a strange clinking sound coming from the slag heap that stretched from the coal mine where our shelter was to the coke furnaces to the east. We called the slag heap, Steinberg. The Steinberg was made of the rock excavation from the mines and had tracks on top. Coal was transported in trams from the mine to the coke furnaces. A string of lights ranged from one end to the other. I strained my eyes to see if I could detect through the flurry of snowflakes what was making this sound.

Something moved on top of the Steinberg. Illuminated by the dim glow of the lights through the misty winter air, I saw silhouettes shuffling toward the mine where Father worked. Did the noise come from them?

This was a different sound, not like the low-pitch metal on metal squeal the trams made when filled with coal or the high pitch when they returned empty. This sound was eerie.

The next day I cornered my father. "Pappa, I saw moving shapes on the Steinberg and heard eerie sounds. What are they?"

"Ach!" said he. His face looked grim.

"Tell me, what makes that clinking sound?"

"I think you saw Russian war prisoners being taken to work in the mine."

"But what is making that strange noise?"

"It comes from the chains."

"Pappa, why are they carrying chains?"

"They're not carrying them—they're chained together so they can't run away."

I was horrified.

After that day, I often had nightmares of moaning silhouettes with bowed heads dragging the chains around their ankles to the edge of the mine shaft and falling in.

Mother would wake me and say, "It's just a dream."
I pleaded with her not to leave the room. "Think of something beautiful. Take a deep breath and skip through the open fields and green forests in southern Germany where Pappa grew up."

Visit, 1944

Chapter 20

My brothers didn't like having to sleep in their day clothes again and had trouble waking up when the sirens wailed announcing an air attack. Alfred's angina was flaring up. He was always out of breath when we ran to the bomb shelter. I could hear him wheezing.

The boys missed going to school and roaming freely through the fields with their cousins. They were home only a week when Alfred's best friend was killed. He was distraught and kept to himself in his bedroom. Sometimes I heard him crying. Jürgen would go upstairs and stay for a while.

I was disappointed that they didn't play with me and jealous when they met their friends in the courtyard and tell them stories about life on the farm. Some days I'd go into their room and leaf through their school books or go to Oma's house for a short visit.

Tante Grete, Mother's middle sister, wasn't there anymore. I missed her. Why did she have to move away? One day she was gone and Oma never spoke her name again.

Tante Grete had worked at Öttinger's, our neighborhood store. It had recently relocated closer to where we lived because the big store on Harbor Strasse had been bombed, flattened to the ground, with all the goods in the store and those in the storeroom now buried under a heap of rubble.

I liked the old store, because it carried so many wonderful things. Colored pencils, coloring books, wooden shoes, school supplies, aprons, and in the corner, a big barrel filled with salted herring from the North Sea.

The cabinet on the back wall had shelves on top and bins below. The bins were filled with bulk sugar and flour, and the shelves had tins and jars of all sizes on them. On the counter were blocks of butter and cheese to be cut into chunks for the customers. Sausages dangled from broomsticks that hung from the ceiling on ropes. They carried darning yarns and needles, shoelaces and almost everything one might need on the spur of the moment.

Tante Grete had been gone for a long time.

One day, when I went to Oma's house, to play with little Manfred, I was surprised to see a soldier standing in the middle of the kitchen. He looked familiar, but I didn't recognize him. He was tall and very thin.

"Guten Tag, Ulla," said the soldier. "You don't remember me, do you?"

I shook my head.

"I'm Manfred's father."

Then I remembered the wedding in the potato-cellar-church, with the plain wooden cross on the wall.

"Aren't you fighting in the war?"

"Yes, I am. I'm just passing through town to my new assignment and stopped for a short visit to see Tante Änne and Manfred."

Tante Änne came in and placed Manfred in his father's arms. He lifted him high above his head, threw him in the air and laughed with delight. Manfred squealed and reached for his father's hair.

Opa relaxed on the sofa puffing on his pipe. I climbed on his lap and watched Onkel Kurt play with Manfred.

"Time for your nap," Tante Änne said and took the toddler from his father's arms. She carried him upstairs.

Onkel Kurt turned to me and said, "Ulla! Öttinger had a barrel of salad oil delivered to the store when I walked by this morning. Would you go and buy some for me? It's a quiet day and the store is not far away."

"You want oil?" I said

"I haven't had fat for so long, I'm craving it."

"I'll go."

He pressed money and rationing cards into my hand and closed my fingers around them.

"Don't lose these," he said.

Then he gave me an empty wine bottle with a cork in it.

"Ask the saleslady to fill it."

I ran all the way to the store. When I stepped inside, I was shocked. The shelves were empty and the counter had nothing on it. I didn't see any wooden shoes or coloring books. Hardly any goods for sale piled on the counter. No sausages on the brooms-ticks. I looked around for the barrel of oil. It was sitting on a stool behind the counter.

A few women stood in line, each holding a bottle. They talked with the saleslady in hushed voices. I stood in behind them.

"When is this war going to end?" One woman said.

"Too bad they didn't get our Führer in June."

I recognized some of the women form the shelter.

When it was my turn I said, "Please fill the bottle with oil all the way to the top."

"Ulla, I can only give you half. I have to make the oil last so everyone can get a little," the saleslady said.

"But Onkel Kurt is visiting just for a day," I said. "He's craving fat."

The saleslady grinned, held the bottle under the spout and filled it more than half. I gave her the money, the rationing card and thanked her. I ran back home to Oma's house and felt relieved I heard no sirens.

Onkel Kurt smiled when I gave him the oil. He pulled the cork off the bottle and drank gulps of oil as if it were beer.

"Ach!" he said wiping his mouth with the back of his hand. "That was good."

I didn't know oil tasted so good. He pushed the cork back in and gave the bottle to Oma. She took it to store in her pantry.

Later that day, when everyone was busy, I sneaked into Oma's pantry unseen. It was actually a cabinet placed on the landing of the steps to the cellar. The top of the cabinet had doors with fine wire-mesh so flies couldn't get in. The bottom part had open shelves. I found the bottle with oil on the bottom, removed the cork and took a big gulp.

I gagged and spit it out. It landed on the wire-mesh doors and ran down the wall. It sprayed out my nose and went down my throat. I couldn't stop gagging and spitting until the last bit was gone.

My mouth felt fatty and slimy. Every time I closed it, I felt like throwing up. Quickly, I drank a swig of water from the faucet next to the cabinet. That made it worse. Then I drank milk right out of the milk can. That didn't help.

Finally, I pinched my nose and started breathing through my mouth. That took the awful taste away. For the rest of the day, I pinched my nose and stayed out of everyone's way.

The next day the family said good-bye to Onkel Kurt. He wasn't a stranger any more. Everyone gathered on the sidewalk and waved. He walked away with quick steps, looking sharp in his uniform.

Manfred gurgled. Tante Änne cupped her lips with one hand and whispered, "Come back whole."

Cold and Sad Winter, 1944

Chapter 21

Tante Änne had received a notice from the housing authority with the news that she was allotted a room at a farm in the Sauerland. Heavyhearted, we said goodbye to her and little Manfred. Even though the Sauerland was not that far, we didn't know when we would see them again.

The housing shortage had become severe in Essen. Opa said that our city had been destroyed and was flooded with homeless families. People who still had a home had to take in those who had lost theirs. A family moved into Oma's upstairs bedrooms. Oma and Opa brought their bed down into the living room. Tante Ruth slept in the little room half-way up the stairs. It was a very cold and damp room in the winter because it had three walls exposed to the elements.

The weather turned cold early that winter and it snowed more than ever. I liked the snow, but couldn't go outside because I needed to keep my only pair of hand-me-down shoes dry.

One blustery morning, at breakfast, Mother said, "I can't fire up the cannon stove in our bedroom because our coal supply in the cellar is almost gone. I wish I knew when we'll get our delivery."

Father looked up from his newspaper. "I put a request in a while ago. We probably won't be able to heat the bedrooms this winter because our allotment has been decreased."

After weeks of cold, slush and sleet, the windows in the upstairs bedrooms were covered with a permanent sheet of ice. The ice thawed a little during the day and became opaque but froze again at night covering the window with a design of beautiful ice flowers by morning. To Mother's amazement the wallpaper on our thick brick walls upstairs had ice crystals on it.

Father said, "The dampness seeps in through the mortar between the bricks."

When I went to bed, I could see my breath turn into a white fog. Mother filled our only hot water-bottle with hot water and put it under our covers before my brothers and I went to bed alternating between their bed and my parents' bed where I slept. The heat from the hot water-bottle made our feather comforters less clammy.

I made a peephole on the sheets of ice by breathing on one spot. Through it, I could see the strings of lights on the slagheap and the trams transporting coal to the coke furnaces.

I was glad our house didn't burn down last year when the rafters in the attic had caught fire during an attack. I remember Father was at work and Mother wouldn't let us in the house when we came home from the shelter. She and Tante Grete went into the house and carried our china cabinet outside, down the stone steps and set it in our front yard. I was surprised our china was still in the cabinet and none of it had broken.

I missed Tante Grete. Why didn't she come to visit us anymore? Maybe it was too dangerous now. I loved listening to her stories about her work in the grocery store. Usually she told us the news she heard from women coming to the store shopping for groceries, darning thread and other miscellaneous items. But one story she told was so sad and upsetting that I could not forget it.

She told us about the two sweet, old Jewish sisters who owned the millinery shop on Harbor Strasse. They made beautiful hats and all the women enjoyed wearing them. Tante Grete thought that under the Nazi regime they didn't get rationing cards. They were thin and hungry.

After dark, they knocked on the back door of the grocery store looking scared, begging for food. Herr Öttinger let them in and gave them bread, cheese, butter—whatever he could spare. But before he let them go, he asked Tante Grete and other clerks to go outside and check if the Gestapo lurked behind corners or in door-ways. When they came back inside and reported that it was safe to let the ladies out, they went home.

It was against the law to help Jews and Herr Öttinger worried about being reported. He would go to prison and lose the store. What would his wife and eight children live on?

Those old ladies wouldn't have harmed anyone. But they were picked up by the Gestapo anyway and Tante Grete never saw them again.

I missed Tante Grete. Maybe she'll visit for Christmas.

Why is the Sky so Red? 1944

Chapter 22

My father and I walked home from the coal miner's business office. The wind howled through the poplar trees and the temperature had dropped to freezing. I shivered. My nose felt frozen—my lips dry and sore. I skipped along the sidewalk, happy because the day had passed without bombing attacks.

A glowing shimmer in the evening sky caught my attention. Enchanted by its beauty I asked, "Pappa, why is the sky so red?"

We stopped. My hand cradled in his, both looking up over the brick houses and poplar trees that lined our street. The sky, aglow in shades of red, streaked with patches of gray, captivated me. I clapped my gloved hands and jumped up and down. Father looked at me and smiled.

"The *Christkind* is baking cookies for Christmas Eve," he said.

"I don't see an oven!"

"It's hidden behind those gray clouds," He pointed to bunched together silver-lined clouds.

"When Mamma bakes cookies, there is no red glow."

"You're seeing the radiance of hot coals in the oven reflected in the sky."

He turned the collar of his wool coat up, removed his gloves and stuffed them in his coat pockets. He bent down toward me and closed the top button on my coat. Then he pulled my cap over my ears. The tip of his nose and cheeks looked red and our breath turned into white puffs.

"Let's go home. Mamma is waiting," he said.

I reached for his hand. The snow crunched under our shoes on the frozen sidewalk.

"Pappa, when does the *Christkind* bring the cookies to our house?"

"When the candles are lit on the Christmas tree."

"I've never seen the *Christkind*."

"That's because he never makes a sound. After he rings the Christmas bell, he leaves quickly through the window."

My steps turned into skips, and the tail of my scarf danced behind me.

"Is that why the window is still open when we go into the living room after we hear the Christmas bell?"

"That's why," he said.

"Why isn't the sky red anymore?

"Because the fire in the oven has gone out."

"Trudy told me that the *Christkind* grants your wish if you were good. Is that true?"

"Ja," he said.

"How do I tell the Christkind my wish?"

"You mention it in your prayer."

My heart started to pound and my chest burst with happiness.

"Trudy has seen a bicycle, just big enough for little kids."

"I've read about them."

"That's what I'll wish for. I'll promise to be really good."

Father stopped and turned to me. The flickering streetlight behind him illuminated the edges of his hair like a halo. He looked sad.

"During the war it'll be impossible for the *Christkind* to bring you a bicycle."

"Why?"

"That's the way of war," he said softly.

We continued our walk home in silence. I didn't feel like skipping anymore. Sobs built up inside me.

"I wish the war was over," I stammered.

"This may be the last Christmas of the war. Allied forces have already captured the city of Aachen south of here, near the Belgium border"

"Is that bad?"

"No, Ursula, that is good. It may mean that the war will be over soon."

☙

Finally, it was Christmas Eve, the night the *Christkind* brought cookies and gifts. I was excited all day. I skipped through the house, up and down the wooden stairs, filled with anticipation. I knew my father couldn't know which gift the *Christkind* would bring.

"Ulla, sit down. You're wearing yourself out," Mother chided pulling a cake from the oven. The kitchen filled with the aroma of Christmas.

It was dark outside. Snowflakes whirled past our window illuminated by the glow from the kitchen lamp. The door to the living room was closed.

Mother had made the table especially festive with her embroidered tablecloth and good china.

"When is the *Christkind* coming?" I asked.

"Usually he comes when we're in church. But it's too dangerous to go that far from home—he'll probably come while we eat dinner."

The family gathered around the table. Father and Alfred sat on the sofa, Jürgen and I across from each other at the heads of the table, and Mother to my right.

I couldn't take my eyes off the living room door and listened.

Halfway through our meal, Mother excused herself and left the kitchen to go outside to the drop-closet. Finally I heard the Christmas bell and Mother returned. My brothers and I stormed into the living room. I dashed, past the candle-lit tree perched on our sewing machine table in the corner, to the window and searched the sky.

"I see him! Mamma, Pappa, kommt schnell. The *Christkind!* I saw him flying up there in the sky."

My parents joined me at the window. Father stroked my hair. Alfred and Jürgen giggled behind me. Father gave them a disapproving look.

We sang Christmas songs and my brothers and I had to recite poems before we could see what was hidden under the white cloth on the living room table.

While Alfred recited his poem, I looked around the room for my bicycle. It wasn't behind the Christmas tree, and not under the table. I craned my neck to peak behind the living room door, and looked to see whether it was behind the cast iron stove in the corner.

"Ursula, it's your turn to say a poem."

The verses I had practiced for days were gone from my memory. I couldn't remember the title, the author or a single word. Mother looked at me in disbelief.

"You knew it yesterday," she said.

After an agonizing eternity, she excused me and reached for the tablecloth.

Could the bicycle be hidden under there? No it wasn't. I saw only five Christmas plates filled with cookies, walnuts, apples and a pair of socks on each.

"Where is the gift I wished for?" I blurted. "Where's my bicycle?"

My parents looked at each other and said, "This year the *Christkind* couldn't bring one because all metal in Germany was used for the war."

I turned to Mother feeling disappointed. Her eyes looked sad. My chest tightened and tears gushed uncontrollably.

Mother pulled me close. "Let's be grateful that we are together. Remember last year Alfred and Jürgen were far away on the farm in East Prussia. Maybe next Christmas, the war will be over."

Sharing our Home, 1945

Chapter 23

In January one day, when we were all sitting around the kitchen table, everyone engrossed in their own activities, Father said, "I have something important to tell you."

Alfred and Jürgen stopped playing checkers. I had been watching them.

"In two days, a couple will be moving into our upstairs bedrooms."

I stared at my father. Jürgen's mouth dropped open.

"Who?" Alfred asked.

"It's someone I know from work and his wife. When I heard they had become homeless in yesterday's attack, I suggested it to them. It's better to have someone you know move in, instead of strangers."

"Where are we going to sleep?" I asked.

"Tomorrow, we're moving our bed into the living room but we'll leave Alfred and Jürgen's bed for them upstairs.

"Where are we going to sleep? The boys asked at the same time.

"Jürgen, you'll sleep on the couch in the living room. We're going to push it under the window to make room for our bed at the back wall. Ulla will sleep with us. Alfred will use the sofa in the kitchen."

"We'll be really crowded," Alfred said.

"Do they have children?" I asked

"Ja, a boy. I believe he lives with relatives in the Sauerland where he can go to school."

I was disappointed.

Mother looked up from darning socks. "Actually, we're lucky it's only two people. The housing authority could have sent us a family with several children before now. In these bad times, where so many people have lost their homes, we must share ours. They'll be cooking in our kitchen, store items in the cellar, use our coal bin and drop-closet."

"Where did they live?"

"On Harbor Strasse—the only belongings they have were in their emergency bag they had at the shelter. Herr Verschleuss is from Holland—his wife, I think, from the Sauerland. You might know them from the shelter."

Strangers living in our bedrooms unsettled me "Now I can't make a peephole on the ice flowers on the upstairs window any-more and look out," I complained.

"It will be a big adjustment for all of us." Mother said.

The next day I watched Opa and Father carry my parents' bed and wardrobe down the steps. They had trouble getting the war-drobe around the corner on the landing half-way down. They put the vanity with the mirror where the sewing machine used to be in the living room. There was hardly room to walk. Oma and mother cleaned the upstairs rooms to get them ready for newcomers.

The next day the Verschleuss' arrived. Mother introduced us and took them to their rooms. I overheard her talking upstairs. "Have a cup of tea with us when you're ready and then I'll show you the rest of the house."

When Mother came back to the kitchen I asked, "Why don't they dig some of their stuff out of the rubble at their house?"

"It's too dangerous. Walls and ceilings can cave in and bury them alive."

While Herr Verschleuss worked in the mine, his wife stayed mostly upstairs. She only used our kitchen rarely. Sometimes, she prepared something small. Mother thought that her husband might be purchasing hot meals from the single-miners-home kitchen. Occasionally, Mother offered her some of our food. Frau Verschleuss usually declined politely.

Mother washed clothes on Mondays. We dried them on lines in the cellar. Frau Verschleuss did her laundry after our items had dried. But it took days for them to dry in the cold and damp basement.

Herr Verschleuss worked in the same mine where Father and Opa worked but sometimes they had different shifts. Herr Verschleuss was friendly. He and Father often chatted in our entrance. Even though Father invited him into our kitchen, Herr Verschleuss never did come in.

I heard Mother complain to Oma once, "She always leaves for the shelter after we do but most of the time she forgets to lock the front door."

We were crowded in the two rooms. There was no place to play in the living room or in the kitchen. I was glad when Father brought a table and chairs for children that fit under the kitchen window. We played there so Mother could use the big table.

Sometimes during the night Alfred tip-toed into the living room to snuggled under the comforter with Jürgen on the sofa.

Jürgen looked grumpy in the morning and complained. "I can't sleep with Alfred on the couch. There isn't enough room to breathe."

Mother looked at Alfred. "Why don't you stay on the sofa? You have more room there."

"It's spooky being in the kitchen all alone," he said.

Sometimes my brothers went into the little room we used for storing things half-way up the stairwell. On one wall stood a bookshelf filled with Father's books. But the boys never stayed there long because it was too cold in the room.

One day when my brothers were in the little room and I looked at a picture book at the little table I heard Mother talk to Father. "You're gone for hours. I'm going crazy with the kids underfoot all day. It's too cold for them to play in the slush outside."

One day Father gave my brother's a book. "I want you boys to settle down in the house. Here, you can read the Max and Moritz book. Every page is filled with drawings and interesting stories. Read it together. You'll enjoy it."

All three of us liked looking at the pictures. Alfred read some stories aloud. Max and Moritz were boys who often got into trouble.

I welcomed Oma's invitation to celebrate our birthday together. "I'll bake a birthday cake for us this weekend and we'll eat it on a quiet day."

One morning, she knocked on the door and said, "Let's celebrate this afternoon. I'll grind real coffee beans for the occasion. We have to celebrate when we can because we don't know if we have to spend our birthday in the shelter."

When we went to her kitchen it smelled of fresh brewed coffee. In the middle of the table was the cake platter with a pound cake. After we were seated Oma poured the coffee and Tante Ruth served the cake.

Opa added sugar and milk to his coffee and turned to me. "You're six years old today."

"I know. How old are you Oma?"

"I was born in 1890. That makes me fifty five."

"That's old!"

Oma laughed and joined us at the table, "Let's give thanks for this quiet day."

We bowed our heads.

The cake was delicious. Oma dunked hers in her coffee.

Opa said, "This child's only memories are of war and catastrophe."

I looked from face to face. The grown-ups sipped their coffee in silence.

Oma cleared her throat. "I received a letter from Martha this morning and didn't tell you about it so I could read it while we are together."

Everyone paid attention.

≈

"My dear Family,

In these stressful times, I have wonderful news to tell you. In December, our daughter Ingrid Christel was born. She was baptized on Christmas. We are both well.

Margot and Karl-Heinz are delighted to have a little sister. I have written to Emil and hope he will receive this good news on the front. We haven't heard from him for a long time and I am worried about his health.

We have said goodbye to many friends. With a heavy heart they are leaving their farms and fields and are joining other refugees who are fleeing to the west.

I could not survive without the help of Irene the Russian woman and Eugene the war prisoner from France. I don't know how much longer I can stay. The Russians are closing in. My heart is troubled. I don't want to leave the farm. How could Emil ever find us?

For now we're sleeping in warm beds and have food. May God protect us.

Viele Grüsse, Eure Martha."

February, 1945

Chapter 24

Tante Ruth asked me one morning if I wanted to go with her to the beauty shop on Vogelheimer Strasse.

"Can I go, Mamma?"

"It's a long way and it's very cold outside."

While Tante Ruth helped me into my coat and tucked my scarf in, I slipped my knitted cap over my head and Mother tied the laces of my high-top shoes.

When we stepped outside—the air was cold. Through the bare branches of the poplar trees, I saw black smoke rise from the chimneys across the street. I pulled my gloves from my coat pocket and put them on.

Tante Ruth took my hand. We lowered our heads and walked into the wind.

"What are you carrying in your basket, Tante Ruth?"

"Shampoo and towels."

"Why are you bringing those?"

"The hairdresser needs them. She'll wash my hair before cutting it and then roll it up in curlers. You'll see how it's done when we get there."

On the sidewalk in the Vogelheimer Strasse, we slipped on the icy spots that were hard to see. When I lost my balance and fell, snow stuck to my knitted gloves. My hands got cold fast.

By the time we reached the beauty shop, my toes tingled. Tante Ruth rang the door bell. No answer. She pushed it again. We listened. No movement inside. She went to the window. On tiptoes she peeked inside.

"The lights aren't on. The hairdresser isn't in—where could she be?"

We trudged back home over the snow and ice-covered sidewalks. The wind picked up and chilled me. When we reached our street, my feet throbbed. My gloves were wet and my fingers ached. When I whimpered and complained, Tante Ruth rubbed my hands. I cried out in pain.

"Let's hurry home so we can warm up."

By the time we reached our house, I howled from the pain. Mother knew exactly what to do. She sat me on a chair near the stove and untied my shoes. I cried out when she pulled them off.

"I'm frozen too. I'll go home and warm up," said Tante Ruth.

Mother removed my wet stockings.

"Mamma, don't touch me. It hurts too much."

"Let me put these warm socks on. Your feet will hurt and tingle for a while, but soon they will feel better."

She took my hands and put them in the hollow of her arms. Her warm body made my hands sting and I wanted to pull them away, but Mother held them in place. After a long while, they felt better. Mother heated a cup of milk, added a teaspoon of honey and handed it to me. It tasted good and made me sleepy.

The next day was Sunday, February fourth, a bitter cold day. But our kitchen was warm. So far, it was a peaceful day—no attacks. After dinner, when Alfred returned from the cellar with a bucket filled with coal, sirens howled.

We grabbed our coats, caps, emergency bags and hurried outside. We raced down our street turned at Emscher Weg and ran toward our bomb shelter. The path had turned into a sheet of ice covered with a new dusting of snow.

People rushing in front of us held their arms out like wings trying not to slip. Their dangling handbags swung from side to side. I noticed that some of them wore socks over their shoes.

"Mamma, look, they're wearing socks on the outside of their shoes?"

"They hope they won't slip and fall."

Fascinated, I watched them while running next to Mother. Jürgen and Alfred were ahead.

"They're sliding anyway," I shouted.

"That's because the snow sticks to the socks and turns them into sheets of ice."

The second wave of sirens pierced the air. Mother took my hand and held it tight. The sirens sent shivers down by back. We hurried, slipping on the ice.

We rushed along the snow-covered fields on our right. They sparkled in the moonlight. A moment later, the moon disappeared behind the clouds and it started to snow. Mother ran faster.

The droning of airplanes came from behind. Suddenly, Alfred clutched his chest and gasped for air. He stumbled and stopped in the middle of the road. I heard his wheezing.

Mother let go of my hand and rushed to him. She put her arm around his shoulder and said. "Relax, breathe slowly. We're almost there."

Jürgen rushed to his brother's side.

Mother, with her arm still around Alfred said, "Let's walk slow-ly."

People hurried past us taking tiny steps.

"What's wrong with Alfred?" I asked.

"It's his heart."

The entrance to the shelter was congested with people stomping their feet and shaking off snow.

Once in the shelter and in our seats, I felt my feet throbbing. Melted snow seeped in through the seams of the shoes. My socks were wet.

Many people lived farther away from the shelter than we did. They continued to pile in. They didn't have time to shake off the snow because the first bombs were exploding outside.

"The bombers are diving down, shooting into the folks running to the shelter," an old man said.

That night, Father and Opa worked on the search and rescue team. They had the responsibility of keeping order in the shelter, helping those who needed assistance and accounting for those missing after the attack was over.

"Mamma, Tante Ruth and Oma aren't here."

"Maybe they left late, took the short cut through our garden and went to the entrance near the blacksmith shop," Mother said.

We huddled together.

"The explosions are getting closer," someone said

The shelter shook and rumbled. Lights flickered on and off. Mother seemed restless. She looked worried. Alfred's face was pale and Jürgen's eyes huge.

"I hope we don't have to spend the night," old Herr Stuhrmann said. Numbness came over me and I leaned against Mother.

Explosion upon explosion assailed the shelter. Our benches shook. I recognized direct hits, because they sounded different, but no bomb had ever broken through the shelter's ceiling.

When the lights went out someone said, "That was a bad one."

We sat in the dark. Alfred scooted close to me. His body trembled. I held onto Mother. Across the aisle, someone whispered the Lord's Prayer. Jürgen brushed by me and cuddled up to Mother. We sat in darkness for a long time. Finally, the monotone wails of the sirens announced the end of the attack. People stayed seated for a while. I listened for more bombs. All was quiet.

Someone lit a lantern. People rose from their seats, stretched their necks and shoulders. The man with the lantern guided us out.

When we walked back home along the Emscher Weg, Mother wouldn't stay by my side. She let go of my hand and ran to this neighbor or that asking, "Have you seen our Ruth, have you seen my mother?" No one had.

My brothers ran off looking for their friends. Alfred's couldn't forget his best friend who had been killed only a few weeks ago.

Then my mother said, "Ursula, you go home. I'll catch up with you later." Fear was in her voice.

Panicked, I pleaded, "Please Mamma, don't send me home. I'm afraid."

One of the Ehlert girls took my hand, "I'll walk with you."

I knew that the dark streaks in the snow were blood. I looked away. Was that a person's arm hanging in the tree? Was that a person's leg along the fence? I turned my head and looked at my shoes until we arrived home.

Oma stood in the opened door. I was relieved to see her.

"I never made it to the shelter," she said, wringing her hands. "Bombs exploded before I had a chance to leave. The alarm doesn't give us enough warning anymore."

"Is Tante Ruth here?" I asked.

"No, she was working on a dress at her sewing machine. I urged her to leave for the shelter. Didn't you see her?"

"No, Oma. Mamma is looking for her and for you."

"I'll go back and find Gertrud," Mia Ehlert said. "I'll tell her that you are at home."

"Ursula, go into your Oma's house. You'll be safe now."

I didn't feel safe, but climbed up the steps toward Oma. She only came into the house for a while but didn't sit down. She walked between the kitchen window and the front door, looking out, listening.

"I'll go outside for a moment," she said.

I followed behind her. The snow on the ground illuminated the dark of the night.

On the sidewalk people went back to their houses talked in hushed voices. Many were crying. Oma asked everyone passing by. "Have you seen our Ruth?' They shook their heads. She rushed to another group of people. Her voice, louder, "Have you seen our Ruth?"

No one had.

I recognized Alfred's pale face in the shadows of the poplar trees. Jürgen walked beside him. Instead of going home, they came into Oma's kitchen.

"Have you seen Tante Ruth?"

"No. Mamma and the Ehlert's are looking for her. Opa and Pappa are carrying the bodies back to the mine," Alfred said.

Oma's shoulders slumped. She folded her shaking hands. We waited inside. No one spoke.

After a while the front door opened and Mother walked in. "The team thinks they've accounted for everyone, but no one has seen Ruth."

Oma pulled her handkerchief from her apron pocket and wiped her nose.

"I'll make some peppermint tea." Mother picked up the kettle and filled it with water. She put tea leaves into the little sieve shaped like an egg and put it into the pot.

Oma started to cry. Mother set cups and saucers on the table. When she poured the boiling water into the teapot, Opa walked in. His face looked ashen.

"We've collected forty bodies and laid them down in rows in front of the horse stables,' he said. "Most have been identified. But I haven't seen Ruth."

"Why didn't Anton come home with you?" Mother asked.

"He won't give up until he finds her."

Oma sobbed. "She's only eighteen."

After we finished drinking the tea, Mother took us home. I was glad Jürgen slept on the couch near my parents' bed. Mother tucked me in. Alfred squeezed in next to Jürgen. He didn't complain.

Mother switched the light off and said, "I'm going back to Oma's."

Father worked through the night covering every inch of land between the shelter and our street. He found Tante Ruth's body in a field where no one expected her to be. Shrapnel had hit her head.

I could hear grandmother's agonizing wails all the way into our house. The next morning I heard that my friend Trudy's mother was killed.

The memorial was held in the chapel of the "Nordfriedhof," a cemetery a few miles from where we lived. Unfortunately, Mother's other three sisters, Tante Änne, Grete and Hildegard could not come because they lived too far away. On the morning of the funeral, Oma was dressed in a black coat, black hat, black stockings, black shoes and purse. Opa and Father wore a black band on the left sleeve of their coats. Our family started a procession down our street on foot. A few neighbors and Tante Ruth's boss, Fräulein Hüttemann, filed in behind us.

On the sidewalk across the street another group of neighbors dressed in black marched in the same direction. People spoke in whispers.

The grown-ups in our group walked in silence. Suddenly Oma stopped. Everyone waited behind her. She lifted her fist toward heaven and shouted, "No bomb is going to make me leave the grave of my child." She turned around and continued the procession.

We gathered at the chapel and walked behind the coffin to the grave site. Pale sunbeams pushed through the cloud-covered February sky. When the pastor asked us to bow our heads for prayer, I heard the droning of bombers and tensed. Someone gasped and left quietly. I looked at Oma. She did not move. Her eyes were closed, her head bent down. The engines got louder. People shuffled. I wanted to run away and looked at my parents. Father peered at the sky, Mother sat rigid, the pastor prayed. Over distant roof tops the bombers flew north. The humming grew fainter.

Later that day, when the adults gathered in Oma's house for ersatz coffee and cake and the temperature rose a little, Mother allowed me to play outside for a while as long as I stayed close to the house. I was alone and made designs in the dirt with a stick under the poplar trees in front of Ehlert's house. For no reason, I looked up over Oma's roof. Against the pale blue sky Tante Ruth's beautiful face appeared, bigger than life. Her auburn hair flowed to her shoulders. Her kind, big eyes looked at me. She smiled. I'll protect you forever. I knew it to be true. I looked at her until she faded away. Her calming eyes filled me with peace.

The Trek, 1945

Chapter 25

Our house became quiet after Tante Ruth's funeral. My brothers didn't rough-house as they used to and Oma came over to visit more often. She and Mother sat quietly weeping with their hands folded in their laps.

Oma said, "If I hadn't urged Ruth that night to go to the bomb shelter, she would have stayed at her sewing machine, and she would still be alive."

"This wasn't your fault," Mother replied wiping her nose.

I wasn't as sad as the adults, because I felt Tante Ruth's spirit inside me. I knew she protected me as she had promised when her calm face appeared to me in the sky.

Even though it was March, the days were dreary. Sleet and rain chilled the air.

One day, Father came home from work when my brothers and I had just finished our cabbage soup. He washed up and joined us at the dinner table. Mother had waited to eat with him and filled two bowls with steaming soup.

"The latest news the miners were talking about underground was that the American Army had crossed the Rhine River at Remagen," he said. "That's only fifty miles or so south of here."

Mother's spoon fell into her bowl. Everyone stared at Father.

"After our shift, we were called to an assembly. The situation is bad. We were told to pack our necessities and leave our homes as soon as possible."

"Where will we go?" Mother looked worried.

"We're to meet at the schoolyard on Vogelheimer Strasse the day after tomorrow. Someone will be there with instructions."

"Why do we have to leave?" I blurted.

"The evacuation is not mandatory but we were warned that heavy fighting was anticipated in this area. The Allies are expected to surround the entire industrial Ruhr Basin."

My brothers and I didn't leave the table. We listened to our parents discuss what we needed to pack.

The next morning, Father built a box from bits and pieces of wood and secured it on top of the rusted frame from an old baby carriage. "The wheels are spindly. God knows how long they'll last," he said.

I watched Mother fill the baby-carriage-cart with clothing, food, and the boys' bedding. She spread a blanket over the top and Father secured it with rope. Father brought the two-wheel pushcart into the front yard and scrubbed it. As soon as it was ready, Mother filled it. Father put a tarp over the top and tied it to the wooden frame.

Oma and Opa were busy in the adjoining yard loading up their belongings.

Mother turned to them and said, "Another year the children can't celebrate Easter."

In the afternoon, I wandered around every courtyard in our neighborhood. People were rushing out of their homes, arms loaded with household goods packing them into wagons and carts. I was excited to be going on a trip with our neighbors and ran home to tell Mother who was going.

When I reached our courtyard, I saw my father with a knife in his hand, bent over the sewer grate in the middle of our yard. He held our six-week-old pig down. Blood streamed from a cut in its neck into the drain.

Alarmed, I screamed, "Pappa! What are you doing?"

"Ulla, we can't take this pig with us. We don't know how long we'll be gone. It would starve if we left it here."

At that moment, a neighbor with an empty sack over his shoulder passed on the other side of the street. Father looked up and yelled, "Ludwig, come over here."

I ran into the house and watched from behind the front door.

"Do you want the pig's head?" Father asked. "I can't take it with me."

The neighbor nodded. "Ja, I'll take it. I'm staying here." He put the tiny head into his sack, said, "Danke, and good luck on the trek."

The image of the pig's tongue hanging from its open mouth haunted me. That night I woke up often and was still tired when, at dawn, Mother woke my brothers and me. After putting on our warm clothes, we bounded downstairs into the kitchen, ate jam sandwiches and drank ersatz coffee with the last drops of milk.

"It's time to go," Mother said.

In the front yard, Father took the pushcart and Mother the baby carriage. They pushed them toward the sidewalk. The boys and I followed. We stopped at the corner of Oma's house, turned around and looked at our green front door one last time.

The sidewalks were filled with bundled-up people pulling their wagons or pushing their two-wheelers heaped with household goods. Little children sat on top looking around.

The drawn-out trek walked east and then turned south toward Vogelheimer Strasse. When we arrived, the yard was already crowded with families. People scooted together to let the latecomers in.

Soon a man climbed on top of a heap of rubble and waved his hat. "Listen up! " He shouted.

Everyone stopped shuffling their feet and became quiet.

"We want to leave as soon as possible because we have more than seventy kilometers ahead of us. First, we're heading north to avoid Gelsenkirchen and Dortmund which are also primary targets of the Allies, and then we'll turn east toward Heeren-Werve, our destination. We're staying in a local grade school there."

A woman yelled, "Where will we sleep on the way?"

"In empty schoolyards and market places—let's hope we can find some halls with a roof on top."

Someone shouted from the middle of the crowd. "How long is it going to take?"

"It depends on how fast we can travel. Let's form a line now and stay together. There will be other groups on the road. I'll be in front, you line up behind me."

A light mist settled on us. Women tightened their headscarves and put caps on their children. People turned their carts around and headed out of the yard. We walked east on Vogelheimer Strasse and turned north on a broad street toward the Rhein-Herne-Canal bridge. Slowly we maneuvered through city streets and settled in for the night in a school yard in a damaged gymnasium with half a roof.

We took off the next morning at dawn. It seemed days before we left the cities, and continued on country roads. On the uneven surface Mother's cart broke down.

"What an Easter present," she moaned.

"The load was too much for it," Father said.

The caravan stopped and several men came to help. They lifted the cart and Father knelt down to look underneath.

"This one won't make it. Both axles are broken."

Everyone transferred items onto our other cart. "This one is sturdy—it'll do fine for the rest of the way."

On Easter Sunday we meandered along tree-lined roads. The sun peeked through at times. I looked for the Easter Bunny and ran ahead of our group searching under bushes and behind trees for colored eggs.

"Ulla, the Easter Bunny can't find us here," Father said. "We're always moving."

"I think I saw him jump way in front. He's probably hiding the eggs for all the children on the trek." Unperturbed, I ran ahead.

My brothers smirked when I returned empty handed. "Ulla, the Easter Bunny doesn't hide eggs on April Fool's Day."

"Stop it!" Mother's voice sounded sharp.

When we turned into a schoolyard that evening, a light drizzle made tiny pearls on our tarp. Before it turned dark, Mother had prepared a make-shift shelter under which we huddled. We had settled down next to the fence that separated the schoolyard from a garden that surrounded a white house with a pointed roof. It looked like a beautiful house in the Grimm's fairy tale book.

A lady with blond hair came out of the house and walked into the schoolyard. She stopped in front of our group and said, "I can bed several children in my home." She looked at me with her kind eyes. "This little one can sleep in two easy chairs pushed together. At least she won't be out in the rain."

My parents agreed. We said good night to them, and several children followed the lady through the garden and into the fairy tale house. The fragrance of lily of the valley trailed behind her. The aroma of hot cocoa greeted us in the entrance hall. It was warm inside.

"Hang your coats and shawls on the hooks behind the door and wash up," she said.

We took turns scrubbing our hands and faces in the porcelain sink in a tiled indoor bathroom. I had never seen such a beautiful toilet before.

"Come to the table and warm up with hot chocolate," she said.

It was delicious. Soon my cheeks warmed up. The kind lady took me to the living room and pushed two plush chairs together. "You'll have to sleep in your dress, but that's not so bad, is it?"

I shook my head and unlaced my high-top shoes.

She covered me with a warm blanket. "Sleep well," she said and closed the white lacquered door.

Through the wooden window shutters, I heard people talking outside.

I slept fitfully. The chairs kept moving apart. One time they separated so much that I fell to the floor.

The next morning the lady served us crisp Brötchen with butter, strawberry jam and soft-boiled eggs. "The Easter Bunny left them here," she whispered into my ear. Only he ran out of color."

I detected a faint scent of lily of the valley.

Evacuation, 1945

Chapter 27

After breakfast the next morning, I said, "Aufwiedersehn," to the kind lady in the Grimm's fairy tale house and met up with my parents in the school yard. They had already dismantled the make-shift shelter where they slept and finished loading the cart.

Father lifted me on top, "You're getting a ride today so you won't wear holes in the soles of your shoes."

I was grateful I didn't have to walk but once the cart was in motion, I had nothing to hold on to. The tarp was pulled so tight I couldn't grab any of it for support and worried I would slide off.

"Pappa, I'm slipping."

"Stay in the middle. After a while the bedding will settle and the weight of your body will make a little depression."

The trekkers lined up behind the leader and meandered out of the schoolyard gate on to the tree-lined sidewalk. Sometimes I had to duck to keep low growing branches from hitting my face. It was a dreary, overcast morning and the wind soon chilled my entire body. I shivered. My brothers' noses and cheeks had turned red.

We passed through villages and forest-lined fields. I wondered if we would ever get to our destination. Finally, we arrived in a small town where we marched through narrow streets looking for the school that was reserved for us. People peered from behind white lace curtains; others opened their windows and watched in silence.

The caravan turned into a schoolyard with tall linden trees and stopped between two tall brick houses. From behind the buildings, two camouflaged tanks with gun barrels pointing at us rumbled into view with wide-eyed soldiers looking out the turret hatch. Our group pulled their carts and wagons out of the way.

"What's going on? What are you doing here?" a young soldier asked.

My stomach tensed. I looked at my father but he didn't seem scared and I relaxed.

Several men from our group shouted at the same time, "Go West!"Get out of here. The war is almost over."

"Coming through!" a soldier yelled.

People pulled aside and the tanks rolled by at a snail's pace. When they reached the street, they thundered in the direction we came from.

The leader of our assembly climbed into the fork of a tree and shouted, "Listen up everyone. This is going to be our home until the war is over. We'll sleep in the gym over there and eat in the hall behind me. After you've unpacked, store your wagons in the rear." He pointed to the back of the gym. "A local relief group has prepared supper for us. They'll serve it after we're settled in."

We gathered around Father. Our cart was close to the steps of the gym.

Two women appeared in the door. "We'll help you set up."

Father untied the tarp. "Everyone has to carry something in." He handed a feather comforter to Mother. She climbed the steps. Alfred and Jürgen were loaded up with their bedding and I carried a blanket. We followed Mother into the huge gym. One of the ladies rushed ahead and pointed to a space on the floor. "This is where you can make your quarters. How many are you?"

"Five."

"You can have this much space." She pointed to a place on the wall and went away.

"Ulla put the blanket on the floor and spread it out," Mother said.

I worked hard to align it next to the wall and straightened it. Mother and my brothers piled the bedding on top of the blanket and went back outside to get more. I lay on my stomach on top of the soft comforters and looked around.

People also streamed in through the back door with their arms loaded up to their chins. The corners were occupied first. Soon the spaces against the walls were filled and the ladies instructed new-comers to line-up their bedding through the middle on the floor, leaving spaces for people to maneuver between the rows.

While I watched, my brothers dumped blankets and clothes on top of me and Alfred shouted, "Move, lazy."

"Let her be," Mother said. Father brought in pieces of wood which he had kept from the broken–down cart and built a low par-tition on one side of our space. Mother placed her traveling bags and Father's knapsack alongside.

Children checked out each other's quarters and adults talked. In the far corner, a man hammered nails into the walls, strung up a clothesline from one side to the next and hung a blanket over it.

Comfortable under the pile of blankets, my eyelids became heavy. The next thing I knew, I felt someone shaking me, "You had a nice nap," Mother said. "Come and let's eat."

"I'm warm in here. I don't want to get up."

"You better eat something or you won't make it through the night. Here is your bowl and spoon."

I got up, smoothed my wrinkled coat and followed Mother, bowl and spoon in hand, into the dining hall. People ate at long tables aligned in rows. We lined up at a table under the windows where women dished out bean soup and rye bread. It smelled deli-cious.

We joined Father and my brothers who had kept places for Mother and me. The soup was hot and tasted good. I broke my bread in pieces and floated it on top of the broth.

"I need your attention for a minute." A relief worker stood in the middle of the room waving a piece of paper in the air. "We have to form groups for kitchen duty. You'll alternate between cooking, cleaning and going to the near-by farms for vegetables and any meat products you can get. When you've finished eating, come by this table to sign up."

While the women signed up for kitchen duty, the boys stormed outside.

On the following morning, I woke up late. By the time I stepped outside, girls skipped rope and boys chased each other and climbed trees. Some explored the surrounding area. I loved being there. It was like belonging to a big family. Strangers patted me on the head. I felt safe. No more bombings and many children to play with.

At night, we sometimes heard the roaring of bombers in the distance, but we had no air attacks. At times, during the day, I thought I heard bombs explode far away and I remembered what Opa once said, "The British attack at night and the Americans bomb during the day."

One day, when Mother had kitchen duty, I went down the hill to the cook-house looking for her. But she wasn't there. I walked back outside and sat on the grass at the top of the hill gazing toward the forest. In the distance, I saw her and several other women pulling little wagons behind them. When they got closer, I noticed that they were filled with carrots, onions, potatoes and cabbages. In one wagon lay several white-feathered chickens with broken necks.

"We're eating well today," one lady said.

I followed the caravan to the cook-house where they unloaded the vegetables onto tables near the kitchen sink. The chickens were put into huge tubs. On the long stove, steam rose from a big kettle. Two women poured hot water over the chickens.

"Get out of the way little one," someone said.

I gagged from the horrible smell coming from the chickens.

"Children can't be in here," Mother said. "Go outside and play so you'll build up an appetite. I'll see you at dinner. We're having chicken stew today."

I ran back to the school and looked for my brothers. A man on a bicycle rode into the yard. He stopped under the linden tree where a group of men had gathered, my father among them.

"I've just come back from town," said the man. "People are saying the Americans have taken Essen but heavy fighting continues in the surrounding areas especially in the Sauerland."

"I wonder how long before the Americans arrive here," someone said.

"That's not all," the cyclist announced. "The Allies have agreed to divide Germany into four zones: American, English, French and Russian."

"Let's hope the Americans will hold Essen. God help us if the Rhine-Ruhr region is occupied by the Russians," Father said. I moved closer and cuddled against his leg. He took my hand, "Let's look for your brothers."

As we walked toward the empty field behind the gym, I asked, "Why do you want the Americans to hold Essen?"

He didn't answer for a while. When we reached the corner of the gym, he said, "Because they like children."

"What do they look like?"

"Oh, they're probably wearing brown helmets and coats."

At night, I saw the Americans in my dreams. They were huge brown birds with wide wingspans flying low to the ground along the edge of the forest looking for us. Days went by and I waited for them.

One morning, when I skipped toward the street, I heard a man shouting up the road a ways. He raced into view on a bicycle waving a white flag. "The Americans are coming. The Americans are coming."

Men, women and children came running and lined up next to me along the fence. Across the street, people opened their windows and leaned out.

When the cyclist passed our group he yelled, "They're just a day away," and continued down the street shouting, "The Americans are coming."

I was scared and excited at the same time and searched for my family. The adults talked about what to do. They looked nervous.

That night, I heard a woman's agonizing screams come from the far corner. I jumped up to run toward the sound. Mother's firm grip on my arm pulled me back.

"You can't go there, Ulla." The tone in her voice convinced me not to argue. Ear-piercing screams kept me awake most of the night.

The next morning, before breakfast, I walked toward the corner from which I heard the screams. A baby carriage stood next to a make-shift bed where a woman was sound asleep clutching a baby in her arms. An old woman sat on a wooden crate watching over them. She smiled at me. I rushed out of the back door.

I heard my mother's anxious voice. "Ulla! Where are you?"

Then I saw Alfred running toward me. "The Americans are approaching. We have to hide."

We ran back to our quarters. Mother grabbed her traveling bag and handed Alfred Father's knapsack. "Let's go!' she said. Jürgen put his backpack on and we rushed to the door. Everyone wanted to get out first.

Once outside, the leader of our group waved his hat and directed us into the cellar. We settled on a bench along the far wall and scooted together to make room for others. When everyone was seated, the leader put a finger on his lips, turned around and closed the door. People whispered.

"Where is Pappa?" I asked.

"With the men."

"Where are the men?"

"I don't know."

Then I heard a clicking sound. I looked around and saw that Alfred's teeth were chattering. His face was white, his eyes huge. Jürgen dug his teeth on his lower lip. His eyes were as big as Alfred's. I scooted closer to Mother. She felt rigid.

Then we heard loud voices outside. Everyone stopped talking. My hands started shaking and I dug them into Mother's arm. Pounding against the door. It flew open and crashed into the wall.

I saw the boots first, then the barrels of rifles. Boots descended the stone steps, many of them. I wanted to run away, but they would catch me. Their faces were young and looked scared, too. The soldiers pointed their rifles at us and spoke words I couldn't understand. People squirmed in their seats.

"Get up!" One of them shouted. "Leave your bags on the seats."

Benches screeched on the floor as people rose. "Move over there." We went to the corner he pointed to.

Other soldiers rummaged through purses, knapsacks and cardboard boxes, looked under the benches and moved them aside.

"What are they looking for, Mamma?"

"Guns and German uniforms."

"Why?"

"If they find uniforms, they think German soldiers are hiding among us."

After they examined every bag and every corner of the cellar, they left. We went back to our seat. Mother checked her bag.

"They took nothing," someone said.

I turned to Alfred. Color had returned to his face and his eyes were normal again. He looked at me with a faint smile.

An old man walked up the steps, stopped at the door and listened. "They're driving away." After a while, he opened the door and stepped outside. "The coast is clear," he said.

The boys jumped up and raced up the steps, squinted into the sunshine for a moment and ran outside. Women rose, stretching and smiling at each other.

"It's over," one of them said.

I ran after the boys. In the bright noon sun, they lined up against the fence. From the distance a caravan of war vehicles rolled toward us. When they got closer, we saw the back of the trucks loaded with soldiers. I wasn't afraid of them. When they passed in front of us, they smiled and threw something over the fence into the schoolyard. The kids screamed and scrambled to pick up the loot. "Candy!" someone shouted.

I decided to join the others. Every time I reached for a lump, someone else grabbed it. I tried again and again but ended up with nothing. Angry, I turned my back to the candy telling myself, I didn't want it anyway.

More American vehicles loaded with soldiers passed. Many of them chewed on something.

"What are they eating?" I asked.

"Chewing gum, Dummkopf," an older boy yelled.

"What color is it?"

"Brown, I think."

When the caravan ended, one by one people went back to the gym. Some women strolled toward the cookhouse and the men appeared. I was relieved to see Father, waved at him and went inside the eating hall. I found a brown paper bag, tore a piece off and chewed on it. It tasted ghastly and I spit it out.

When I strolled back to our sleeping quarters, my brothers sat cross-legged on the bedding with candy between them. Alfred handed me a hard ball wrapped in paper. I popped it over my lips. Sweet strawberry flavor filled my mouth.

Journey Home, 1945

Chapter 27

One evening when I went to the eating hall for supper, it was very noisy inside. I recognized the bicycle scout in the corner. Several men had gathered around him. I wandered over to them.

The scout said, "The sky over Essen and Dortmund is in flames. In town, people showed me a flier that had *German Troops, Trapped in the Ruhr Valley, Surrender* written on it."

A woman stood up and shouted, "When can we go home?"

Everybody stopped talking.

"I don't know," the cyclist said. "There's more. The Red Army has reached the outskirts of Berlin before the Americans. There's heavy fighting in the streets and from the air."

I looked around the room. Everyone gazed at the scout.

"It seems to me the Russians and the Americans want to get their hands on the man in the bunker," a burly man said.

"I heard the Italians captured Mussolini and his mistress and hung them in a public place where people could see that they were dead."

"That's terrible," I mumbled. The image of a dead man and woman hanging in a tree made my hands tremble. Where was Mother? She stood behind the tables serving dinner.

"Ulla, come here and have something to eat," she called. "I have your bowl and spoon."

"What are we having?"

"Boiled potatoes and creamed cabbage with bacon bits."

She filled my bowl. "Eat! You want to be strong for our trip home."

Bowl in hand I joined my giggling friends at a table near the door. I scooped a spoon full of potato smothered with cabbage sauce and bacon bits. It tasted good.

"Let's jump rope," Inge suggested. We left the table together and bolted outside. Two girls twirled each holding one end. The rest formed a line. One by one, we jumped over the rope just when it hit the ground spinning out at the other end, singing songs until it was too dark to see.

But the boys didn't stop playing soccer in the moonlight at the other end of the yard. We rushed to the bathrooms and washed our faces, necks and dirty knees. Back inside the gym, we changed into our nightgowns, met at one girl's sleeping quarters and talked until our eyelids got heavy.

During the day we enjoyed roaming through the fields near the school, making wreaths from wildflowers for our hair and laying in the grass watching the clouds float by. Sometimes the local girls joined us. The worry of air attacks had faded.

One morning, during breakfast, the group leader stepped on a chair and said, "Listen up! I have an announcement."

Everyone stopped chewing.

"We can start trekking home."

Cheers and whistling filled the hall.

"We'll leave early tomorrow. We'll stay on country roads going west. I don't know what the cities will look like. Crossing the canals and the river might be challenging. Some bridges have been destroyed. But we'll find a way."

Cheering erupted again then turned into laughter and hand shaking.

The next morning, I woke to the bustle of scurrying footsteps by my bed. To my surprise bedding and clothing were stacked in neat piles all over the gym's floor. My parents and brothers comforters and blankets were gone. I dressed in a hurry and rushed outside.

Wagons were lined up in front of the gym. Women pulled carts loaded with loaves of bread, cheese, sausage and marinated, hard-boiled eggs into the yard. They went from family to family handing them their portion. "This will carry us through the first days."

Across the street locals gathered on the sidewalk; others watched from their windows. Some of our new friends came over and helped load our carts.

The organizer of our group climbed into the fork of the linden tree and waved his cap "Let's make a final inspection."

Several men walked toward the gym, others to the eating hall. The women returned the empty carts to the cookhouse. My friends and I played hop scotch at the side of the school.

Although I looked forward to going home, I felt a pang of sadness at leaving. Here, I didn't worry about air attacks and made many new friends.

We stopped playing when the man in the tree yelled, "It looks like we're ready. Let's go!"

People pulled their wagons out of the yard and into the street. We waved to the locals. They waved back.

"When you get home, the war will be over," a toothless old woman shouted.

The sun peeked through the overcast sky. I turned back for one last look at the school. The tender leaves of the linden trees quivered in the breeze.

The village children ran along-side our caravan shouting, "Aufwiedersehn."

The air was warm. We left the town the way we came, and when we reached the country road, I noticed that the fields we had passed weeks earlier were greener and covered with wildflowers.

But the nights were cold as were the April showers. We slept huddled together under our tarp, sometimes at the edge of a forest, other times under trees in open fields.

Finally we arrived at the canal. The first people who reached the bridge turned around and shouted, "Kaput! Split in half."

The caravan stopped at the embankment and looked at the collapsed structure. It had broken in two even parts with its center under water in the canal.

Whispers arose from the crowd. "How are we going to get our carts across?"

"Let's figure this out," a man said.

Our guide climbed on to a cement block where the bridge's frame was once attached. He waved his cap until he had everyone's attention. "I need some men willing to test the integrity of the structure."

Hands went up.

"If it holds, the strongest will build a human chain, one on each side of the canal so we can lower the wagons here, and pull them up over there." He pointed to the embankment on the other side.

"We just have to figure out how to keep the bedding dry," a woman said.

The men nodded. "That's right." They walked toward a nearby willow tree and talked.

The women spread blankets where we had a view of the canal. It was lunchtime. Father cut a chunk of bread and joined the other men. Mother gave the boys eggs to peel and handed me a slice of rye. It was dry and hard. "These are the last eggs," she said.

My brothers gulped them down, took a slice of bread and ran off to meet other boys. They raced down the embankment toward the water.

"Boys! Stop! Mines!" Mothers screamed, rising to their feet. The boys froze.

The men came running and shouted, "Don't move! Mines are everywhere. You're safe where you are, just come back exactly the way you went down."

The youngsters' faces turned white. They hesitated, and then turned around. With careful steps they retraced the path they had taken before. No mines went off.

One woman slapped her son's face, "Don't ever run off again. I don't want to lose another child."

Women and children returned to their blankets and the men walked toward the bridge head. Two of them climbed down the steep incline holding on to the frame. I turned on to my stomach and watched. Halfway down, they stopped and prodded and pushed. One man jumped a few times.

After repeated testing, they looked up and shouted. "It doesn't budge. But we need to lay logs across the water to keep the wagons dry."

Some men got their axes and felled trees. Others pulled them to the bridge. When they looked stable, the leader waved his cap. "Load your wagons, people, and line up for the crossing."

The men who had wedged the tree trunks into position on the other side, stayed there.

Father fastened the tarp on our cart and pushed it toward the bridge. Mother, my brothers and I went with him. Two families were ahead of us.

Men lined up at the incline. A burly man went to the first cart to be lowered. He laid a rope over his shoulder and tied the ends to the handle bar. "Ready?" he said to the man next him. They linked arms. One man after another locked arms.

"I'll start going down," the first man in line shouted.

With locked arms, the chain of men eased the first cart down bracing against the steep incline of the bridge. Near the water's edge, another crew took the cart and maneuvered it to the other side where men waited to pull it up.

"That went well. Next!"

Then the families followed. Older women and men were assisted by younger, stronger men.

I crossed on my father's shoulders. He handed me to someone half-way across. My brothers didn't want any help.

It was dark when the last wagon was pulled to safety. We made camp for the night near the canal and enjoyed watching the setting sun.

At dawn, our trek home began anew. When we finally entered the first city street, we had to stay in the middle of the road because the sidewalks were covered with broken bricks and debris from bombed houses. A local man came toward us and guided the caravan to a soup kitchen near the train station. It felt good to sit on a bench and eat at a table. Everyone looked tired. Mother's hair needed combing. She had dark circles under her eyes. Some laid their heads on the table and fell asleep.

During our evacuation at the school, I hardly saw Oma and Opa. Their living quarters were on the other side of the gym. Now they joined us at the table and had soup with us.

Oma cried. "Why couldn't Ruth have survived just a few more weeks? She could be with us today."

"Oma, Tante Ruth is watching. She's protecting us," I said.

Oma looked at me surprised and dried her tears.

We continued after we were full. On a building I saw words written with red paint. "Pappa, what do those words say?"

"Tommy, go home!"

"Who is Tommy?"

"Some folks call English soldiers Tommy. We may be in the English zone."

"Why are people saying that?"

"Citizens are tired of conflict and want the soldiers to go home."

I looked around corners and behind trees for English soldiers. Maybe they'd give candy to children like the American soldiers had. But I never saw any.

The soles of my shoes had worn through and I could feel the street though my socks. For a while I walked on the side of my feet, but soon my ankles hurt. When we stopped for the night, Father found a piece of cardboard, traced the outline of the soles on it and cut them out with his pocket knife. He pushed the cut-out soles inside my shoes and said, "They'll work as long it doesn't rain."

Despite the dry weather, my cardboard soles wore out quickly. I took my shoes off and continued barefoot. Soon I had blisters on my feet and couldn't walk any more. Mother tore a sheet into strips and draped them around my wounds. The next morning, Father lifted me on top of our wagon.

My heart beat faster when I recognized houses. At the corner of Vogelheimer and Wiehagen Strasse, the caravan split up. On the way to our street, more houses lay in ruins. Some people seemed to live in them anyway.

"Ruin rats!" someone said.

"I haven't seen any rats."

Father said, "Some people call folks who live in bombed houses ruin rats."

I shuddered.

"God knows what our street will look like." Mother said.

When we turned the corner onto my beloved Wildstrasse, I strained my eyes to see if our house was still there. As we neared our soot-tarnished brick houses, upstairs windows flew open in the first few houses to our left and strangers looked at us. They spoke words I didn't understand.

"They're speaking Polish," Oma said.

Helga's mother sobbed, "They're in our house."

Helga looked scared. Our caravan moved on in silence.

A neighbor behind us said to Helga's mother, "You can stay with us. Our house is still standing."

"Look!" A group of older boys yelled, and pointed down the street. Huge, white chunks lay strewn in the middle of the road. The boys raced toward them, picked them up and smashed them on the street.

"Stop!" One of them shouted. "It's sugar!"

I slipped off the tarp and hobbled on my blistered feet toward the white lumps. "Come back, Ulla, you don't know if they're safe to eat," Mother bellowed.

"Why? Where did the sugar come from?"

"The sugar was probably stolen from the rat-infested ships in the harbor."

I gagged and dropped the little lump I held at my lips.

We pulled into our courtyard, Oma and Opa right behind us. Our front door stood open. "Someone broke into our house," Mother moaned.

"Let me go in first," Father said and disappeared behind the kitchen door.

"Anyone here?"

No answer.

We waited.

After a while, he returned looking grim.

"All our canned vegetable and fruit jars have been stolen. They even took our potatoes. At least they left the coal."

We stood stunned.

"Let's unload," Mother said. "Alfred, build a fire in the kitchen stove and heat water for tea."

Father untied the tarp. Everyone carried something inside. Mother opened the living room window and spread the feather comforters over the windowsill to air.

"Are Mr. and Mrs. Verschleuss coming back to live upstairs?" I asked.

"I'm sure they'll return once the coal mine becomes operational again. I think they went to stay with relatives in the Sauerland."

That night we only had sweetened peppermint tea for supper. Later I snuggled up under the comforter in our own bed.

End of the War, 1945

Chapter 28

Father discovered that the thieves hadn't found the two sacks of feed-grain he had stored last winter in the little room in the house to keep it dry and safe from rats.

"At least we have something to eat," Mother said

"That's true," Father answered. "I'll grind some grain with the feed-grinder. With the pig and chickens gone, we don't need fodder."

"Where are our chickens, Pappa?"

"I freed them before we went on the trek so they could forage for food in the garden and the fields."

"Why don't we look for them and bring them back?"

"Ulla, the chickens are long gone. There're too many hungry people out there."

Mother said, "We're fortunate to have this grain. I wouldn't know where to buy food. The butcher shop and grocery store are gone. Who knows if the baker has flour to bake bread or if the milkman has milk?"

"I'll grind some in the shed right now." Father left.

He returned, with a bowl filled with ground grain. Mother soaked it in water right away. When she cooked it, our kitchen smelled of animal fodder. We ate porridge with a little sugar sprinkled on top—but we had no milk. Mother made enough for three meals.

Father was excited that our vegetable seeds had not been stolen."It's the beginning of May—I better till the garden and get the seeds in the ground—unfortunately, we don't have planting potatoes."

The first few nights back home, I woke periodically. I thought I heard sirens. Even though there were no bombing attacks anymore, the dark hours were not peaceful. We heard men shouting outside and pounding on neighbors' doors a few houses away.

Opa came over one evening and told Father that the Polish soldiers were drunk and plundered homes, demanding schnapps, raiding people's wardrobes, and stealing clothes.

Opa understood Polish. He grew up in the city of Treuburg in East Prussia on the Polish border. My grandparents sometimes talked Polish when they didn't want me to hear what they were saying.

One evening after dinner Opa came over to talk with Father. "Tomorrow, a few men and I are going to the Polish camp to speak with the commander."

"That's a good idea—we're lucky, our house hasn't been raided so far."

The next day Opa reported back, "The officer in charge at the Polish camp is going to put a stop to the looting. But it would be difficult because the soldiers squatting in private homes refuse to go back to Poland. He was awaiting orders from Head Quarters to transport the soldiers in camp back home."

"What can we do to protect ourselves?" Mother asked.

"The commander urged us to report to him right away when we hear the men force their way into homes."

I liked the Polish soldiers. I watched them from the sidewalk. They always smiled at me and waved. Sometimes they walked arm in arm with women. One day, several of them strolled up our street, laughing and drinking from bottles wrapped in brown paper. I especially liked the pretty woman with the long, blond braid down her back. She always wore a colorful dress. All the soldiers wanted to kiss her. But she only giggled and pushed them away.

Days later, when my parents were tending the garden and my brothers had left with their friends, I heard shouting outside and hurried to the corner of Oma's house.

I was horrified to see three Polish soldiers run away from a man chasing them with a gun. The woman with the blond braid ran after the armed man screaming and flailing her arms. Shots pierced the air. One soldier faltered and collapsed on the pavement. He laid face down, legs spread away from his body. The gunman passed where the injured man was and pursued the other two who were running away.

When the woman reached the fallen man, she fell to her knees next to him cradling him in her arms, sobbing. I wanted to run to her but was too afraid. Soon a military vehicle with blaring sirens raced toward the scene. It stopped behind the hysterical woman. Two men in uniform got out speaking Polish.

I started when someone touched my shoulder. I turned around and looked into Father's serious face.

"Come into the house."

Frightened, I followed him into the kitchen.

"Ursula, although the war is almost over, our neighborhood is not safe. When you witness a commotion again, I want you to come into the house right away."

Shaken, I nodded.

But there wasn't much to do, and I liked watching what was going on in our street. One day Father even joined me at the corner of Oma's house.

"It's so quiet, Pappa."

"I know. No sirens or bombs explode—no clanging from the coke furnaces or grinding from the wheels of the mine shaft. All are destroyed."

"Is the war over?"

"It will be soon. Hitler is dead, our troops defeated."

"What will happen to us?"

"We'll be alright. We have each other." He patted my head and walked away.

147

༃

Father listened to the news on the radio every day now. One day I walked into the house and found my parents and brothers standing in front of the kitchen cabinet staring at the radio.

A man said, "The war is over. All fighting has ceased in Germany. Our country is occupied. The power of Government has been transferred to the Allies."

We stood quietly for a while then Father said, "That was Grand-Admiral Dönitz."

We looked at him.

He lowered his head and whispered, "Our country is in ashes"

Mother put her hand on his shoulder. "I'll make chamomile tea. The children are hungry. Let's eat."

No one spoke when Mother filled the bowls with porridge and poured tea into the cups.

She sat down and looked at us. "Thank God the war is over. You will be able to play outside again."

"But I don't have any shoes," I complained.

"It's warm enough to go out barefooted," Alfred said.

"That's not a good idea. The fields and roads are scattered with shrapnel," Mother warned.

A few days later, my brothers burst into the room carrying stacks of brown, enamel soup bowls. "The Russian war prisoners are gone," they shouted.

"Where did you get these bowls?" Mother asked.

"From the building in the forest, where the Russian war prisoners lived who worked in the coal mine," Alfred said.

"You have to take them back."

"Can't we keep a few as souvenirs? There are hundreds left in the kitchen over there," Jürgen said.

Alfred put a bowl filled with a white substance on the table. "I brought you some salt."

Mother looked away. "Keep a few, but take the rest back."

My brothers had fun roaming through the fields with their friends and rummaging through debris in the bombed-out factories on the other side of Harbor Strasse. On washday, when Mother was busy in the cellar, they came home and dumped empty bullet shells, pieces of shrapnel and scraps of metal on the kitchen table.

"What's the metal for?" I asked.

"This is magnesium we stripped from a British bomber that crashed in the field behind the defunct ammo factory."

"You're in trouble if you tell. We're going to have fireworks at New Year's Eve."

"How are you going to do that?"

"We have to find wire and empty tin cans first."

"Can I help?"

"Only if you keep quiet."

"I promise!"

For days I was giddy knowing a secret.

A week or so later, Mr. and Mrs. Verschleuss returned and moved back into our upstairs bedrooms. They carried their belongings in suitcases and a cardboard box.

When our sugar supply ran out, we ate the porridge plain. Even though I was hungry, without sugar, it tasted awful. Mother mentioned that our coal supply was so low and that she could only heat the stove for cooking.

After dusk one day, we heard a faint knock on our door. I went to the entrance and opened it.

A thin boy, Jürgen's age, held a small bucket out. "Can you spare a little coal? My mamma is sick. She's had a baby."

Mother lined up next to me and said, "Where do you live?"

"In a bombed-out house near Lüschershof."

"Where is your father?"

"He was killed in the war."

"Give me your bucket."

The boy looked at me and then over his shoulder. He seemed nervous. Mother returned with the pail and an old tin covered with a rag. "Here is a little coal and some porridge. Are you alone out here in the dark?"

"My brother is waiting over there."

An older, slender boy peered at us from under the poplar trees, holding a sack.

149

The little boy said, "Danke!" and scurried away.

I watched him pour the coal from his bucket into the sack his brother held open—then they disappeared. As Mother closed our door, I heard knocking at another house.

I couldn't fall asleep that night. The image of the boy with the big blue eyes and his mother holding a baby flashed through my mind.

Overnight, the Polish soldiers were gone and our neighbors were able to move back into their homes. The rooms were left in shambles. Wallpaper had been stripped from the walls, mattresses were on the floors, dirty clothes piled in the middle of the rooms, furniture chopped into firewood, and the corners in one room had been used instead of the chamber pots.

My spirit lifted when Father came in from the garden handing Mother a bouquet of lily of the valley.

"The mine is operational again and I've been called back to work. This is perfect timing. I just finished putting the vegetable seeds in the ground."

Tante Ruth, fourteen years old

Tante Ruth, 18 years old, killed February 4, 1945

Oma and Opa Schmidtmann

Parents with Jürgen and Alfred

Mother and Ursula in the Field, 1940

Alfred, Ursula and Jürgen, 1944

On the Farm in East Prussia, 1944
Tante Hildegard, Manfred, Tante Änne, Jürgen and Alfred

Margot, Jürgen, Karl-Heinz, Alfred

Edelgard and Margarete

Ursula, ten years old, 1949
Photo taken by door-to-door Photographer

Farm house in Bavaria where Father grew up.

House on the Wildstrasse

Nights After, 1945

Chapter 29

The nights were quiet now, no more plundering of homes. A curfew had been imposed on the population. No one was allowed outside after dark. Even though we were not supposed to be out late, my brothers, their friends and I often played hide and seek long after the sun had set.

I wanted to see what the English looked like but saw only American military patrols on our street.

Daylight lasted longer and the sun broke through the clouds between showers. Every day, Father meandered through our garden to see if the vegetable seeds had sprouted. When the seedlings were big enough, he thinned them out and planted rows of carrots, peas, beans, kohlrabi, onions and parsley in raised beds.

Mother could hardly wait to pick the first tender vegetables so she could make spring soup.

Everyone was glad that the men had started working in the coal mine again. The wheels of the mine-shaft squealed and flakes of soot settled on our houses, plants and fields as before.

After several peaceful nights, the pounding on doors started again. One evening, not long after our family had gone to bed, I heard men shouting outside. My parents sat up in bed.

Someone yelled, "Stop! Halt!"

Shots echoed through the night.

Alfred tiptoed into the living room from the kitchen where he slept, and said "Did you hear that?"

"Don't turn the light on," Father said. "They're close by."

Jürgen who usually slept through noise sat up on the couch under the window. A woman's agonizing screams pierced the night. "Hilfe! Please, someone help."

"Was that Frau Witten?" Alfred whispered.

My stomach churned.

Men's voices shouted in a foreign language.

"Americans," Father said. "I'll have to get iron sheets from somewhere to install on our windows and the front door to protect us from stray bullets."

We heard approaching vehicles and screeching brakes near Oma's house. "Over here!" A man shouted.

"They're across the street," Father said.

Alfred slipped under the covers on the sofa next to Jürgen.

"Go back to sleep," Mother insisted.

I cuddled up under the feather comforter, shaking. I listened to my parents and brothers whisper long after the vehicles from across the street had driven away.

When I awoke the next morning, I was alone in the house. I hurried outside in my nightgown to find my parents. I saw Mother standing next to Oma and Opa at the corner of their house and ran to them. Nearby, under the poplar trees, my brothers stood with their friends. All our neighbors seemed to be on the sidewalk.

"What happened?"

"Gisela Witten was shot," Mother said.

"Why?"

"It was an accident. The Americans were chasing a fugitive last night. They thought he was hiding in Witten's house. When he didn't come out, they blasted rifle shots through the front door. Gisela was sleeping in her crib. She's not even five."

"Is she dead?"

"We don't know."

"Gisela's uncle told us that the Americans were horrified they had shot a child and rushed her to the hospital," Opa said.

One by one, people went back to their homes.

"Let's go inside and eat," Mother said.

After I had dressed, I returned to the sidewalk many times that day hoping to hear news of Gisela. When a military jeep drove up and stopped across the street, people came to the sidewalks again. Two American soldiers got out and went to Witten's house. After a while they returned, accompanied by Gisela's mother. They got into the jeep and drove away.

Later we heard that a bullet went through Gisela's stomach but didn't damage other vital organs. She had lost much blood but had come out of surgery well.

~

One afternoon, I saw my brothers come into our courtyard carrying rusted tin cans and pieces of wire. They were so busy talking, they didn't see me. Instead of coming into the house, they rushed past our front gate to the back alley. I followed them.

They disappeared in the empty chicken-coop. I watched through an open slit in the door. They sat cross legged on the dirt floor and arranged several tin-cans in front of them, straightened the wires and laid them in a pile. I recognized the pieces of magnesium they had ripped from the crashed British bomber a few days ago.

Alfred got up. "I'll get some nails and a hammer." He pushed against the door. It banged into my nose before I could jump back.

"What are you doing here?"

"I want to help."

"If you tell, you're in trouble." He hurried away and returned with Father's hammer and rusted nails.

I slipped in to the coop behind Alfred. He handed the nails to Jürgen, kept the hammer and arranged the tin cans upside down on the ground.

Jürgen held the nail on the tin and Alfred pounded it with the hammer. They made holes in the bottom and all around the side.

"Ulla, give me the wires," Alfred said.

He twisted two pieces together, made a long loop and fastened the ends in holes on opposite sides near the rim of the rusted can.

"That's a great Schleuderbüchse." He stood up and swirled it around overhead.

159

"What are these for?" I asked.

"Fireworks!"

"But it's not New Year's Eve."

"We're practicing tonight after the American patrols are gone," Jürgen boasted.

"Hand me the metal cutter," said our older brother.

"What are you doing now?"

"Ulla, go back to the house. Mother might get suspicious. We'll come in after we finish cutting the magnesium into strips so they'll fit into the tin cans."

The boys didn't talk while eating their porridge. After we finished, Mother soaked the dishes in hot water in our big enamel bowl. My brothers left the table and went outside.

Father leaned back on the sofa and filled his pipe with tobacco from a leather pouch. "This is the last of it. But I'll enjoy it to the last puff."

"I have to use the drop-closet," I said and left. Once outside, I raced into the back alley where I saw my brothers and their friends a few houses away each holding a tin attached to a wire loop.

Alfred struck a match and held it to a rolled-up piece of paper. When it caught fire, he put it under his can filled with magnesium until it ignited and started to sizzle. He gripped the wire and twirled the can, sparks spewed through the holes. It looked like a Ferris wheel of dazzling stars against the darkening sky.

Soon Jürgen and the other boys also made Ferris wheels of stars. They smiled, their faces radiant. I watched in amazement. After a while, the tins glowed bright orange.

"Can I try once?"

"You're too short."

"Hush everybody," a boy whispered. "Did you hear that?"

Everyone stopped and listened. The sparks dimmed. Smoke rose toward the roof tops. A man shouted words I didn't understand followed by pounding on a door.

"They're in the back alley across the street."

"Run! Don't make any noise."

Everyone ran in the direction they had come from. We raced to the next house and peered around the corner.

"All's clear," Alfred said.

We hurried to the next house and the next until we arrived home. My brothers dunked their hot tins in a bucket of water in the chicken-coop and hid them.

"You go in first."

Mother was drying the dishes, Father smoking his pipe.

When the boys burst into the kitchen Alfred looked at my parents. "Did you hear the pounding on the doors?"

"Maybe they're Polish soldiers raiding homes again," Father said. "There! I hear it."

Herr Verschleuss who lived upstairs knocked and came in. "Did you hear that?"

Father nodded.

I climbed on the sofa behind the table and folded my hands in my lap.

Opa rushed in. "It's time to report them to the Polish military commander."

Father put his blue work jacket and cap on.

"Be careful." Mother said.

The three men left. I heard them in the back alley rushing by our window.

Mother turned around. "Where did you kids get so dirty? Wash up!"

Alfred poured hot water into a bowl and scrubbed his hands, face and neck. Then Jürgen and I did the same.

We all sat at the table listening.

Alfred said. "They're knocking on Borschart's door."

Mother rose, "I'm going down the cellar—I put a chamber pot down there. It's too dangerous to go outside to the drop-closet."

Mother left and my brothers went into the living room, kneeled on the couch under the window listening.

Sitting alone in the kitchen frightened me. The wooden floor planks creaked upstairs. Frau Verschleuss paced back and forth.

I heard men shouting in the distance, "Halt! Stop!" After a while again, "Halt!"

Then I heard rifle shots. Some ricocheted off the brick walls, more shots from a different direction.

Alfred and Jürgen whispered in the living room. I wondered why Mother was taking so long in the cellar.

Then I heard scratching at the kitchen window. "Open up," a familiar voice whispered.

I jumped off the couch and on top the table under the window. Frantically I pulled the shade up and opened the window. Herr Verschleuss' white face stared at me. His bloodless hands gripped the window frame.

"My wife! Call my wife."

I raced to the entry way and yelled up the stairs, "Frau Verschleuss! Come down," and hurried back to the window.

Herr Verschleuss' head had sunk to his chest and his fingers slipped away from the frame. He rolled down the bomb-protection mound he had been standing on and landed in the gutter.

Frantically I screamed, "Mamma, komm schnell. Herr Verschleuss is hurt."

Mother and Frau Verschleuss rushed into the kitchen at the same time.

"Where is he?"

"Out there!"

The women raced to the window. I heard gurgling sounds and labored breathing.

Frau Verschleuss screamed and climbed on the window sill. Mother pulled her back.

"You can't go out there like that. We'll bring him in together," Mother said.

Frau Verschleuss pressed her hands against her mouth and wailed.

My brothers came running, peered out the window and gasped. "We have to help him."

Mother said, "Shut the window and pull the shade down. Frau Verschleuss and I will go outside and bring him in. I'll switch the

162

lights off before I open the door. Lock it behind me and don't open it unless you hear my voice."

Mother took the weeping woman by the hand and pulled her along. The gurgling sounds grew faint. Alfred closed the window. I climbed back on to the sofa. My body trembled and I had trouble breathing. Then I heard the women outside.

"Take his ankles. I'll take his shoulders." Feet scuffed on the ground.

After an eternity, a tap on the door, Mother spoke softly, "Open up."

Shuffling in the entry way. Swift steps into the kitchen. The lights came on. They laid Herr Verschleuss on the floor. I peeked at him from under the table. Blood pulsated out of a hole in his neck and made a puddle on the wood planks.

Mother pressed a towel against the wound. Frau Verschleuss sank to the floor at his feet, holding her head, her mouth contorting into a soundless scream.

"Alfred, fill the big enamel bowl with water and bring me more towels." He scurried off and returned in a flash.

Strands of hair had fallen into Mother's face. She ignored it. Jürgen stood at the end of the table holding on to the edge. His eyes huge, his face pale.

We heard men's voices outside below our kitchen window. "Americans," Alfred said.

Steps in our front yard, pounding on the door.

"Open up!"

"You three, go to bed. Schnell!"

We scrambled into the living room. I sat up in bed and saw Herr Verschleuss' body through the open door.

Mother stopped mopping up the blood and went to the entry hall. "Who is it?"

"American security! Open up!" a demanding voice shouted.

The key turned in the lock. The door scraped over the tiles. Uniformed men rushed into the kitchen.

"Who is this?"

"Her husband."

"Why was he outside?"

"To report marauding soldiers, who were breaking into our neighbors' house, to the Polish military commander."

"Where are the others?

"We don't know of others."

An American knelt on the floor and touched Herr Verschleuss' wrist and examined his wound. "He's dead."

Frau Verschleuss sobbed.

"There were no Polish soldiers out tonight. The American security forces are conducting a door to door search" one of them said.

An older American looked into the living room and saw me. He came closer. His face was kind like Opa's.

"Children shouldn't be witnessing this." He closed the door.

My back stiffened. I gasped for air and tried to scream but my throat went dry. I wanted to jump out of my skin but remembered that I must remain whole. Then my body calmed, I fell back on the pillow. Blackness engulfed and protected me.

Everyone Worried about Someone, 1945

Chapter 30

The next morning Herr Verschleuss' body was gone and the wooden floor-planks in our kitchen were scrubbed clean. A bowl of porridge stood on the table. But I couldn't eat. Soap-laden vapor drifted up from the cellar. Mother must be washing the blood stained towels. I heard her clamber up the steps and into the kitchen.

"You slept for a long time. Eat your breakfast."

"Where is Pappa?"

"He's at work."

"Why didn't he come home last night?"

"The American military security suspected that there were more men outside. He thought it was too dangerous to come into the house."

"Where did he go?"

"He hid outside in the drop-closet and stayed there until it was safe to come in this morning."

"Pappa only wanted to go to the Polish commander."

"The American's didn't know that. They probably thought that Opa, Papa and Herr Verschleuss were fugitives."

"Did Opa hide, too?"

"Yes, he did."

"What did they do with Herr Verschleuss' body?"

"They took him to a mortuary. Eat! I have more laundry to do."

For weeks I had no appetite and was uncomfortable being alone in our kitchen. The smell of blood seemed to linger in the air. Frightened to step on the area of the floor where the body had lain, I made a detour around it every time Mother asked me to fetch something from the pantry or the cellar.

At breakfast one morning, Mother looked at me longer than usual. "I'm worried about you. You're losing weight. Your dresses are hanging loose on your body. If you don't eat, you'll get sick."

After Father finished breakfast, he took my hand. "Let's go into the garden."

"I don't want to go."

He put his hand on my shoulder. We went down the garden path. When we reached the flower beds, he stopped. "See the lilacs? They're blooming late this year. Look over there. The peonies are in full bloom. Let's pick a bouquet for Mamma."

He cut lilac branches with his pocket knife and gave them to me. They smelled good. Then he added long-stemmed peonies. When my arms were full, we went back to the house and arranged them in a porcelain vase. The sweet fragrance filled the kitchen and masked the smell of blood.

Days later, Frau Verschleuss said good-bye, "I'm going back to my family."

Mother scrubbed the floors and windows upstairs and Opa and Father moved our furniture back up.

"Sleeping upstairs will be safer," Father said. "Bullets can't hit us in our sleep."

Downstairs, Father and Opa installed rusty metal panels on the front door and the living room window.

"I think we're protected from stray bullets now," Mother said.

After that day our living room looked gloomy, because the metal panels blocked light from coming in.

☙

Everyone worried about a loved one. Father didn't know if his brother Franz, whose troops had been fighting on the eastern front, was still alive. And Tante Änne, living away from the family in the Sauerland, didn't know if Onkel Kurt had survived the war.

166

She wrote that the two spinsters who owned the farm were happy that she could help. Jan, the Polish war prisoner, who had worked on their farm during the war, stayed in Germany. The sisters were grateful.

Oma didn't know if her brother Emil had been captured by the Russians, or if Tante Martha and her three children had been able to escape from East Prussia before the Russian army rolled in.

Our neighbor, Frau Bach, hadn't heard from her eldest son Helmut, who was drafted during the last throes of the war. From her kitchen window she waited for the mailman every day.

One sunny morning while playing hopscotch under the poplar trees, I saw Frau Bach leaning out of her window talking to Anneliese Haus.

"I can't stand not knowing if Helmut is dead or alive," she said, "Maybe he is in an army hospital or prison camp somewhere. Tonight I'm going to find out."

"How are you going to do that?" Anneliese asked.

"I'm having a séance at my house."

"A séance?"

"Yes. Do you want to come?"

"I don't know. Do they really work?"

"Oh yes, they do. Frau Herbs and Lottie are coming and many other neighbors who are worried about their men."

"We don't know if my brother Ewald has survived. He was drafted when Helmut was. Maybe I should come."

Excited, I ran home. "Pappa, Frau Bach is having a séance tonight. She's going to find out if Helmut is dead or alive. You should go. Then you'll know what happened to Onkel Franz."

He shook his head, "Ulla, you can't find out from a séance if someone is alive."

I didn't believe him. After dinner that evening I thought about the séance while barely listening to my parents and brothers talk about the food shortage.

"I must take a trip to Bavaria, visit Kathel and scrounge food from the farmers." Father said.

Mother looked up. "I've heard the trains are more crowded now than during the war. People are standing outside on the footboards. Starving folks from the cities are flocking to the country, begging. They barter for morsels with jewelry, even their wedding rings, family silver and china."

"It's bad, I know, but the farmers I went to school with will have something for us." Father said. "I'll take Alfred with me. He can carry a knapsack and a suitcase."

Alfred eyes lit up. While everyone talked, I slipped out of the kitchen and headed to Frau Bach's house. I hurried along the sidewalk close to the houses, peeking around every corner for patrols until I reached the courtyard where the Bach's lived.

I crouched behind a fence and waited to see who else was coming. Frau Herbs and Lotti rushed by. Anneliese and others followed. I slipped inside after them unnoticed and stayed behind the grown-ups.

The kitchen was filled with people. After a while, I squeezed between them to see what everyone was looking at. No one paid attention to me. In the middle of the room stood a little table covered with a floor-length tablecloth. On it, silver candle sticks with candles, a black Bible and a rectangular board with holes along its edge. Little pegs lay next to it on the tablecloth. I spotted Frau Bach. She wore a black dress, her hair combed neatly and tucked behind her ears.

"I think we're all here." She lit the candles. "Someone turn the light out."

The flickering flames made shadows on the ceiling and the walls. The room became quiet except for Mr. Bach's pigeons cooing in the attic.

A tall, dark-haired woman behind the table put a black lace scarf on her head. In a deep voice she said, "Let's begin." She wrapped a long cord with shiny tassels at the ends around the Bible and pushed a ring down to hold the book in place.

With a serious expression, she handed it to Frau Bach who gripped the cord below the tassels and straightened her arm so the Bible dangled in front of her.

The dark-haired woman's eyelids fluttered, her raspy voice said, "The Good Book has to be completely still. Then you can ask your question. Be patient. Wait until it gives you a sign. A clockwise motion indicates he is alive. A counterclockwise turn means he is not."

Frau Bach gazed at the Bible. Her face looked grey. Everyone stared at her. I was nervous. Shuffling on the floor stopped.

The tall woman closed her eyes, waited. "I feel a presence. It's weak but getting stronger." Her head tipped back. "Come closer, someone wants to talk to you."

"Helmut, is that you? Can you hear me?" Frau Bach whispered. "Please give me a sign."

Everyone waited, staring at the Bible. The room was quiet. The doves cooed. The air was warm and stuffy.

With a breaking voice, Frau Bach pleaded, "Helmut! Please talk to me."

"There!" someone said. "It stirred ever so slightly."

I strained my eyes. Was that a tiny tug?

"There! —Again! See?" People mumbled.

I couldn't tell in which direction it had moved.

Frau Bach slumped on a chair clutching the Bible to her chest. Her eyes rose to the ceiling. "He's alive!"

Feet rustled on the wooden planks. People whispered. "That's amazing," someone said.

I couldn't stay in the eerie room another minute. Shaken, I slipped out running all the way home looking over my shoulder.

Once inside, Mother looked up from her mending. "Where have you been? You look like you've seen a ghost."

Dangerous Games, 1945

Chapter 31

At dawn our street was deserted as we said goodbye to Father and Alfred when they left for the train station. Train schedules were unpredictable and the trip to southern Germany where Father grew up might take even longer than during the war.

"Heaven knows when you'll be back," Mother said.

"We'll bring eggs and sausages back for you," Alfred boasted.

Mother smiled. "That would be nice."

With his older brother gone, Jürgen took off with his friends and Mother told me not to trail after them. Lonely and bored, with no one to play with, I went up the stairs to the boys' bedroom and looked out the window. I had not been able to do that while the Verschleuss' lived upstairs.

In the field behind our garden, a big bomb crater had drawn ground water. It looked like a little pond with grasses and reeds growing around its rim. Father wanted to leave it that way.

In the sky, above the coal mine, I saw two wild ducks flying in for a landing. They'd been coming to the pond for a while.

Father told me they were Mallards. The one with brown feathers and orange bill was the hen and the bigger one, with a shiny green head and a white stripe at its neck, was the drake. He thought that the hen was probably looking for a suitable nesting area in the surrounding rushes and weeds.

I loved observing the pair swimming side by side, flapping their wings and dunking their heads into the water with their tails sticking up in the air.

From the corner of my eye I noticed something orange flicker in the distance. I strained to see what it was. Are those flames? Flames have no legs and flailing arms. Oh my God, it was a person on fire, running toward the pond. The ducks flew off when he jumped into the water. Men raced after him, dove in and helped him.

Frightened, I shut the window and ran downstairs. Mother wasn't in the house. When I opened the front door, I saw her with a policeman in the courtyard. I froze.

The policeman said, "Several boys were seriously burnt last week when they ignited magnesium strips in tin cans. Some are hospitalized. One of them will be disfigured for life."

"That's horrible," Mother said. "The boys are bored because they can't go to school, and there are no youth activities at church."

"True," the policeman said. "That's probably why they're combing through the fields looking for war mementos. They don't realize how dangerous that can be. One youngster was killed when an incendiary bomb exploded in his hand."

Mother's hand flew to her mouth. "How terrifying!"

"That's why we're going from house to house warning parents. You need to talk with your sons. Tell them the police will pick boys up who are collecting bombs and take them to the station."

"That'll scare them. I'll ask my husband to speak to them."

"Auf Wiedersehen, Frau Fischer, I hope our schools and churches will be rebuilt soon."

Quietly, I stepped back into the entrance, rushed inside and jumped on the sofa waiting for Mother to come in.

I was nervous. Did she know that I had followed my brothers and their friends a few times when they rummaged for bomb shells and shrapnel with interesting designs. One afternoon we saw two boys carrying a heavy log, "Look! We found a bomb," they shouted beaming.

"Ja, ja, ja!" The boys in our group answered.

A few days later we heard that the person who jumped into the pond was an older boy who lived not far from us. We all knew him. He had been scraping the dirt from the shell of a fire-bomb. Then it detonated. He incurred severe phosphor burns and was in critical condition.

We didn't see him for a long time. Months later, a tall boy came toward me on the sidewalk. I knew who he was. His face looked like it had no skin, just gnarled, shiny, red scars. Part of his nose was missing and his head was covered with thin patches of hair. I looked down and noticed his burned fingers when he came near me. They must hurt when he moved them I thought.

Father and Alfred were gone for a long time. I missed them. We would have a lot to tell them when they returned. I knew Jürgen felt lost without his older brother. He walked forlorn through the rooms and didn't talk much. Mealtimes were quiet.

"Mamma, when is Pappa coming home?" I asked.

"They've been gone for over a week. I expect them any day now. Why don't you watch for them from the corner of Oma's house?"

Every morning and afternoon I'd go to the corner looking up and down our street. I wondered when Herr Tennagel would return with his horse drawn wagon filled with vegetables and when the baker would be delivering fresh baked bread again. It would be nice to hear the fish man's bell ring on Fridays announcing the arrival of fresh herring from the North Sea. Even the rickety old dump truck delivering the allotment of coal Mother was waiting for would be welcome.

But no one came.

Then I recognized Father's floppy hat and Alfred, next to him, carrying a knapsack and suitcase. I ran toward them waving and laughing. I threw my arms around Father and kissed his hand.

"Pappa, you've come back."

Even Alfred looked happy to see me. Father cradled a chicken wrapped in a checkered shirt in the crook of his arm.

"Pappa, you were going to bring us eggs."

"I did. But I also brought a hen. If we're lucky, we'll have little chicks soon."

When I tried to pet her, she snapped at my hand and struggled to get away from me. Her red wattle jiggled. Father stroked her back and she settled down.

"Let's go home and make a nest for the hen in the empty pigpen in the stall." Father said.

"Why not in the chicken-coop behind the house?"

"Because someone would steal it in the night."

When the three of us walked into the kitchen, Mother mended socks and Jürgen played with wooden blocks on the floor. Jürgen jumped up and ran to his brother and Mother took a deep breath, "You're home," she sighed.

Father removed his hat and hung it on a peg. His curly black hair looked disheveled. The hen struggled. After a few gentle strokes on her head, she calmed and Father removed the shirt. He lifted the hen and showed Mother.

"She started brooding just before we left and fought Kathel when she took her from the nest. I brought the hay from her nest and all her eggs. This is an experiment. She may reject the eggs and throw them out of the nest"

"Did you bring food?" Jürgen asked. He never seemed to get enough to eat.

"Yes I did, but first I'll prepare a box for the hen and help her get used to her new surroundings, then I'll unpack. Boys, come and help me."

While my brothers and Father were gone, I stayed in the kitchen with my eyes glued to the travel bags. What was in there?

Eventually they returned and Father unpacked. He placed two round farmers' bread on the table and a ring of smoked blood sausage. Jürgen moved closer and smelled it.

"These eggs are for eating," Father said.

Mother brought an enamel bowl and put the eggs in.

"Frau Kraus gave me this piece of bacon and Kathel wild blueberry jam, a few rutabagas and potatoes.

"We won't have to eat porridge tonight," Jürgen said.

173

"We only have enough grain left for one or two more meals." Mother said. She closed all the windows in the house. "We can't let the smell of frying bacon escape outside. It would torture the people who have nothing to eat."

Without being asked, my brothers set the dinner table as soon as Mother started cooking. The aroma of sizzling bacon made my mouth water and I joined my brothers at the table. Father came in when Mother put the pan heaped with fried potatoes, diced bacon and scrambled eggs in the middle of the table.

"Let's fold our hands and thank the Lord for our good fortune." We bowed our heads.

She filled our plates with the most delicious dinner we'd had since returning from the trek. Alfred and Father told us about their trip.

"Hungry people are dragging themselves from farm to farm begging for food. Many are only skin and bones. We saw women trailed by young children roaming along country roads," Father said.

I listened to every word.

After dinner Alfred and Jürgen went outside. I cuddled next to Father on the sofa.

"When will we get little chicks?" I asked.

"If the hen won't reject these eggs, in about three weeks," Father said. "I hope one will be a rooster so he can fertilize the eggs the new hens will lay when they're grown. If we're fortunate, we'll have many chicks and give some to our neighbors."

"I can hardly wait to hold one," I said.

"Why don't you play outside for a while," Mother said. "It's staying light longer."

Through the kitchen window I saw the elderberry bush in front of Opa's chicken coup sway gently in the breeze. White petals from its blossoms swirled through the air.

As I left the kitchen, I heard Mother say, "The boys have been playing dangerous games."

I didn't think it was dangerous when we played because no one got hurt.

Registering for School, 1945

Chapter 32

Mother guarded the bounty Father had brought from Bavaria. She stored the bacon and blood sausage inside a pot in the pantry to protect them from mice. Then she marked the top of the two round farmer's breads with a knife indicating where to make a cut. I watched her count each slot she had marked on the crust with the tip of the knife.

"A loaf yields twenty five slices. Two yield fifty. Each of us can have one slice per day for the next ten days."

"That's a long time," I said.

"It may seem that way to you but it really isn't. The sausages and bacon will soon be gone too. But if we have a few more sunny days, the first tender vegetables can be harvested. Then I'll make spring soup and add a piece of the smoked bacon."

"That sounds so good."

"It is a good meal to celebrate the end of the dreary cold days with the vegetables of spring.

Mother never used a cutting board for slicing bread. She always held the loaves in place with her left hand and pressed it against her bosom slicing toward her body. The knife never slipped. This day, she cut five even slices from the bread and arranged them on the wooden serving board. She fetched the blood sausage from the pantry and cut five pieces of different lengths, the biggest one for Father, and the smallest for me. My mouth watered watching her prepare supper.

"We're fortunate to have such a plentiful meal," she said. "So many people don't have relatives with farms who can help them."

While we ate, Father said, "Reconstruction of a school in Berge-borbeck has begun. Classrooms will be ready in the fall for the higher grades. Monday is registration."

The boys cheered.

"In Bergeborbeck?" Mother said. "That's three kilometers from here. "

"I know. But building materials are scarce. They chose a school that accommodates students from several districts."

"Can I register too?"

"We'll try. You were supposed to start first grade in the spring but the war was still on."

"I'm concerned," Mother said. "The children are so slim. It's more than an hour each way. I don't know if they have the strength to walk so far. Until now they've been eating mostly porridge every meal since we returned from the evacuation."

I didn't care how long I had to walk. I wanted to start school.

Father left the dinner table and took his cap from the peg behind the kitchen door. "I'll go to the pigsty and check on the hen. I wonder if she's thrown the eggs out of the nest. Alfred, go to the field behind our garden and pick a pail full of greens for the hen. Later, I want you boys to polish your shoes for school registration day."

"I suggest all three of you run off some energy outside before bedtime." Mother said as she cleared the table.

After Father and Alfred left, Jürgen tugged on Mother's apron and looked at her with his big brown eyes, "I'm still hungry."

She took something from her apron pocket and put it in his hand. I had seen her break a piece from her bread at supper and put it in her pocket. "Go and play now," she said.

Father had repaired my high-top shoes with soles he had removed from Tante Ruth's pumps. When Alfred and Jürgen polished their shoes on the stone landing outside, he handed them mine and said, "Shine these too."

On Monday morning Mother combed my hair longer than usual and tied a white, satin bow in my braids. My brothers wore knee socks, navy blue shorts and short-sleeved shirts. Mother looked pretty in her light grey dress with a tiny white flower design and a hat with a feather on the side.

We walked down the Harbor Strasse hill over the Emscher River Bridge and passed the potato-cellar-church we had attended during the war. On both sides of the street houses lay in ruins.

I saw an old man sitting on a stool between heaps of debris chiseling the mortar from bricks. He tossed the cleaned-up ones into a wheel barrel next to him. Children collected pieces of wood and stacked them on a cleared spot on the sidewalk. A few steps further, a bent-over woman rummaged through rubbish in a bombed out kitchen. A dangling stovepipe barely attached to the collapsed ceiling swayed over her head

We walked in the middle of the street most of the time because the sidewalks were covered with broken bricks. In front of us children dressed in school clothes and their mothers wearing hats or head-scarves walked in the same direction we did.

When I thought I couldn't take another step, we made a right turn and the ghostly ruin of the bombed-out Rosenkranz church looming into the sky across the street caught my attention. The destroyed façade, crumbling walls and gaping holes in the ceiling made an eerie silhouette against the grey morning sky. Dangling wooden beams clanged against the shattered windows.

Mother hurried her steps and pulled me along. After we trudged through a few more winding streets, we entered the gate to the fenced in schoolyard and passed by stacks of bricks and terracotta tiles. Men hammered on the roof. Others worked in windowless classrooms. Once inside the building, we followed the stream of mothers and students along a hallway to a big room where a row of rectangular tables were set up against the far wall.

"You stay here," Mother said. "I'm going to find out where we need to line-up."

When it was our turn, a lady asked for my brothers' names, birth dates and grades last attended. Finally it was my turn and

Mother recited my name and birthday. I could barely stand still, I was so excited.

The lady put her fountain pen down and looked up. "We don't have a classroom for first graders yet. You'll have to come back later when more rooms have been finished."

"She's so ready," Mother said. "How am I going to keep her occupied all day?"

"You can try registering her for kindergarten. One will open soon near where you live at the corner of Wiehagen and Wildstrasse. They have to accept first graders first."

I was sure everyone in the room had heard that I couldn't start school and was certain they all thought I wasn't smart enough. The boys were probably smirking behind my back. I kept my head down and looked at the floor boards. My mother took my hand and dragged me out of the room.

Once outside the held-in tears spilled down my cheeks and an agonizing howl burst from deep inside. I sobbed all the way home. When we turned on to Harbor Strasse, Mother tugged on my arm, "Ursula, that's enough. Everyone is looking at us. Your brothers are embarrassed and went across the street."

I let go of her hand, walked behind her and kept my distance. When I saw a billboard, I stopped in front of it and looked up. I moved my lips mimicking reading the words and hoped someone would see me and think I could read.

Once I arrived at home I had no more tears left. Mother had already changed into her work dress and apron. She looked at me and said, "Put your play clothes on and come with me into the garden. You can help pick vegetables for spring soup."

Back in the kitchen, I watched Mother from my favorite seat on the sofa peel and dice the vegetables. She added them to the boiling water in the soup pot on the stove.

She closed our window. "We don't have enough to share with others."

Then she diced onions and bacon and fried them in a pan. "I'll add these later to the soup."

Soon the kitchen smelled wonderful. When Father came home from the mine, the boys came in from playing. They took a deep breath.

"What smells so good?"

Father looked at me and said, "I have good news. Ursula has been accepted in kindergarten. She can start next week."

The spring soup tasted especially good.

Tante Martha, 1945

Chapter 33

On my first day at kindergarten, the teacher showed me where girls and boys were making patterns with wooden blocks. I had never seen flat, colorful blocks like that before.

Mother turned to leave and said, "I'll be back at eleven."

"I'll go with you."

"Ursula, you stay here."

I sobbed.

"She's not been away from me for a while," Mother said.

The teacher came to me. "Let me show you how to make a star." She spread colorful blocks on the table.

I looked toward the door—Mother was gone.

Through the veil of tears I watched the teacher align red and yellow triangles into a starburst. "Now you make a design."

The girl next to me had made a tree and the boy across the table a house. I put some blocks together to make a flower. It looked nice. Later the teacher showed us how to make a necklace with wooden beads and allowed us to put them around our necks. At recess, we played hide and seek in the yard. Back inside, we held hands and formed a circle. The teacher taught us a song we were going to sing every day before going home, "Heim wollen wir gehen."

Mother returned. I skipped next to her all the way to our front door.

After lunch, my brothers left for school. Because there weren't enough teachers or classrooms for a full day of lessons, their classes started in the afternoon. The minute they closed the kitchen door, it opened again, and Oma came in holding a letter.

"From Martha," she said wiping her red eyes with a white handkerchief. "Here, read it."

Mother took the letter and sat down on the sofa. I scooted next to her.

She read aloud.

"My dear Anna and family,

I know you must be worried about us. I often wondered if you received the announcement I sent you before Christmas with the happy news that our little daughter Ingrid Christel had arrived. Much has happened since then. I hardly know where to begin.

Back in January when everyone was worried about the approaching Russian army, many of our neighbors left East Prussia. With Emil at war, a newborn baby and Margot and Heinz still so young, I hesitated to abandon our farm. The weather was bitter cold, the snow meters high.

One morning, Margot went to school as usual. When she entered her classroom, no children were there. Her second grade teacher stood behind her desk packing the schoolbooks into boxes.

She looked alarmed when she saw Margot and said, "What are you doing here? There is no more school. Everyone is leaving."

Frightened, Margot hurried home and told me what the teacher had said. That's when I began to worry, too. If we left, Emil wouldn't know how to find us. You know your brother; he would have been beside himself.

On January 19, I heard the public announcement to leave immediately and go west. The Russians were only a few days away. It seemed I had no choice. My heart was heavy thinking about leaving our beloved farm and fields, the farm where you, dear Anna, grew up.

You remember the Frenchman Eugene, and the Russian woman Irene, who had been assigned to work on our farm after they were brought to Germany as war prisoners? Without them, I would not have been able to tend the farm. They were so helpful and kind to us when the baby was born and did not abandon me when it was time to leave.

They wanted to go west, too. Together, we planned what to take. I stuffed warm clothes and bedding into sacks and Irene packed food into boxes. Eugene filled sacks with oats and feed for the horses to last for a long trip. We loaded the wagon while Eugene readied the horses.

At four o'clock in the afternoon, in four degrees below freezing temperatures, we climbed onto the wagon and Eugene took the reins. Irene sat next to him on the driver's seat, and the children and I huddled under fur-wraps in the back. When we pulled out of the barnyard, a paralyzing silence set in, and I watched the farm fade in the wintery mist.

We traveled throughout the night and the next day to gain distance between us and the advancing Russian army. We stopped the next night in an abandoned farm. Eugene fed the horses and rubbed them down. Irene laid out our nourishment. We rested for a few hours, then continued during the night steering west throughout the next day.

In the evening, we joined other refugees and stayed with them overnight in an abandoned barn. The following day was slow going. The country road was congested with streams of refugees and wounded soldiers. The Russian army was gaining on us. We decided to drive north toward the Baltic Sea to the city of Elbing. The Russian army arrived there about the same time we did. They fired into the refugees killing two children and wounding many others.

We headed for the train station and decided it was best to split up. The children and I were to take the train and Eugene and Irene were going to take the horses and wagon west. At the station I noticed a freight train. The conductor told me it was the last one out of Elbing. I rushed into the station and found an empty room where I changed the baby's diaper. Margot and Heinz watched our belongings.

When I returned to the platform with Ingrid in my arms, the train had started to move. With the help of a female station attendant, the children and some of our belongings were pushed through an open window into a freight car. People on the inside pulled them in. At the last minute, I jumped on. The baby carriage stayed behind on the aisle.

We shared the freight car with the sick, wounded, old and young and slept huddled together on the floor. The next morning we found four pillows from the baby carriage the station attendant had thrown in after me.

The train progressed slowly on the way to the city of Dirschau, often stopping to repair tracks. On one of those stops the engineer told me we would have at least a one-hour layover. I took the opportunity to venture with Margot to a nearby farm hoping I could boil water to make fennel tea for the baby. She had developed a worrisome cough. A lady in the freight car offered to look after Heinz and little Ingrid. When we returned to the tracks twenty minutes later we watched in disbelief the train was already moving.

People inside the cars yelled frantically out the window to stop to no avail. We raced after it. Folks stretched out their arms and pulled Margot in. With a burst of energy I jumped on to the running board and held on until I was pulled in, too. With a grateful heart, I thanked God for uniting me with my children.

During the night shots were fired at the train. At dawn we stopped. The engineer announced there were no more tracks. I folded a blanket into a pouch, put it over my shoulder and tied the ends behind my neck. I wanted to keep the baby close to my body. We disembarked, carrying a suitcase in one hand and a travel bag in the other.

At the edge of the forest, I saw the outlines of three Russian tanks. The lady who had looked after Heinz and the baby said, "It's only three kilometers to Dirschau. She joined us and together we hurried toward the Weichsel River. German soldiers helped us cross the bridge just before they dynamited it. We were thirsty but had no water and sucked on icicles instead.

When we arrived at the train station in Dirschau, it was overflowing with refugees. Loudspeakers announced names of missing persons. Somehow Heinz became separated from us. I was frantic. Everyone helped to locate him. Thankfully, he was found quickly. The only train on the tracks was getting ready to leave. Exhausted and scared, Margot started to sob which caught the attention of the good-hearted engineer. He saw my predicament with three children and took us to a passenger compartment with one available seat. Margot and Heinz sat on the suitcase.

The lady who had helped us decided to head north to the city of Danzig on the Baltic Sea. We hugged and said goodbye. She was an angel sent from heaven. After riding for a day and night without stopping, we arrived in the city of Stargard in Pomerania. Kind people from the village served us hot food in the station. They tended sick and feeble travelers and offered them a place to stay.

We continued to the city of Stettin on the Baltic Sea. There we switched trains to Berlin. On January 27 we reached the capital and looked up distant relatives on my mother's side, hoping their apartment had not been bombed. They were home and took us in. We were all exhausted. The baby's cold had settled in her chest. For a few days we did get some rest until bombing attacks occurred day and night. Often we barely made it to the shelters and I was certain we were going to meet our end in Berlin. I prayed to God to take us all together. When we left the shelter one day, the Reichstag was in flames. It was time to leave.

On the second of February, after a six day stay, we said good-bye to our relatives in Berlin and boarded a train to Hanover. During the night, the train was shot at but it didn't stop. In the morning we disembarked in a small village. We were the first refugees to arrive from the eastern front and were taken to a house in a nearby village where a widow and her daughter took us in. By this time, the baby was very sick. We called a doctor who said she had pneumonia.

My sweet baby Ingrid Christel, just three month old, died on February 10 never having met her father. The mayor of the town made all the arrangements for a Christian funeral.

Margot started school there in the spring. On April 10, American troops arrived and two days later English tanks rolled into town.

My heart stopped when in August a letter arrived from my beloved Emil from an English prisoner of war hospital. Margot and Heinz rejoiced when they heard their father was alive. Even though Emil was very sick, the British released him so I could take care of him at home. The children were happy to see their father. But I could see that he was not well. Soon his illness took a turn for the worse and he was taken to a hospital near Hamburg.

I was worried being so far away from him. Weeks later, the doctor called me to come soon, saying Emil was gravely ill. The children were taken in by a farmer's wife and I traveled to the hospital. The doctors allowed me to take care of him. After ten days, he too closed his eyes forever. His last wish was to be buried next to our baby daughter. Distraught I walked into the heather the next day and wove two wreaths from heather *branches and placed them on his coffin for the train ride to his final resting place. I'm grateful that I could accompany him.*

Weeks later, Eugene and Irene somehow found us, exhausted but safe, with tired horses and the wagon. It felt like being united with family but they didn't want to stay and headed west toward France, Eugene's homeland.

I know this is not news you wanted to hear, dear Anna. You have lost your youngest brother. The war is over. May God give me strength to go forward and provide loving care to the two children he has left me.

Your sister-in-law, Martha"

New Chicks, 1945

Chapter 34

The letter from Tante Martha saddened everyone. Alfred was especially grief-stricken. He had enjoyed working beside Onkel Emil on the farm and in the fields.

But Father captured our attention one day when he came into the kitchen holding a tiny chick in his hands. Mother, my brothers and I were still at the supper table.

"The eggs are hatching," he said. "But the hen has thrown this chick out of the nest, because it's deformed."

Alfred and Jürgen jumped up. "Let's see!" They shouted.

Father came to the table. Nestled in the hollow of his hands was a tiny yellow body. It had two heads. Its eyes were closed and its chest moved rapidly.

"When a chick is born like this, it won't survive—but I wanted you to see it." Father said. "Usually they are too weak to crack the shell and die inside the eggs."

"That's amazing," Alfred said. "

"How do the chicks know when to come out?" I asked.

"They know instinctively when they're ready. They peck at the shell from the inside until it cracks. When the hole is big enough they'll jump out. I better go back and see how many have hatched." He left cradling the fragile creature in his hands.

The next day Father told us that all chicks but the one with two heads had survived. Mother cared for them when Father worked.

The chicks grew fast. One warm afternoons, Father opened the door of the animal stall so the hen and her young could venture out into our fenced front yard. Alfred gave them the greens he had picked in the field behind our garden. At night, Father put them back inside and locked the door.

The chicken-coop behind the house had a leaky roof and the mesh in the door was torn. Father said, "If I could find a piece of corrugated metal in a bombed-out building, I could make repairs. I also would like to fix the fence around the run behind the coop."

Soon the yellow chicks had little white feathers growing on their backs and wings. We put them in the chicken-run during the day but locked the door.

Father said, "They need light and a little sun so they'll lay eggs."

I liked watching the chicks scratch and peck in the dirt and scurry around in the run. Sometimes the rooster chased them. They seemed to grow a little every day. One afternoon, when I peeked at them in the run, Father was there spreading fresh greens on the ground.

"Pappa, when will they start laying eggs?

"Oh, Ulla, when they're about five or six months old. It may take longer for these chickens because we haven't been able to feed them any grain."

One day, I played after kindergarten with my friends and came home late. My brothers had already left for school and Mother was not in the house. She had kept the porridge warm in a pot on the back of the stove for Father and me.

While I ate, I heard a commotion in the back alley through the open kitchen window. I went outside. A crowd had gathered in front of the Bednuts' house. The front door to the home was to the alley. Inside the house, a woman screamed. The sound of glass crashing against a wall and shattering to the ground surprised me. What was going on?

As I got closer, I saw canning jars fly out of the cellar window and smash into pieces in the alley. People jumped back to keep splinters of glass from hitting them, or fruit and vegetables from splattering their clothes. The jars came fast. That must be Frau Bednuts having one of her spells. Her slurred words were frightening.

A woman next to me whispered, "She just came home from the hospital."

"Maybe having a child every year was too much for her," someone said.

"That and the war."

Several of the Bednuts' children appeared in the entry way. The little ones looked frightened. One clutched a blanket to his cheek, sucking his thumb. I smiled when I saw Irmgard peek over her brothers and sisters heads. She gasped when she saw the onlookers and stepped back into the house.

Her oldest brother Ewald rushed down the stone steps. People made room for him to pass.

"Can we help?" a neighbor asked.

"I have to get Pappa from the mine," he shouted.

He mounted a bicycle that had been leaning against the wall and rode away.

His Mother started cussing. I felt sad for him and his siblings. I didn't see Helga who was supposed to be in my kindergarten group, but she didn't come to class very often.

For a while it was quiet and no jars flew through the window. Then I heard bursts of angry shouts and glass smashing into pieces inside.

Herr Bednuts pushed through the crowd.

A man asked, "Should we send someone for an ambulance?"

"Ewald is already on his way." Herr Bednuts grimaced when he saw the mound of glass and food in the alley and rushed up the stone steps into the house.

The screams turned into agonizing moans when I heard Herr Bednuts talking in the cellar. Jars stopped flying out. The moans turned into sobs and eventually stopped. No one spoke.

The ambulance arrived. Men rushed into the house. Someone grabbed my arm from behind and pulled me away. I turned around and looked into Mother's serious face. "Come home! I don't want you to gawk when someone is in so much pain."

Mother wouldn't let go of my arm. Unwilling, I stumbled away with her, but turned around and saw men carrying a stretcher up the steps.

"How do you think the Bednuts children feel seeing onlookers staring at them?" Mother sounded angry. "They're frightened and their mother is very sick."

I felt awful. "What will happen to them?"

"They'll probably be taken to an orphanage."

That evening I didn't feel like eating and put my fried potatoes on Jürgen's plate without Mother seeing. He ate every bite.

My brothers were upset too when they heard how sick our friends' mother was. They played with the older boys, but Ewald, the oldest, often couldn't come out because he had to take care of the little ones.

Alfred said, "Ewald hasn't been coming to school."

We didn't see the Bednuts children again.

☙

Caring for our new chicks helped take our minds off the sad event. When the chicks were four weeks old, they had lots of feathers and the hen started laying eggs again.

When Father removed eggs from the nest, the hen pecked his hand. It bled. "She wants to brood again. Too bad we have no grown rooster to fertilize the eggs," he said.

When we had collected enough eggs for a meal, my brothers and I watched Mother scramble them. She added a little flour and water and made a thin batter.

"This will fill your stomachs."

The aroma of green onions frying in the pan made my mouth water. Mother added the eggs to the pan and stirred them with a wooden spoon until they were cooked but still moist.

While we ate our delicious dinner, Father said, "If the young rooster survives he'll fertilize the eggs of our new chicks. Then we can let the hen breed again and we have another set of chicks."

"Thank God for that," Mother said.

Days later, the mailman delivered an envelope with a black border around it. Mother looked shocked. "It's from Tante Kathel."

When Father came home from work that day, Mother gave him the unopened letter and asked me to play outside for a while.

That evening Father looked sad. He told us that his youngest brother Franz had died. I remembered being at his and Tante Fannie's wedding in Bavaria.

"Franz was severely wounded in the last days of the war when his battalion retreated," Father said lowering his head. "He lost so much blood that he became too weak to walk. A soldier in his troop loaded him into a wheel barrel he had found on the way and pushed him. But he never made it home. He died in a nearby hospital when the war was already over."

I climbed under the table, into Father's lap and kissed his cheek.

Summer, 1945

Chapter 35

When the days became longer we had a stretch of warm weather and some of our vegetables could be harvested. All seemed well for a while until alarming reports came from neighbors at the end of our street. Someone had been stealing vegetables from their gardens during the night.

One evening, there was a knock at our door, and Father invited Herr Lamm in. He removed his cap and said. "Guten Abend Anton." He turned to my father. "We're having a meeting at my house after supper tonight."

Father nodded.

"Last night," our neighbor continued. "I watched over our garden from my upstairs bedroom window. Around midnight, shadows climbed over the fence and crawled on the ground into my vegetable patch. I hurried outside. But when I got there, they were gone. My garden gate scratching on the ground must've warned them."

Father said, "I'll be there."

Throughout the summer, at night, the men took turns keeping watch over the neighborhood gardens for thieves.

Father called them poor devils. "They have nothing. Many are refugees from the east who are looking for food and work."

So far no vegetables were stolen from our garden. Father thought we were lucky that we lived in the middle of the block. It would be harder for thieves to get away.

Even children at kindergarten talked about the vegetable thieves. In the sandbox, at recess, a boy said, "Do you know there are starving people in the city who are stealing children and making sausages out of them?"

"That's not true," a little girl said.

"Yes it is. My brothers told me."

After kindergarten class ended, I was frightened walking home and looked behind me every few steps to see if someone followed me. That evening, I was too scared to go to bed and Mother asked my brothers to let me sleep with them until she came up.

A few days later when I was sitting on the hole in our outside drop-closet, I heard Opa talking to someone. I pushed the window open and saw my father and Herr Lamm.

"The men on night watch found a dead body slumped over in Wolf's potato patch."

I gasped. My hand flew to my mouth. My arm scraped against the metal hook on the wall which held newspaper squares for wiping. I wondered why there were only three pieces left.

Rubbing the scratch on my arm, I heard Herr Lamm say, "He was just skin and bones."

"Although I was upset, I stayed inside the drop-closet until the men left. Then I ran into our house, found Mother in the kitchen mending, and jumped on her lap.

"What's going on?" she asked.

"We're out of newspaper in the drop-closet," I stammered.

"That's because no papers have been printed in Essen since we returned from that long trek in April."

"What are we going to do?"

"I don't know. Papa heard that the American army command is publishing a paper called Die Neue Ruhr Zeitung. But I don't know where we can buy it."

When I heard a knock at the door I forgot to tell her about the dead man in the field. A friendly woman with curly blond hair came in.

"My name is Ingrid Müller. I'm a seamstress and lost my sewing machine when my apartment was bombed. I'm doing alterations for families on your street. Your neighbors let me use their machine. I could set it up in your house. Do you need something done?"

"Ja! I do. You can use my machine." Mother pointed at me. "This one needs a new coat and cap. Can you alter my sister's winter coat? She was a seamstress too. Unfortunately she was killed in February."

"I'm sorry for your loss. Where did she work?" The friendly lady asked while taking a little notebook from her purse.

"At Hütteman's in Bergeborbeck."

"What was her name?

"Ruth Schmidtmann."

Frau Müller's face turned pale and she sat down on a chair next to the stove. With a quivering voice she said, "I knew Ruthy. I met her when I helped out at her work sometimes. She was so young."

Mother wiped her eyes.

No one spoke as the seamstress leafed through her note book. "I'm just beginning work in your street. I'll be able to start your coat before the weather turns cold. I can begin earlier, separating seams, washing and pressing the pieces at my home. I'll come by one evening to take measurements."

"You're that busy?" Mother asked.

"It seems everyone needs something altered. Children have outgrown their clothes and men have holes in their pants. Please don't give the work to someone else. I have no other income."

"I won't." Mother said.

"You can trust me with the coat. Can I pick it up tomorrow evening?"

Mother agreed and accompanied the seamstress to the door.

"Aufwiedersehn," they said and smiled.

After our vegetables were harvested and Mother canned a few of them, it started raining. It was a warm downpour. Several girls and I danced barefoot in puddles on the sidewalk singing, "Regen, Regen Tröpfchen...." We believed that would make our hair grow faster.

On my way home from kindergarten one day it rained hard. But I didn't mind. Like the boys across the street, I jumped into every puddle. My braids already seemed longer.

But Mother was upset when I got home dripping. "Stay in the entry and take your clothes and shoes off."

A puddle formed on the tiled floor. Mother took my shoes, stuffed them with old rags and placed them on the opened oven door to dry. She gave me a cup of her hot ersatz coffee and stirred a little milk into it. It tasted good.

The next morning, I couldn't find my shoes and asked Mother where she put them.

"Ach, meine Güte," she gasped, rushed to the stove and opened the oven door.

Inside were my shoes all curled up, only half their size.

"I intended to leave the door closed only while I cooked last night but forgot to open it again. I've never done that before." Her face turned red. "Ulla, you can't go to kindergarten today. You have no other shoes."

One afternoon, Gisela Moore from across the street wanted me to play outside. I said, "My mother only lets me play in the courtyard because I have no shoes."

"I have an extra pair of wooden shoes. Let's go to my house. I'll give them to you." Gisela said.

Inside, her house was dark. The drapes were drawn. I had never been there before. In the entrance, aligned in a row, were three pairs of wooden shoes. One of the pairs was small and red with an edelweiss painted on top.

"How come you have so many?" I asked.

"Shush! My mother is napping."

She pointed to a pair. "You can have these."

"Don't you have to ask your mother?"

"No, I don't like those. I have new ones."

"Where did you get them?"

"From my aunt in Holland."

The floorboard squeaked upstairs.

"Here, take them. Go quick! But don't put them on until you're home."

I grabbed them. She opened the door and pushed me out. I ran across the street and into our back alley. There, I stopped slipped into the wooden shoes and strutted home. I was surprised how hard and stiff they were inside not soft like leather shoes. I liked the light wood and pointed tips and paraded up and down the alley. They clacked with every step. After a while, I had blisters on both feet. I took them off, went home barefooted and hid them under my bed.

The next day Gisela and her Mother came to our house. "Ursula took wooden shoes from our house," Frau Moor said.

"Gisela gave them to me," I said.

"I wouldn't have allowed her to do that," Frau Moor said.

"Ursula, do you have these shoes?" My mother asked.

I nodded sheepishly and fetched them from under the bed. Frau Moore grabbed them and huffed away.

Autumn, 1945

Chapter 36

Autumn winds rustled through the poplar trees and yellow leaves tumbled through the air covering the sidewalks and street with a thick, colorful blanket.

Up the street, men wearing blue work suits and caps swept the leaves into huge mounds. I enjoyed watching them. Gisela Witten appeared across the street. I had not seen her since she was released from the American hospital. Her blond hair had grown but she looked thin and pale. I wondered if the bullet was still inside her body.

When the workers had made several piles of leaves in a row, they swung the brooms over their shoulders and walked back to their truck. I jumped into a pile of leaves in front of Ehlert's house. My bottom hit the ground. Unperturbed, I bolted up and down twirling leaves into the air. I was surprised when my hand brushed against someone else. It was Gisela. We laughed and jumped and ran to the next mound piling leaves on our heads.

We stopped when we heard the revving of a motor. The truck was moving closer. A worker looked out the window shaking his fist and shouted, "You darn kids are ruining our work."

I grabbed Gisela's hand and pulled her along. We ran into the back alley and crouched behind our garden gate. My heart pounded. The motor idled and the truck doors slammed. Soon rakes scraped over the pavement. "If I catch you, I'll take you to your mother," a worker yelled.

"Let's wait until they're gone," I said.

After a while the scraping stopped and the truck drove down the street. Guilt ridden, we went to Ehlert's house and peeked around the corner. The workers picked up the leaves with rakes and shovels and loaded them into the back of the truck. To my surprise they were talking and grinning. Relieved, I looked at Gisela. We giggled.

"Is the bullet still inside you?" I asked.

"Ja!"

"Why didn't the doctors take it out when you were in the hospital?"

"They said it was too dangerous. The bullet is too close to my heart."

"Is it going to stay there forever?"

"Ja."

"Does it hurt?"

"No—I have to go now."

Gisela went home. I ran into my house and told my mother about her bullet.

&

A rumor spread from house to house. The milkman had received a shipment of fresh milk but he would only sell it from his store on the Vogelheimer Strasse.

Alfred volunteered to go. "I'll leave at four o'clock. There will be a long line."

"I'll go with you," Mother said.

"You don't have to do that, my buddies are getting milk for their families too."

Mother agreed and went into the pantry, returning swiftly with our navy-blue enamel milk can with white speckles on it. "We haven't used it for a while. It's covered with dust." She scrubbed the milk can in soapy water.

The next morning Alfred had returned from the milk store before I got up. We ate porridge cooked in milk. It tasted chewy, almost sweet. "This is a special treat because the milkman doesn't know when he'll have another delivery," Mother said.

197

Alfred didn't even look tired. He grinned as he spoke. "You should've seen the line. It was blocks long, past the pharmacy and the barbers shop. When the milkman opened at six he said he didn't have enough for everybody. That's why he gave us only half a portion."

"We're grateful for every drop." Mother said.

Jürgen licked his bowl. Mother looked away.

❧

Finally Frau Müller, the seamstress, came to our house to take my measurements for the coat. She asked me to step on the wooden footstool. She stretched her measuring tape across my back from the neck to below my knees and wrote it down in her note book. She put the tape around my chest and said, "Breathe in," and wrote that number down. "Bend your arm." She measured from shoulder to wrist, from one shoulder to the other, around my neck and wrote it all in her notebook. Mother watched while brewing ersatz coffee and putting cups and saucers on the table

When the seamstress finished, Mother filled the cups. Frau Müller poured milk into her coffee, stirred and said, "I'll start tomorrow. I've taken Ruthy's coat apart, washed and pressed all the pieces. The material of the sleeves was too worn to use. But I found a remnant of brown cotton velvet I can use for the yoke."

Mother said, "Thank you."

Frau Müller looked at me. "When you come home from kindergarten tomorrow, I'll be ready for the first fitting."

"I'm not going to kindergarten anymore because I have no shoes."

Mother said, "Ulla, the hen started laying eggs again. Father was able to barter with them for a pair of shoes for Alfred. Jürgen will get Alfred's old ones and you can have Jürgen's and go to kindergarten again."

I was elated, could hardly contain my excitement. "When will he get them?"

"Soon."

Father had positioned our Pfaff sewing machine under the window in the living room and oiled the mechanical parts. Frau Müller didn't have to bring a sewing machine to our house. She started sewing early the next morning. From my seat on the sofa in the kitchen, I watched in amazement how she pumped the foot-treadle with her feet and at the same time pushed the fabric over the sewing machine table. I liked listening to the click-clack of the needle.

The seamstress ate the midday meal with us. Mother made scrambled eggs and fried potatoes.

"This is delicious," Frau Müller said. "I'll get the coat done today. I only have to finish the bound buttonholes and sew the buttons on."

Mother smiled.

"As promised Ursula can wear it when the cold weather sets in. I'll finish the cap at home. I have to look at my remnants to see if I have enough fabric to match the yoke."

One day Father brought a pair of men's shoes home for Alfred, and on the same day, the seamstress delivered my cap. I was ecstatic about the shoes because I could return to kindergarten.

The next morning I was excited to get ready. It was a cold day. After breakfast, Mother helped me into my new frock. Suddenly I felt uncomfortable in it because it was made from my dead aunt's coat. I took it off quickly and handed it back to Mother.

She looked at me knowingly and knelt in front of me. "It's too cold to go out without it. Tante Ruth would be pleased and is probably smiling down at you."

Then I remembered her beautiful image, relaxed and put the coat back on. But when Mother slipped the pointed cap on my head and I saw myself in the mirror, I was horrified. I ripped it off my head and threw it on the floor.

"I'm not wearing this. I look like a gnome."

"Ursula, you will have to get used to it. It'll keep your head dry in the winter when it snows."

"I'll never wear it—ever!" I ranted and stomped my feet.

Mother looked distraught. I pouted and cried.

After I calmed down, I left for kindergarten with my head uncovered.

Winter, 1945

Chapter 37

The wind howled around the corners and eaves of our house and blew snow under the front door into the entry way. We could feel the icy draft all the way in the kitchen. Mother laid rags in front of the doors and around the window frames to keep the cold and dampness out.

Many people who lived in make-shift quarters of bombed-out houses died from hunger or the frost. Grave diggers couldn't dig holes in the frozen ground fast enough. Bodies piled up in mortuaries and sheds at graveyards.

We only had enough coal for the stove in the kitchen and stayed inside most of the time. Our windows were covered with permanent sheets of ice flowers.

Father brought a knee-high wooden work bench with a shoe-anvil mounted at one end into the kitchen. "It's time I repaired some shoes."

The stitching had frayed on Jürgen's high-tops and the soles had separated from the top leather. His toes peeked out and the soles flip-flopped with every step. He complained that his socks were always soaked.

Father straddled the bench in the middle of the kitchen and adjusted the anvil. He held a chunk of wax in one hand and pulled string over it.

"What are you doing that for?" I asked.

"The wax coats the thread so it'll glide easier through the holes when I sew the top leather to the sole. It also plugs the holes so water won't seep into the shoe."

He slipped a shoe upside down on the anvil, attached clamps to keep it in place and threaded a big, curved needle. He pushed a metal spike through the holes in the leather and the sole so the needle would pass through them with ease. Then he put the shoe on the bench and started to sew. When the needle got stuck, he pulled it through with pliers. He worked all afternoon.

When sweat beads formed on his forehead, Mother said, "It's time for a break." She handed him a cup of steaming ersatz coffee.

He came to the sofa and sat next to me. I cuddled up to him.

Our neighbor, Frau Kersting, who had no children and lived with her husband in old Frau Mahr's upstairs bedrooms, often visited us. Sometimes she helped Mother with the wash or ironing. She liked to knit. When she visited, she usually brought a basket filled with yarn and needles and sat opposite Mother on a chair at the other side of the stove.

Mother mended or darned while Frau Kersting knitted stockings, shawls and mittens. Some days they'd sit and work until dusk. When it was too dark to see, they talked or Frau Kersting started singing a song of the blue lakes and dark forests of East Prussia where she grew up. Mother chimed in. I loved listening to them.

One evening Oma came to the door, tears streaming down her face. "My brother Otto is dead. Emmy sent me a letter. It took a long time to get here. The envelope was postmarked in Berlin months ago."

Teary eyed, Mother pulled a chair close to the stove. "Come and sit down where it's warm."

Oma reached for her handkerchief and blew her nose. "Emmy wrote that his papers only said he died in the service of his country. She wants to know what really happened to him but doesn't know who to turn to. Otto's job was to guard Count York von Wartenburg, at the Plötzensee prison. The count was a Resistance fighter and was involved in the unsuccessful assassination attempt on Hitler last year. After the count's execution, Otto became depressed."

"Poor Tante Emmy," Mother said.

I remembered Onkel Otto in his police uniform from when we stayed overnight in his house in Berlin when Mother, Jürgen and I traveled to the farm in East Prussia in 1943.

Oma looked so sad. Her voice quivered. "In just a few months, I've lost a child, two brothers and a three-month old niece to this wretched war."

⁊

In kindergarten we learned Christmas songs. At home, we celebrated the four Advent Sundays before Christmas. We sang songs by candlelight in the evenings. Mother had exchanged a few eggs for a little butter and used it for baking spritzgebäck cookies. Our house smelled so good. After we finished singing, everyone received a cookie.

One Sunday after our cookie treat, Frau Kersting said, "I saw the Polish war prisoners, who had squatted in houses in our street after the war, down the hill on Harbor Strasse. They bartered handmade wooden toys, carved ornaments, small bowls and plates for food."

Father said, "If Ursula is a good girl, maybe the Christkind will bring her a doll on Christmas Eve this year."

"Last year, the Christkind didn't bring me the bike I wished for," I said.

He stroked my hair. "During the war that was not possible. Now we have peace."

I remembered Tante Hildegard's beautiful doll with the light blue dress and white lace collar. Secretly, I wished for a doll just like that. I tried to be very good and didn't upset Mother or old Frau Mahr.

My parents wondered where they could get a small Christmas tree. On Christmas Eve afternoon, Father came home with a few fir branches. Mother arranged them in a tall vase, decorated them with colorful ornaments and left-over candles from the previous year.

She placed the bouquet on the sewing machine in the corner of the living room and closed the door. We were not allowed to open it.

Too excited to sit still, I roamed through all our rooms until Mother told us to get dressed for the festivities. I wore a clean, white pinafore over my dress and all our newly repaired shoes were polished to a high shine.

After dinner, the living room door was opened and the candles lit. While we sang Christmas songs in front of the decorated fir branches, I peaked to see if I could detect the shape of the doll under the cloth that covered the table. First my brothers and I recited Christmas poems. Then Mother lifted the cloth. Five plates filled with a few cookies and walnuts, one apple and a pair of hand knitted stockings were on the table. No doll. I turned around so no one could see my tears.

"Look under the table," Father said.

I bent down and searched for the doll. In the shadow of the table I saw a stuffed, gray sock with buttons for eyes and a black mark for a mouth. It sat slumped over in a little cart made from old wood. My knees buckled. I sat on the floor and sobbed.

Father kneeled next to me and pulled the cart from under the table. "You can take the doll for a ride. Look the wheels turn." He pushed the cart back and forth.

"I was a good girl. I wished for a doll with a light blue dress," I hollered. "You said it was peace time now, but the Christkind didn't listen."

Father looked sad. "You'll enjoy playing with it any way."

Behind me Mother said, "We gave a whole loaf of bread for this?"

❧

The next week my brothers didn't go to school and there was no kindergarten. Although I stayed inside most days, because it was too cold to go outside, I never played with the doll.

One day when the wind was especially blustery, it pulled loose a corner of the corrugated roof on the chicken-coop. It creaked and struggled against the wind flapping up into the air then slamming down again.

"We have to do something about this," Father said.

He and Alfred put their warm coats and caps on and went outside. I watched them through the kitchen window climb onto the roof. Father's coat flapped in the wind while hammering nails into the metal. Alfred pulled his knitted cap over his ears and placed bricks on top of the metal for extra weight.

Across the window, the branches of the elder tree in the alley whipped wildly back and forth. I thought they were going to break.

Father and Alfred came back inside shivering. Their noses and cheeks shone bright red. They rushed to the stove and held their hands over the warm cooking plate.

When the weather warmed a little, the boys' school friends came calling and my brothers bundled up and went with them. I always wondered what they did outside because the police had forbidden the collection of bombs and magnesium from crashed bombers a long time ago. Sometimes they all came inside to warm up. When Mother was not in the kitchen, they talked in hushed voices.

"What are you talking about?" I asked.

"Boy stuff. "

When Mother came back in, they put their caps back on and clambered toward the door.

"Can I go with you?"

"No!" They all said at the same time and left.

One day, I put on my new winter coat and followed the boys. From old Frau Mahr's corner, I watched them run down the back alley. When they disappeared in Lamm's garden path, I hurried to catch up to them. When I reached the gate, I heard their voices coming from the shed. On tip-toes, I inched closer and peeked in through the grimy window.

The boys stood around a workbench with a pile of white chunks on it that looked like chalk. Päule stacked bricks two high on the ground and his brother Ewald took a clump, put it on the bricks and smashed it with a hammer. Pieces flew in all directions. My brothers picked up the pieces and put them into a rusted canister. Jimmy Bach lined up empty bottles in a row against the wall.

"We need more stoppers," he said. "Can anyone get wine bottle corks from home?"

"We could also try old cans with lids and see if they work."

"We're going to have a great New Years Eve," Alfred said.

He and his friends were so busy they never looked up at the window where I was. After a while I backed away slowly and headed home. A snowflake landed on my nose. I looked up into the sky. Thousands of flakes glided through the air and covered the soot-stained back alley with a dusting of white snow. When I got home my parents were sitting on the chairs next to the warm stove.

"When is New Year's Eve?" I asked.

"Tomorrow," Mother said. "Imagine, you're almost seven years old but this is the first peace-filled New Years Eve in your life."

"We will celebrate along with the entire country," Father said. "I heard that all the church bells in Germany are supposed to be ringing in the New Year. You can stay up until midnight."

"Our church and the Rosenkranz church in Bergeborbeck were bombed," I said.

"That's true, but I don't think all church bells in Essen were destroyed. Take a nap so you'll stay awake." he said.

Mother got up, stoked the embers in the stove and added a shovel of coal. I remembered how nice the bells sounded from the church next to Tante Kathel's house in Bavaria. The next day, I took a nap on the sofa in the warm kitchen. After dinner, the boys bundled up and went out.

I waited for a while then I said, "I have to go potty," put my coat on and left. I rushed into the back alley and saw my brothers and their friends near Ewald and Päule's home. Their parents were celebrating New Years Eve with the Kornblum's, a few houses away.

I moved toward them in the shadow of the houses. They didn't notice me. The empty bottles were on the ground and the canister with the white chunks stood next to them.

Jimmy dropped several pieces into a glass bottle and spit into it. He held the bottle at eye level and swirled it around. "Look!"

Everyone scooted closer to him. I sneaked behind them. White vapors swirled inside.

"Pour some vinegar water on it," someone said.

Ewald grabbed a jug and trickled a little into the bottle. Jimmy pushed the stopper down, stirred the white chunks with quick motions. They began to bubble. He shook the bottle. A burst of milky clouds churned wildly inside.

"Quick, put it on the cellar window sill."

"Everyone hide!"

Some jumped into the drop-closet and closed the door. I followed the others around the corner.

Bang kablam! The bottle exploded. Glass fragments hit the brick walls and clinked onto the ground. When all was quiet, the boys came out of hiding and inspected the site. The bricks inside the cellar window sill were stained with white splatters. Shard glass lay strewn in the alley.

"What are you doing here?" Alfred yelled.

"I want to watch!"

"This is dangerous."

"I know. What is this white stuff?"

"Gypsum!"

"Where did you get it?"

"We found it behind the old plant near the excavation pit."

"That was fun," I said.

"The big bottle's gonna blow! Run!'

We jumped for cover, and a much louder explosion followed. Splinters lodged in the wooden wall of the shed.

"That was a great one!"

"Let's try this old can with the lid."

A boy filled it with gypsum, spit on it, swooshed the can, poured liquid on it, shook, and closed the lid. "Run!"

From behind the corner, I only heard a little puff and the lid rolling into the gutter.

"That didn't work."

After several more explosions, a boy said, "Someone sweep up the glass and put it in the trash can."

Jürgen grabbed the broom and handed me a shovel. "You can help."

When we were done, I saw the shadow of a person in the distance. "Someone is coming."

"Hide!"

The boys grabbed the bottles and canister and put them behind the garden gate. Then I heard Father's voice. "It's time for you to come home."

On the way to our house he said, "You're playing dangerous games. You can get seriously hurt that way."

Mother served us hot peppermint tea and a spritzgebäck cookie. While we sipped the tea, Father warned the boys not to play with hazardous materials again.

We watched the hand of the clock on the wall move close to midnight, Mother opened the kitchen window. We gathered in front of it. Father turned the light out.

We waited. A church bell rang in the distance. Another chimed in from further away, then still more. They sounded faint. We heard high-pitched bells and deep sounding ones ringing through the night. All together, they sounded like a far away chorus.

"They're announcing peace and freedom," Father said.

I smiled. We stood close and listened. The bells chimed for a long time. When they stopped, Father said, "Now they'll ring once for every hour."

Together we counted, "One, two, three, ...twelve."

Alfred cheered, "Happy New Year—It's 1946"

Mother closed the window. We hugged and laughed.

Surviving Peace, 1946

Chapter 40

In January, a policeman again showed up on our street and warned parents about the dangerous activities some of the boys had been involved in. He said that over the holidays several youngsters were injured when they made gypsum bottle-bombs. When they exploded, shards of glass hit their faces.

Father had another talk with us after dinner that night. "The policeman told us that one boy nearly lost his eye. I don't ever want you to go near the plant where you found the gypsum."

Later that month was Oma's birthday. She couldn't bake a cake because she didn't have all the ingredients. One day Mother put a little white flour into a sack and two eggs in her apron pocket.

"Let's take these to Oma," she said. "It's your birthday too, you know."

Outside, the air was crisp. Oma's front door was unlocked. We brushed the snow from our shoes in the entry and knocked on the kitchen door. Inside, a child squealed.

Tante Änne smiled at us from the sofa. She held two year old Manfred on her arm. Oma poured hot water into the coffee pot.

"What a surprise," Mother said. "When did you arrive?"

"An hour ago, we've barely warmed up."

The sisters shook hands. Their eyes sparkled.

"I'm upset and wanted to be with family," Tante Änne said. "I still don't know what happened to Kurt. The war ended eight months ago. What could have happened to him?"

"Have you gone to the authorities?"

"All I could find out was that he had been stationed in Berlin during the last battles of the war. It seems the Russians are taking over the city now."

"You know, the mail delivery is very slow," Mother said. "We're glad you've come. How was your train ride from the Sauerland?"

"More than six hours—it was twice as long as I expected. "

"Was it crowded?" Mother asked tickling Manfred, who wiggled in his mother's arms.

"Not as bad as the trains going in the opposite direction. You should have seen how many people were hanging on from outside the trains."

Mother gave Oma the sack with the flour and the eggs. "Do you have enough for a birthday cake?"

Oma smiled. She served the ersatz coffee. "It is! Änne brought fresh butter from the farm. We'll bake a pound cake tomorrow."

The next afternoon, the entire family gathered at Oma's house to celebrate our birthday. Even Opa's sister, Tante Lotti and Onkel Wilhelm who lived up the street came. The table looked festive. Everyone relished the delicious cake and the coffee with a little milk and sugar.

After we finished, my brothers left. Cousin Manfred went down for a nap and Opa poured a jigger of schnapps for the men. They talked about the collapsed tower of the second mine shaft. The women chatted about friends and the empty store shelves.

I leaned back on the sofa and gazed at the brown streaks on the wallpaper across the room. I followed along the rows of tiny flowers up to the big, brown water stains on the ceiling. Rain had been seeping in since roof tiles were shattered from shrapnel during the war.

Everyone seemed to have a good time. Then Oma broke into tears. "Next week, Ruth will be gone a year."

The smiles faded from everyone's face.

Oma's red eyes looked angry, "Women should refuse to have children. Then they can't draft boys as soldiers and innocent girls won't be killed by bombs."

No one spoke for a while.

When I heard a truck from the mine rumble down the street, I got up and went to the window.

"It's about time for our coal allotments to be delivered," Opa said. "We're running short."

"So are we," Father said and Onkel Wilhelm nodded.

A few days later, a truck from the mine stopped in front of Oma's house and dumped two mounds of coal on the street. Part of it spilled onto the sidewalk. One pile was for us and one for my grandparents.

After Mother signed a paper and the delivery man left she said, "Put your coat and shawl on. I need you outside."

We dressed in a hurry and left the house.

"Watch over the coal on the street. If anyone comes near it with a pail and shovel, call me. I'm going to get equipment from our shed."

Soon she returned with a wheelbarrow and shovel. She transported load after load to the alley behind our house and dumped them in front of the coal-chute door.

Oma opened her kitchen window. "I'm going to wait for Opa to come home from work. I'll watch the coal on the street and Ursula can guard in the back."

"Good idea. Ulla, go to the alley."

Mother's face looked flushed. Every time she emptied the wheelbarrow, she straightened up and massaged her lower back with both hands. Then Opa and Father came home. Mother wiped her brows with her jacket sleeve when she saw them.

"I haven't even started cooking," Mother said.

"No matter," said Father. "We'll take over from here."

Opa got his tools and transported his stack to the chute in the front of his house. After Father had taken our last load to the back, I watched him sweep the street from my post in the alley. Then he came to the back and shoveled the coal into the cellar. When it piled up on top of the chute, he pushed it down. Then he went down to the cellar and shoveled the coal to the back wall in the bin.

"Ulla this coal is as precious as black diamonds."

When Father put his tools away, I went inside. Mother looked clean and wore fresh clothes. Fried potatoes sizzled in the pan.

"There's warm water in the bowl in the sink. Wash up before Pappa comes in."

Father took his clothes off in the entry way and came in wearing only his long johns. He scrubbed his hands and arms with a brush. Then he lathered his face and neck. After he dried himself and put on clean clothes, he sat down next to me.

Mother said, "You look tired. I fried a piece of the smoked bacon Änne brought us. Jan, put it in her bag when he carried her suitcase to the train station. Remember, he isn't going back to Poland. He's doing a good job running the farm for the sisters."

That evening, Mother fired up the stove with extra coal and opened the kitchen door so the heat could rise to our bedrooms.

Father said, "We can't do this often. We received only a partial allotment of coal. The mine may never be fully operational again. There is no steel to fix the war damaged wheel tower."

One quiet afternoon when my brothers were in school, and my parents were busy, I rummaged through our living room cabinet curious to see what was inside. On the bottom shelf was our blue and white china. I remembered Mother telling me that she had purchased it with coupons over several months before the war. On the other side, behind the stack of ironed tablecloths, I found a piggy bank made of shiny steel. It was heavy. I took it into the kitchen and showed it to Mother.

"You can use the money to buy bread," I said.

She shook her head. "I can't open it. The key to the piggy bank is at the Sparkasse where your savings account is. They'll open it when it's full and add the money to your account. Someday, we may be able to fill it with coins again."

Spring, 1946

Chapter 40

The April air was laden with moisture. Occasionally, the sun peaked through the clouds on my way home from kindergarten and raindrops dangled from the tips of budding poplar leaves. They sparkled in the sunshine.

In kindergarten, we learned songs about Spring and memorized the lines of a play to be performed for our parents at Easter. I always got excited when our teacher, Fräulein Lange, arranged the chairs in a circle in the middle of the room and read one sentence aloud and had us repeat the words together. It became my favorite time at kindergarten.

I remembered how sad I was last Easter when we were on the trek getting away from the bombs in the city, and the Easter bunny never found me.

At home, I practiced the sentences of each character. Secretly, I hoped I would get to play the part of Hansel. I liked his role best because it had the most lines.

One day, Fräulein Lange asked, "Does anyone have a pair of lederhosen at home? We need them for the play. They could be your older brother's."

No one answered. I didn't even know if my brothers had any.

"Ask your mothers when you get home and report back to me in the morning."

Soon I had memorized the entire play and whispered the lines to others when they forgot them.

One morning the teacher announced which role each student would play. Ingrid, who couldn't remember her lines, was assigned the role of Hansel. I was so disappointed that I cried the entire way home and pleaded with my mother to talk to the teacher.

The next morning, Mother came to kindergarten. She talked with Fräulein Lange in the entrance where we hung our coats. I stayed near the door.

"Frau Fischer, Ingrid was the only child who had lederhosen. Her mother insisted that only she can wear them."

When Mother said good-bye, I rushed back to the table disappointed. Now I would never be able to play the role of Hansel.

The day before our celebration Fräulein Lange announced, "Easter vacation starts the day after tomorrow. Some of you will not return. The students, who couldn't start first grade last year because there weren't enough classrooms, will begin classes at the Haus Berge School after the break."

I wondered if I would be going there. On the day of the festivities, parents came and sat on chairs in our classroom facing the area where we were going to perform. The walls were decorated with drawings of colorful eggs and flowers. In the corner stood a tall, stoneware vase filled with fresh cut birch branches from the tree in the back yard.

During the play, I whispered to Ingrid, who played Hansel, when she forgot her words. After the performance, the teacher announced that we had a surprise visit from the Easter bunny. My heart beat faster.

"Search for baskets in the other rooms or outside. Look around tree trunks and in bushes and bring them back. Go!"

Some of the boys jumped up and raced out of the room right away. I followed with the rest. As I hurried through the hallway I saw a basket in a high windowsill but didn't stop. Then I remembered that I didn't get any candy when the American soldiers had thrown them to us, I turned around and ran back. The basket was still there. I reached for it, and was the first to return to the classroom where the parents waited. They laughed.

Bursting with joy, I showed it to my mother. Inside was a brown egg decorated with colorful lines and tiny blossoms, a cutout paper doll and a few candies.

After the Easter break, spring storms and cold showers set in. The morning when Mother and I went to the school to register for first grade, we bundled up in warm coats.

We walked down Harbor Strasse hill past the bombed-out butcher shop and a row of destroyed homes. I huddled close to Mother under her umbrella when we crossed the Berne River Bridge. By the time we reached the soccer stadium, my socks were soaked.

I recognized the building across the street with the vaulted entrance to the potato-cellar-church. When we crossed the rail road tracks, my feet hurt. "How much further do we have to go?"

"I know it is a long way. But we're almost there."

I felt uneasy when I saw the spooky ruins of the Rosenkranz church. A few streets beyond the church, was the fenced school yard.

Inside the school, we signed up with Fräulein Meirich. "Welcome to my class," she said. "You can start on Monday morning."

Mother looked toward the other tables. "Is that Fräulein Birkenstock?" she asked.

My teacher craned her neck and searched the room. "That's her."

"She was my teacher," Mother said. "She retired years ago."

"They called her back because we don't have enough instructors. Too many of our men have been killed or are missing in action."

The teacher smiled at me as we turned to go and said, "Aufwiedersehn."

My legs cramped all the way home. When we reached the bottom of Harbor Strasse hill I sat down on the sidewalk and said, "I can't walk anymore."

Mother stopped and looked at me with concern. "You've grown too big for me to carry. We don't have far to go."

She took my hand. Slowly we labored up the hill side by side, not saying a word.

On Sunday Father showed me my leather school-satchel and slate board. It had a crack in one corner and crocheted cotton square fastened to a hole in its wooden frame and he showed me the two small pieces of white chalk for writing.

"The cotton square is for wiping the slate. You're ready to practice you're A, B, Cs," he said.

It was drizzling when I left for school. When I arrived in class, I was tired and my coat and shoes were damp and heavy.

Many students already sat in chairs attached to desks. I found an empty seat in the third row and took off my wet satchel.

Fräulein Meirich looked at me and said, "The pegs on the wall are full. Drape your coat over the radiator under the window—you won't get burned—the central heating isn't working. Then put your shoes in front of the cast-iron coal stove in the corner. They'll dry quickly."

When I walked back to my seat, my wet socks made footprints on the floor. I took my slate board out and put my writing chalk in the pencil groove at the top of the desk next to the inkwell.

Fräulein Meirich stoked the fire in the round, cast-iron stove in the corner and added a few shovels of coal. The heat from the stove warmed my front but the rest of my body was cold.

"We'll start the morning with the song 'Der Mai ist gekommen' and then we'll learn the names of all forty-seven students."

I loved school.

New Friends, 1946

Chapter 40

At school I met a new friend just before summer vacation, her name was Ilse. She lived on Förder Strasse just one street apart from where I lived. One day after class we walked home together.

"Where did you live before you moved here?" I asked.

"In Bad Mergentheim. We were evacuated there after our house was hit by a bomb at the beginning of the war."

"Why did you come back? All the houses here have been destroyed in the war."

"My dad got his old job back at the coal mine."

Ilse invited me to her home. Her father had fixed up two rooms in a bombed out, abandoned apartment where six families used to live.

"We're the only family in the house now."

Their kitchen was small and narrow. Ilse's mother always greeted me with a smile.

I met her two older brothers and two sisters.

"We all sleep in one room for now," Ilse said.

In the bedroom, a blanket hung over a clothesline in the middle of the room.

"Why is the blanket there?" I asked.

"It gives my parents privacy."

Ilse showed me the area in the basement that her father had cleared where the family could bathe. The sun streamed in through the little window covered only with wire mesh to keep rodents out.

An aluminum tub was on the floor. Next to it, soap and a brush were laid out on a wooden stool. I didn't say anything to Ilse, but I felt a little envious because we took our baths in the kitchen.

Later Ilse told me, "My mother won't let me take a bath in the basement anymore. A water rat tried to push the drain-guard up when I was in the tub. It disappeared when I screamed."

I shuddered. Suddenly taking a bath in the kitchen didn't seem bad at all.

During the summer, displaced families from the Russian occupied eastern provinces moved into abandoned buildings in our area. They fixed up living quarters with scraps from bombed-out houses and factories.

The ruins had become infested with rats that had moved in from ships stranded in the city harbor. Father said they were multiplying fast because there was so much food buried underneath the rubble of bombed out homes, the grocery store and butcher shop. Rat poison could not be purchased anywhere.

"People are fighting them off with rakes and shovels," he said.

I hardly played with Ilse during the summer because her mother wouldn't let her go exploring with me. She said it was too dangerous.

One afternoon while I picked wildflowers in the tall grass in the field behind our garden, I came upon two older girls at a little pond.

"What are you doing?" I asked.

The girl with long blond braids looked up. "Catching tadpoles."

I knelt down next to them at the water's edge. Tiny shadows wiggled their tails close to the surface.

"Renate, use the tin can," the blonde said.

Renate's black curls tumbled over her forehead when she bent down to dip the can into the water.

"Look, Inge, I got some," she shouted.

All three of us watched two little tadpoles swimming inside the tin.

"Put them in the glass jar with the others," Inge said.

I followed Renate to where a jar leaned against the trunk of a willow tree. I saw several tadpoles swimming in murky water.

"We have enough to put on the window sill and watch." Inge's golden braids flipped through the air when she jumped up. "Let's go home."

"I've never seen you before. Where do you live?" I asked.

"We just moved here from the eastern provinces. I was born in Pomerania," the blonde said.

"And we came from Silesia," said Renate, her dark curls bouncing.

"Do your dads work in the coal mine?"

"No, my father was killed in the war."

"And mine is missing in action. My mother doesn't know where he is."

My shoes were wet and my socks were damp. I noticed that the girls wore no shoes.

"My mother thinks it's too dangerous to go barefoot," I said.

"My mother said if I wear my shoes in the summer, the soles will be worn out by the time I start school in the fall."

We often met in the grassy field. The girls usually carried a canning jar and tin can. One day we meandered into the forest behind the mine's slagheap. I never told my mother where we were going.

In the forest, we came upon a pond larger than the one where we caught tadpoles. Frogs jumped into the water when we neared the reeds at its shore.

"Look! There are little fish in there," Inge said.

We lay on our bellies and watched the little shadows flit through the water. We tried and tried to catch some in our cupped hands but they were too fast. Then we used the glass jar. But we had no luck. Inge even waded into the pond and stood very still for a long time but no fish came near her.

"Let's go home and get my mother's sieve," Inge said. "It'll be easier to catch them."

We left the forest and stomped through the field toward our garden path. Suddenly Renate screamed and collapsed in the grass.

"What happened?" Inge and I shouted rushing to her. Renate held her left foot in both hands and wailed. Blood ran down her fingers—she rocked back and forth, her eyes wide and filled with fear.

"Tell us—what happened?" we yelled.

"I stepped on a broken bottle."

Next to her lay a beer bottle broken in half. A shard of brown glass still stuck in her foot. Blood dripped down onto the grass. I felt sick to my stomach.

"Renate, we have to go to a doctor, get up and put your arm around my shoulder."

"No!" Renate screamed. "I can't get up and I won't go to a doctor."

"Then we'll take you home and get your mother."

"No! You can't get my mother—she's going to kill me."

"Ulla, help me pull her up."

Inge took one of Renate's arms and I the other and put them over our shoulders. She clung to us. Together we hobbled through the field to Renate's apartment. She had the key on a string around her neck. Her flushed face was bathed in tears. Her body was shaking.

On the kitchen table, dishes soaked in an enamel bowl. Inge took the plates out and put the bowl on the floor.

"Put your foot in."

"Don't do that," I shouted. "The water isn't clean."

"It has soap in it."

Renate screamed when she eased her foot into the water. Her black curls stuck to her forehead.

When she removed her foot from the water, Inge pulled the splinter from the wound and blood gushed out. A piece of flesh dangled from the sole. Renate turned pale.

"We'll wait until your mother gets home from work," Inge said. She wrapped a dishtowel around the foot. The towel turned red. Renate whimpered digging her hands into her thighs as if that would ease her pain.

Scared but not knowing what else to do, I waited for a while before going home. I never told anyone about the accident. Weeks later, Mother told me about a young girl who had moved here recently and was in the hospital.

"She has a severe infection resulting from a bad cut in her foot," she said giving me a questioning look.

I never saw these two friends again.

Repairing the Schoolhouse Roof, 1946

Chapter 41

I looked forward to starting the fall semester but not so for my brother Alfred. He had outgrown his shoes and my parents couldn't find any shoes in stores or for barter. Alfred was upset. Father solved the problem by cutting the leather away at the tip of Alfred's old shoes so his toes could peek out.

"You can wear them like this for a while," Father said.

On the morning of the first day of school, Alfred fussed. "I'll look stupid going to school like this. Everyone is going to laugh at me."

Mother was still talking to him when I left. When I arrived at the school, I was surprised to see the yard filled with stacks of red shingles. On the roof, two bent-over old men were throwing broken tiles over the edge into a fenced-off area. They crashed into pieces when they hit the ground.

Once in the classroom, the teacher said, "Don't take off your coats. We're going back outside and together with other students we'll transport the tiles to the men on the roof."

In the yard older students had formed a line from where the tiles were stacked to the stone steps into the school house. Another teacher directed each first grader to stand between two older students.

Our teacher, Fräulein Meirich, stood in front of us and shouted into a bullhorn, "Everyone, pay attention! The roof of the schoolhouse is leaking. It needs to be fixed and there are no workers for hire. That's why we need your help."

The kids all along the line shuffled their feet and murmured.

"Listen! We're going to hand one tile at a time from student to student all the way to the roof. A teacher will pick up a tile from the stack and hand it to the first student in line. He will give it to the person to his right and so on. Do you understand?"

"Ja!" we yelled. I was excited and waved to my friend Ilse.

"Here comes the first one," the boy next to me said. "Don't drop it."

The tile felt rough and heavy. I gave it to the girl to my right. Soon I was handed another tile and another. We worked for a long time. I looked at the roof. An old worker went to a place where someone handed him a tile. He added it to a stack on the roof. My fingertips began to hurt.

I was relieved when Fräulein Meirich shouted through the bullhorn, "Let's take a break and wash up. The men have enough tiles on the roof to do repairs all morning. The afternoon students will transport more tiles to them."

When we returned to the classroom, we sang a song before starting our lessons. The teacher said, "Singing will help us concentrate on our work."

I was glad to be sitting and looked out the window. The sky had turned dark and raindrops trickled down the glass. My fingers ached when I used my chalk to write a new letter from the alphabet on my slate.

By the time school was over, the rain had stopped and the potholes in the street were filled with water. I was hungry. My stomach growled all the way home.

My parents and I were eating fried potatoes when my brothers burst into the kitchen.

Alfred looked miserable. His soaked socks hung out from the hole in the front of his shoe. "These shoes are killing me. The leather is cutting into my toes." He sat on the wooden stool and took off his high-tops and socks. His toes were rubbed raw. "I can't wear these anymore."

Mother handed him a towel. "Dry your feet and come to the table."

Father said, "Our neighbor, Otto Mahr, gave me a pair of his old, worn out shoes that have no soles. I'll start chiseling soles from two wood planks and then nail the leather from Otto's shoes on. They'll be ready for you in the morning."

After dinner Father brought his workbench into the kitchen. "Alfred, come over here and put your foot on this plank."

With a pencil, he traced around Alfred's foot leaving additional space for the nails. With a saw, Father cut along the pencil marks and then used a chisel and hammer to shape the platform to fit Alfred's foot. Woodchips flew through the air and landed on the floor. I watched from my place on the kitchen sofa while Mother washed dishes and the boys did homework.

After a while, he held the plank up and said, "Look at its shape. The place for the heel is lower than the arch."

The wood was light where Father had chiseled and dark in other places.

"Alfred come over here and try them on."

He put his foot on the wood platform and said, "It's bumpy."

I heard Father hammer downstairs in my parents' bedroom until I fell asleep.

The next morning, I was surprised to see Alfred wearing the strange-looking platform shoes. He practiced walking in the kitchen back and forth. He looked stiff. I covered my mouth to hide my laughing. He shot me an angry look.

That afternoon, Alfred came home barefooted with the top leather of his shoes hanging over his shoulder and the wooden soles in his hands. "The nails didn't hold."

Father said, "I was afraid of that. I couldn't find the right kind of nails anywhere."

"I'm going to school barefoot tomorrow. Lots of kids have no shoes." Alfred looked determined.

Battle with Rodents, 1946

Chapter 42

One rainy morning Mother said, "Ulla, I'm going to the baker to see if I can buy an extra loaf of bread. Jürgen isn't the only one who's always hungry. I know you and Alfred are too."

That day, she came home with two rye breads in her shopping bag. She put one into the bread box in the kitchen cabinet and asked Alfred to take the other one to the cellar where it would stay fresh.

After we finished the first loaf, Mother brought the other one up from the cellar. It had holes bitten all over its crust.

"Mice," she said.

With her potato knife, she cut away a little bread from each hole and put the crumbs into an old tin can. "We'll save these for the chickens," she said. Then she cut slices for our breakfast.

"When will I be able to buy all the bread allotted to our family on the rationing cards again?" Mother said shaking her head.

Alfred wore the shoes with the leather cut away at the front to school again. Father couldn't find the right kind of nails to attach the leather back on to the wooden soles he had hand-carved. Alfred stayed inside after school most days, "I don't want to wear out the only shoes I have," he said.

He often sat at the kitchen table sketching soaring eagles among clouds or deer grazing in the forest from pictures he saw in Father's books. I liked watching him draw the outlines and then sketch in the faces and bodies making them look alive with his pencil. Sometimes he spent hours in the little room we called kleines Zimmer. He closed the door even though it was cold and damp in there.

Curious to see what he was doing, I went up, opened the door a little and peeked in. He sat on the old cot, his back against the wall, a drawing pad on his lap. He studied a picture in an opened book propped up on a chair.

I tiptoed in, climbed on the cot next to him and glanced at his paper. He had drawn a farm house surrounded by trees. There was a hay-wagon in the yard with a cow coming out of the barn.

"That looks like the farm in East Prussia." I watched him pencil in chickens and a rooster. Sensing that he wanted to be left alone, I slipped out of the little room.

At dusk, Father read the newspaper, Mother darned socks, and Jürgen and I did homework. I jumped when Alfred burst into the kitchen.

"Come upstairs and see what I found."

We followed him to the little room. Alfred rushed to the wardrobe. The bottom drawer was open. "Come over here."

Inside the drawer in a nest made from old rags, squirmed tiny, blind, pink mice like the ones I had seen at the farm.

"We need a cat," Father said.

"What will we feed it?" I asked.

"Ulla, the cat will eat mice and then they won't eat our bread anymore," Mother said.

The next morning terrible screams outside woke me.

"You can't get away from me, you beast!" Mother shrieked.

I stumbled downstairs and opened the front door. Mother stood legs apart in front of the wooden bench on the patio, clutching a pitchfork with both hands. A huge rat cowered under the bench staring at her.

"Close the door," she screamed.

I slammed it shut and ran into the living room to watch from the window. The rat arched its back and retreated into a corner under the bench.

"You won't get into my house," Mother shouted. The rodent squirmed. Mother lifted the pitchfork and jammed it down. Metal screeched on the cement, the rat squeaked and struggled. Blood squirted from its side. Mother freed the pitchfork. Before she could smash it down again, the rat scuttled by her, squeezed under the fence and limped away leaving a trail of blood drops on the ground.

Strands of Mother's hair had come loose from the bun at her nape and hung wildly in her flushed face. She stood completely still, holding her weapon, staring at the spot where the beast had disappeared.

A few days later, Father brought a black and white cat home. "Let's keep her in the house for a while until she knows she belongs here. Then she can go outside and hunt."

"I think Mietze can start hunting in the house," Mother said.

The mice had gotten into the little bit of grain we had left for porridge and Mother told us that we had run out of sugar.

Changing Times, 1946

Chapter 43

Fräulein Meirich started our lesson one morning with an announcement. "Something very important happened on Saturday, October 13 in our city."

I wondered what that could be and paid attention.

"For the first time since the war, democratic elections for a new city government were held in Essen. Our new system is based on the English model of government. The citizens have elected a new mayor. His name is Gustav Heinemann."

"What does the mayor do?" someone asked.

"He'll try to rebuild our city."

When my grandparents visited, they also talked about the elections and the deteriorating living conditions of the people in our city. After dinner my parents discussed news they had heard during the day. Sometimes Father read parts of newspaper articles out loud.

"Here is what our new mayor said before he started his job, 'Our people are hungry, our people are freezing and our people are homeless'. He seems to understand how grim conditions are in Essen."

The adults used big words like de-Nazification of our officials and democratization of the population. Often my brothers joined in the conversation. I enjoyed the long winter evenings because our family was together at the kitchen table talking.

Mother said, "We're fortunate, to have a roof over our head even though it is leaking. Many don't have a dry place to sleep."

I thought about what Mother said on my way to school and noticed that more families had moved into the ruins and more rats scuttled among the debris. I hurried along. By the time I arrived at my desk, I was tired and hungry.

The weather had turned very cold. The newspaper reported on the sub zero temperatures and Alfred couldn't go to school anymore with his toes poking out of his shoes. One day Father took the bus downtown to look for a store that had shoes for sale. He returned empty handed and upset. The lines between his brows had become deeper.

"The destruction of department stores, government buildings and houses is enormous. Clean-up and rebuilding is going to take years," he said.

More people were vying for the little food that was available for purchase in stores or for barter. Hundreds of people froze to death in their make-shift living quarters or died from hunger. Burying them had become more difficult than in the previous year. Digging graves in the frozen ground was impossible and there were not enough warehouses to store the bodies.

Even our chickens were affected by the cold. They laid fewer eggs. Father built a cage for them inside the pen and covered it with rags to keep the chickens from freezing. Then he heard of a widow who was willing to barter her dead husband's shoes for food. We ate fewer eggs until we had saved enough for barter. Mother added more flour to the scrambled eggs for dinner. Soon Alfred had a pair of shoes. They were too big, so he stuffed rags in the front.

School was cancelled during a long cold spell and we spent most of the time indoors. I don't remember Christmas or New Year's Eve that year. There was no cake for Oma's and my birthday in January.

When the cold spell broke, it rained during the day and froze at night. Our street was covered with a solid sheet of ice in the mornings. One day, the ice was so thick, that boys skated on it.

My brothers found the rusted, clamp-on skates in the cellar. While Mother ironed on the kitchen table, and I practiced subtracting numbers on my slate-board, they sharpened the blades with Father's tools and smeared grease on the screws that would tighten the clamps. They worked an entire afternoon but the screws didn't budge.

Alfred put his finger over his lips and whispered, "I have an idea."

When Mother took a stack of ironed bed sheets upstairs, my brothers scrambled into the cellar and returned quickly stuffing old rubber seals from Mother's canning jars into their pockets. They bundled up in haste, grabbed the skates and went outside.

I put my coat and scarf on and followed. On the sidewalk, they used the rubber bands to fasten the skates to their shoes. When they straightened up, their feet kept slipping from under them and they clung to the trunk of a poplar tree to keep from falling.

Older boys skated up and down the street swinging their arms.

Alfred tested the ice with the tip of one skate. Then he let go of the tree and inched toward the middle of the street struggling to keep his balance. Then he glided down the road until he hit a dip, his ankles buckled and he fell to the ground.

An older boy stopped in front of him, pulled Alfred up, and said, "The road has a little slant, that's why the skates take off before you're ready. Watch how I swing my feet. You'll get the hang of it soon."

Alfred watched the boy then tried his moves. He struggled but stayed on his feet. Jürgen and I looked on from under the poplar tree. It was freezing cold.

Alfred steadied himself and glided down the incline. At the end, he turned around triumphantly and waved, then lost his balance and fell again. Unperturbed, he straightened his cap, got on his feet and continued down the road. After a few trips up and down the street, he scooted back to us.

"Come on Jürgen. Take short steps, keep your ankles stiff and hold on to me."

Hand in hand they inched onto the ice and skated away.

More children came out bundled up in shawls and gloves and watched from the sidewalk. We stomped our feet to keep warm.

I watched my brothers. Suddenly Alfred skates got lose and skidded away from him. He fell forward. His face hit the ice. I ran toward him. He held his bleeding nose. Other boys stopped and surrounded him.

"The rubber bands wore out," he said and looked embarrassed.

I picked up the skates and pieces of rubber.

Then Jürgen limped toward us one skate in hand the other on his shoe. Alfred got up and we went home together.

New Challenges, 1947

Chapter 44

My brother Alfred spent the winter evenings reading books about the lives of animals and drawing them in their natural habitat. He often talked with Father about hunting and fishing.

One cold evening, I came home from Oma's house before my parents and Jürgen. I was surprised to see Alfred sitting on a chair facing the kitchen window. I walked behind him and peeked over his shoulder. Propped up against the window frame was a magazine with pictures of various rodents. To his right, lay pages ripped from a magazine with the title *Taxidermy* written in big black letters. Below the title were drawings of a hawk with its wings spread and deer heads with antlers, mounted on a wall.

"What are you doing?" I asked.

He spun around. His eyes sparkled. In his right hand, he held mother's potato peeling knife. "I'm learning how to stuff animals. I'm starting with a small one."

He turned around and continued scraping. I stepped closer. Stretched out, in front of him, on Mother's wooden cutting board, lay a ghastly little gray head, with its mouth open. Drops of blood had stained the board.

"What is that?" I gasped.

"It's a mouse. I caught it without damaging its fur. I'm going to stuff it. See, you spread the legs and nail them down. Then you cut the belly and chest open and clean it out."

I saw the little curved tail still attached to the body. A bloody blob of the innards lay on a piece of brown paper next to it. My stomach churned and I pinched my nose.

"The tail will be the hardest to do," he said.

"What are you going to stuff it with?"

"With sawdust and wire. Then I'll mount it and put it on my dresser."

When my parents and Jürgen came home Mother said, "What's that awful smell." She came closer and examined Alfred's work station. "What are you doing with my cutting board and paring knife? Are you out of your mind?"

I cleaned my hands and face at the wash basin in the corner. Father stepped next to Mother and put his arm around her shoulder. While drying my cheeks with a towel, I noticed a faint smile creep over Father's face.

"Alfred, you shouldn't use Mother's things," he said. "There are pieces of wood in the shed you can use."

"How am I going to clean the cutting board so I can use it again?" Mother thundered, her eyes flashing with anger. "You better clean up right now."

Father said. "I'll use my plane tomorrow and clean your board."

"How!" Mother yelled.

"I'll shave off a layer of wood. Then I'll scrub it with Persil."

Alfred freed the nails from the creature's limbs with care and laid it gently aside. He crumbled the innards up in the brown paper and took them outside to the trash can.

Days later I asked him when he was going to finish stuffing the mouse. "I ruined the tail," he said. "The knife slipped and I cut it off."

I didn't tell Alfred, but I was relieved that I didn't have to look at a stuffed mouse on his dresser when I passed through his room to go to bed in my parents' room.

≈

We attended Sunday services again with the big church congregation once the minister, who had been a Nazi sympathizer, was replaced. He was the reason my family had left the big church during the war and joined the small congregation that worshipped in the potato cellar. I remembered how upset my parents and grandparents were after the war when this pastor was allowed to lead the congregation again.

They were pleased when a new minister was installed. He moved into the sister dormitory because the pastor's house had been destroyed in 1943—the same year the big church had also been hit by bombs. The only part that was not gutted was a room in the back where fourteen-year-olds met to study Bible verses and Psalms in preparation for their confirmation.

That is where we met now for services on Sunday mornings because the big church had not been rebuilt. People crowded into this small space and didn't mind if they had to stand. Latecomers listened through the open door from the outside stoop and steps. Most of the time I didn't understand what the pastor talked about, but I liked listening to the harmonium and the hymns.

One Sunday, at the end of the sermon, the new pastor said, "Many of our parishioners are forced to live in squalor and many do not have enough to eat. One of our esteemed church elders even announced that stealing food for survival was not a sin."

I peeked at Mother. Her eyes focused at the cross on the wall.

The pastor continued, "We have received a shipment of CARE packages with food from America."

People turned to their neighbors and smiled.

"Because there are not enough for each family, we will divide them into smaller portions and distribute them on Wednesday. Everyone will receive something according to the size of their family."

Later that week, Father came home with a package under his arm. We gathered around the table when he opened it. "This is food from America," he said.

Inside were a few tins and packages with words I couldn't read. Father tore the wrapper off a thin package.

"Chocolate!" Alfred said.

Mother broke it into pieces and passed them around. "Let it melt on your tongue."

Fresh Herring and Sparrow Soup, 1947

Chapter 45

We loved the canned meat from the CARE package. Mother cut it into thin slices and fried them until they were toasty brown. I had never tasted such delicious meat before and after I swallowed the last bite, I licked my plate. We also liked the crackers and raisins that were in the package. All too soon the last of the American food was gone.

A few days later, Alfred came home from school very excited, "I heard that a truckload of fresh herring from the North Sea will arrive at the market plaza next to the swim hall early Friday morning. I'm going to buy some for us."

"Alfred, the market is too far and the streets are not safe for children in the dark." Mother said

"I'll be thirteen in July. Besides, my friends are also going. We're meeting at four in the morning in front of our house."

Mother shrugged. "If you insist on going, take the enamel bucket with you. Our kitty Mietze will devour the scraps."

On Friday morning the front door slammed and woke me. It was still dark. Then I heard Alfred and his friends whispering outside. They're leaving for the market, I thought. I snuggled back under my comforter and looked forward to a fried herring dinner that night.

Later that morning, when I got ready for school, Alfred returned almost in tears. "Empty! No fish heads for Mietze," he said tipping the bucket for Mother to see. "By the time we got to the swim hall, the line was blocks long. The fishmonger ran out of herring before it was my turn."

Mother took the pail and said, "You tried your best. Maybe there will be another shipment soon."

"I would have to leave by three in the morning to get any. There was still a long line behind me when I left."

Food was always on my mind and the adults talked about how to get it.

❧

Spring was coming. The weather was mild and the poplar trees had sprouted new leaves. Their shadows danced on the sidewalk when the sunrays penetrated through the branches. I liked jumping on the shadows and counted aloud how many I caught. Women chatted in small groups under the trees and toothless old men sat on benches or chairs in front of the houses. When my mother and I stopped to visit with a group of neighbor ladies, they only talked about the difficulty of buying groceries.

"But we're lucky that our men have work and earn money, even though we can't buy enough food for them or shoes for our children," Frau Bach said.

One morning Father was writing a letter when Mother returned from the milkman clutching the empty pail to her chest.

"No milk today." She looked concerned. "The war ended two years ago and I can't get milk for the children." She wiped strands of hair from her forehead and sank onto the chair next to the stove looking troubled.

Father dipped the fountain pen into the inkpot and looked at Mother. "I'm writing to Kathel letting her know I'm coming," he said. "I'll chance another train trip to Bavaria as soon as I can get time off from work. I know she'll try to get cheese and butter from the farmers before I arrive."

"Thank God for Kathel and farmers you went to school with," Mother said. "I feel sorry for the poor folks who have no garden and no one to help them. No wonder tuberculosis is on the rise."

"I heard that too," Father said. "I also heard that the Americans are working on a plan to rebuild Europe. I wonder if they'll reconstruct Germany."

"A plan? What kind of a plan?" Mother asked.

"It's an assistance program developed by Secretary of State George Marshall."

"That plan isn't going to help me feed our family this year." Mother lamented.

While my parents continued talking, I left and walked down our garden path. The fragrance of lily of the valley always made me feel better and I skipped toward the back gate. Then I heard someone whisper my name. I looked around, but couldn't see any one.

"Psst! Ulla! Over here."

A hand motioned frantically between the fence posts.

"Ulla! Come here."

It was Jürgen.

When I arrived at the gate, he said, "Come behind the fence and duck down so Mother can't see you from the upstairs window."

"She's downstairs in the kitchen," I said.

Next to Jürgen crouched my brother Alfred and two of their friends. On the ground were bricks, stacked three high and arranged in a square with one side open. Inside the bricks a little fire smoldered. I recognized the red haired boy from the school yard. He blew on the embers until they spewed sparks and shot crimson flares into the air.

Ewald, who lived on our street, put a dented enamel pot filled with water over the fire.

"What are you doing?"

"We're making sparrow soup." Ewald said beaming.

"I shot these sparrows with my sling shot," said the redhead. "When the water starts boiling, you can help us pluck the feathers. I'll clean out the insides." He grinned and showed me his pocket knife and flipped it open.

Jürgen grabbed my arm. "Ulla, while the water is heating, go back to our house and get some salt. Put it in this empty match box."

"Why don't you do it?"

"Mother will get suspicious if she sees me one more time going in and out. I already went to the cellar a few times sneaking coal out under my sweater."

'She's going to see me taking salt from the kitchen cabinet," I said feeling very nervous.

"She won't see you. I just saw her put our comforter out to air in the upstairs window."

"The sparrow soup will taste better with salt in it. Besides, we'll give some to Mother. She's always looking for meat to put in her pot." He threw chunks of black coal on the fire with his bare hands and watched my face, waiting for an answer.

"I'll try," I said and left.

When I opened the front door I heard Mother singing one of her favorite songs, "For meinem Vaterhaus steht eine Linde."

I tip-toed to the kitchen cabinet and slowly opened the bottom door so its hinges wouldn't squeak. Mother kept the salt in the back of the shelf in a brown enamel bowl. I took the small box Jürgen had given me from my apron pocked and scooped salt into it. As I put the partially-filled box in my pocket, Mother opened the kitchen door. I jumped up.

"Ah, Ulla," she said. "You can bring me some potatoes from the cellar."

I rushed down the wooden steps, turned the light on, glanced around the corner to see if anyone was hiding in the coal bin and pushed the door open to the back cellar where the potatoes were. I filled the pail and put a few into my pockets. When I put the potatoes on the kitchen table Mother wasn't there anymore and I hurried out of the house.

Once in the garden path, I stopped and took a deep breath before continuing to where the boys were hiding.

Then I heard Mother calling my name. I turned around and saw her in the upstairs window shaking the comforters.

"Ursel, pick a handful of green onion tops from the garden and bring them to me."

I nodded and waved. When she left the window I ran to the boys, gave Jürgen the salt and dumped the potatoes on the ground.

"Prima," he said.

Ewald held four sparrows by their feet with heads dangling down and Alfred poured hot water over them. When they were soaked, Ewald gave a bird to each of the boys. They started to pull on the feathers but they didn't come out easily.

"We might as well cut the wings off, they're nothing but bones," one of them said.

It smelled awful and I pinched my nose. "Mother is waiting, I better pick the onions. I'll bring some for our soup too," I said and rushed away.

Mother was still making beds upstairs when I put the onion tops on the table and hurried back outside.

When I returned to our hiding place, the sparrows twirled in water in the dented pot perched on the make shift brick stove. Redhead peeled the potatoes. On the ground lay a few small carrots covered with clumps of soil. Ewald rubbed them clean against the fabric of his pant leg. I tossed the green onions in the pot, added a little salt and could feel the rising warmth from the boiling broth on my face. The flames from the hot embers stained the side of the pot black.

Ewald pulled a handful of leaves from his pant pocket and tossed them in. "I picked these from the maggie bush in our garden. My mom always adds them to soup."

The boys called the redhead Rudi. He cut the potatoes and carrots into chunks with his pocket knife and dropped them into the pot. Water splashed up and burned his hand. He jumped back and rubbed it against his shirt. He showed us the red blotches on the side of his hand.

"It's nothing," he said.

The boys' fingers were filthy and their cheeks smudged and flushed. Steam rose from the brew—it began to smell good.

"Let's wash up," Ewald said. All four peeked through the fence toward the houses. "All's clear. Ulla, stir the soup with this stick while we're gone."

239

They raced toward our duck pond. I churned the chunks in the pan while I watched the boys dunk their hands in the pond and clean their faces. They returned in a flash.

Rudi removed small aluminum bowls from inside his jacket.

My brother Alfred speared a bird in the pot with the stick and pulled it out. Broth dripped from its cavity. "Give me a dish," he commanded. "Let's test if it's done." He pulled the sparrow's leg away from its body and a tiny bone came out. "Our dinner is ready," he said lowering his voice to sound like a man.

He dunked the dish into the pot and scooped up broth with some vegetables and meat that had come off the bones.

"Ouch, that's hot," he said setting the dish on the ground. He quickly filled the rest.

"Ulla, you taste it first," Rudi said handing me a teaspoon.

"Why me?"

"Come on. You're a girl," he said.

I grabbed the corner of my apron and reached for the steaming bowl. A tiny bone with a sliver of meat on it twirled among, carrots, potatoes and wilted green leaves. "I smell the onions," I said. "It smells good."

"Taste it!" All four said at the same time.

"It's hot—I have to let it cool."

"Blow on it."

I scooped up a bit of cloudy broth with dark specs floating on top and blew. The boys sat cross-legged in front of me and stared at my face. Four bowls filled with soup sat on the ground in front of them. Each boy held a spoon in one hand ready to dip.

Slowly I guided the spoon to my lips, looked from boy to boy and noticed my stomach churning before trying it. Then I slurped a little brew from the tip of my spoon.

Mud came to mind. It tasted like mud, like the wild duck eggs Alfred had scrambled for us a while back that no one could eat. With pursed lips, I swallowed, waited a few seconds—then smiled.

"Good!" I said. "Good! But I have to help Mother now." I jumped up and sprinted up the garden path. I knew they wouldn't let her taste that awful soup.

It's a Goat, 1947

Chapter 46

When I went down to the kitchen for breakfast, Father stood in the middle of the room next to his suitcase, already dressed in his coat.

He turned around and said, "I'm getting ready for another hamstern trip."

"What do you mean?" I asked.

"People call the trips to the country where they barter or beg for food from farmers, hamstern. It reminds them of the way hamsters collect food in their cheeks to take to their burrows."

"I've seen people with sacks over their shoulders coming from the train station." I said and watched Mother wrap jam sandwiches in brown paper, then fill the thermos with hot ersatz coffee and put them in Father's knapsack.

He took a bite from his bread and slurped his coffee standing up. "I'll be back in a week. I don't have much time off."

The sky was overcast when Father and I walked together as far as the corner of the street to the station. I hugged him.

"Mind your mother," he said stroking my hair.

I mumbled, "Aufwiedersehn," and continued on my way to school.

❧

It seemed no time at all had passed when on my way home from playing with my friend Ilse, I spotted a man in the distance with a big brown animal pulling against a leash.

Up the street, boys pointed to the person and yelled, "Look, Herr Fischer brought a horse."

Was that my dad? He wasn't wearing his cap. I strained to see and hurried along until I recognized him—then I ran. As I got near he put his suitcase on the sidewalk and pulled the animal in tight. The brown creature bucked its hind legs and rammed its head into Father's side. The boys ran toward him too, but stayed on the other side of the street.

"Pappa, that's not a horse," I said.

"No Ulla, that's not a horse. It's a goat," he said pulling the rope even tighter.

"Are you going to butcher it?"

"No. I got her for the milk."

"Goats give milk?"

"The females have udders to feed their young."

We walked home side by side. I put my hand next to Father's on the suitcase handle and helped him carry the heavy load. The boys across the street pointed and laughed when the goat kicked and fought against the tight-held line.

'It's not a horse," I yelled at them annoyed. "It's a goat!"

They stopped laughing.

When we reached our courtyard, Mother appeared in the door and beamed. "What did you bring us this time?"

"This is Lore. Kathel got her from Pongratz for us. It's sure nice to have farmers as friends."

Mother came down the steps and took the suitcase from Father. They shook hands and gazed into each other's eyes for a second.

"I'll put her in the pigsty for now. It's safest there," he said.

In the house, Mother unloaded the suitcase. She put two farmer's breads, a chunk of butter, blueberry jam and a piece of smoked bacon on the table.

While we ate dinner, Father told us about his train ride home. "I had to travel with Lore in the freight compartment. It was packed with gaunt people returning from hamstern. They eyed Lore with envy. I couldn't sleep for fear someone would grab her and disappear. People complained when she kicked and bleated during the night."

Father rubbed his eyes.

"You will enjoy sleeping in your own bed tonight." Mother said.

While we ate, we heard Lore kicking the wooden partition that separated her space from the chickens'.

Father said, "It'll take a while before she calms down, but her udder is full and I have to milk her tonight."

"Can I watch?" I asked.

"Ja, you can watch."

He turned to my brothers. "You boys have to help me hold her down so she won't kick the pail from my hands. It won't be easy. Just listen to her banging against the wall."

"Great!" my brothers chimed together. "We'll have fresh milk tonight."

When we opened the door to the stall, Lore kicked the gate with her hind legs. On the other side of the partition, the chickens flew into the air and made a ruckus. The rope was twisted around Lore's horns so she couldn't straighten her neck.

Father said, "Easy. Easy," and reached out to stroke her rump. She bucked. "Calm down Lore, take it easy."

He took a broad broom and maneuvered her against the wall. She tugged on the rope. He opened the gate, slowly moved toward her and unwound the rope from her horns. Father held the goat's neck tight with one hand, stroked her back with the other, talking to her in a low voice. When she had relaxed a bit, he offered her a handful of the hay he had brought back from the farm.

"Alfred, come here and hold her by the horns."

Father pulled twine from his coat pocket and tied her hind legs together. She jumped and fought against it but eventually tired.

"Gertrud, bring me the stool and bucket. Move slowly."

Mother handed Father the equipment.

He gave her the twine. "Hold it tight and keep her against the wall so she can't pull away."

Jürgen and I stayed behind the gate and watched.

243

Alfred struggled to hold her head by the horns. Father sat down on the stool close to her flank and put the bucket between his knees. When he touched her udder, she struggled and kicked. Mother held her tighter. Father squeezed the teats and a stream of milk flowed into the bucket.

"She's full. I couldn't milk her on the train. This is harder than I thought. You can't milk her like a cow," he whispered and continued with even strokes. After a while, Lore settled down.

When Father finished, he handed the bucket to Jürgen. Gradually he rose and pushed the stool aside. He took the rope from Mother and nodded for her to leave. He untied the goat's legs. She kicked so hard that Alfred let go of the horns. The goat chased him and he jumped over the partition out of the sty. Father evaded her and slipped out.

"We won't drink much of the milk at one time. We are not used to so much butter fat and would get diarrhea." Father said.

Back in the kitchen, Mother filtered the milk through a cloth-lined strainer and put five enamel mugs on the table. When the family sat down, she poured a little into each cup and handed them around. The milk smelled like the goat. Butterfat rose to the top. I took a sip. It tasted strong, but creamy, and I had trouble swallowing it. I wiped my lips with my sleeve and hoped that Father didn't notice me gagging.

By the next day, the word had gotten around that Fischer's had a goat. It was a warm day and we kept the front door open to let fresh air into the house. In the afternoon, I saw Frau Witten talking to Father in the front patio. He told us later that her sister had come to live with them until a bed became free in the overfilled tuberculosis sanatorium.

I had seen a sick woman across the street several times but didn't know it was Gisela's aunt. Her gaunt face was so grey and her body so thin that she leaned against the brick wall when she watched the activities in our neighborhood for a while.

Every evening, Mother sent one of us with a glass jar filled with goat's milk to the Witten's house for the sister with tuberculosis.

Summer's Coming, 1947

Chapter 47

I was grateful for the warm weather because I didn't have to wear my bloomers and long-stockings, and the sun made everything in our garden grow. Almost every afternoon, I saw Mother hoeing and raking the vegetable patches. She pulled weeds in the flower beds and watered them with rainwater caught in buckets.

I was sad that my brothers didn't want me around anymore. They had many friends and Mother told me to leave them alone. But I wondered where they went after school. They usually met under the poplar trees and then disappeared for hours.

One day I heard the boys in the courtyard. I went to the living room window and listened from there. They seemed excited but I couldn't hear what they were saying. Some of them had rolled-up towels tucked under their arms. My brothers raced back into the house and returned with towels under their arms too.

After they left the courtyard, I went outside and watched them head toward Harbor Strasse. They're going swimming in the canal. I followed them but stayed far enough behind so they wouldn't think I was trailing them. But I didn't have to worry, they talked and kidded around so much, they never turned around.

On Harbor Strasse, I stayed close to the wooden fence that enclosed the bombed houses to keep people out of the rat-infested ruins. I peeked through a hole in the fence. Parts of soot-stained walls were still standing, ceilings had collapsed and roofs were gone. Debris piled high where people once lived. The debris seemed to be moving. Rats! Thousands of rats climbed over each other and rummaged for food. I shuddered. Shaken, I hurried away.

The sun felt good on my back. The boys had turned on to the street with the harbor gatehouse at the corner. How did they get past the gatekeeper? A dump truck pulled up at the gate and stopped. A man in a blue uniform came out of the house and talked with the driver. Then he lifted the barrier and the truck rumbled through. Once the gatekeeper was back inside, I sneaked by his window and raced after the boys.

Father had talked about the different harbors along the canal where barges picked up coal in one harbor and delivered wood to another. Across the canal, was a warehouse where groceries were delivered by ship and trucks later transported them to wholesale markets. The harbors past the gatehouse were like bays with docks for smaller boats.

The boys had passed the first bay where a row of abandoned and decaying boats were tethered to dilapidated docks. I rushed by the tall crane to my right that stood on rusted iron tracks. Halfway to the sky was the operator's cabin, riddled with bullet and shrapnel holes from the war. Its door hung loose and clanged against the steel frame. The boys turned a corner at the next bay. I hurried by mounds of scrap metal and heaps of junk. They walked all the way to the last dock at the edge of the canal. I hid behind a stack of empty oil drums and watched.

The boys undressed and stuffed their clothes under a bush. They huddled together in their underwear, arms folded over their white chests. Then one of them ran across the wooden planks of the dock and jumped into the water making a big splash. The other boys ran to the end of the dock cheering. Several jumped.

Others went down the incline and looked underneath the wooden planks. My brother Alfred reached above his head and held on to something. He pulled his legs up like a frog and dangled in the air. Then he let go of one hand and quickly grabbed a hold in front of the other hand. Repeating this action he swung his body from side to side, moving away from the shore.

When he reached the end of the dock, he paused for a second then plunged into the canal. I didn't know he could swim. When he climbed back up the incline, the other boys cheered then some of them copied what Alfred had done. Some boys jumped into the canal from above the dock, others from underneath. They yelled and jumped and splashed. Only my brother Jürgen stood back and watched.

"Come on, Jürgen it's fun," someone shouted.

"I can't swim."

"Do the dog paddle—like this."

Jürgen inched toward the edge of the water, dipped his toe in and then lowered his body into the canal. He flailed his arms wildly splashing water into his face.

I grew tired of watching the boys and decided to learn how to swim too. But first, I had to find a place where they couldn't see me. I went back to Dock 3, took off my clothes except for my underwear and put them under the nearby willow tree. Feeling a little uncertain, I crawled down to the water. Sunlight made the oil spots on the surface shimmer in light-green and blue hues. The water felt cool and refreshing on my toes. Since I had nothing to hold onto, I was too afraid to go in.

Above my head I noticed that the wooden planks were held in place by rusted rail road tracks. I climbed back up and latched onto them like Alfred had done. I pulled up my knees and suddenly swayed in mid-air. My shoulders ached from the pull of my weight. This was harder than I expected. I could only hold on for a few seconds then slipped and tumbled onto the incline.

Determined, I clambered back up and repeated the maneuver. By holding my fingers a little differently, I was able to latch onto the tracks and practiced moving one hand in front of the other as my brother had done. I inched away from the shore and dangled above water. Halfway out, my arms began to ache. I pushed on. My shoulders felt as if someone were wrenching them from my body. My fingertips burned and slipped off the tracks.

I plunged into the water. It felt good on my sweaty, hot back. I sank deep into the canal and was grateful when my toes touched gravel. The impact made the gravel give and I slipped lower. I looked up and stretched my hands to the surface. There was nothing to hold on to. The sun rippled through the murky water. I pushed away from the gravel again, but it didn't hold and I slipped further under water. I needed air and was tempted to open my mouth and breath but instead clamped my lips tight. I knew that I would drown if I opened my mouth.

Frantically I searched with my toes for something to hold on to. My gaze never left the rippling image of the sun. It was getting smaller. Dear God, I don't want to sink into the darkness. At last I felt something solid under foot and stepped on it. I gathered all my strength and pushed as hard as I could with arms reaching for the sky. I heaved out of the water as if someone put wings under my arms. When my fingers felt the iron rails I held on to them. Frantically I pulled myself to shore. Overjoyed I let go and fell to the ground. Tears washed over my drenched cheeks. Someone had helped me, I knew.

I crawled to the willow tree breathing hard and collapsed on the grass next to my clothes. After a while, I sat up and hugged my knees to stop shaking.

In the distance, the boys jumped into the canal splashing water high into the air.

In the Canal, 1947

Chapter 48

We all welcomed summer vacation and slept late every day except on Sundays when we went to church. After Sunday dinner, Father told my brothers the chores they needed to do during the week.

"Keep the garden in good shape," he said. "Weeds take moisture and nutrients out of the soil that the vegetables need. Once a week, remove the dirty straw from the goat's stall and clean the droppings from the chicken coop."

Alfred nodded and said, "We'll do that."

Before going downstairs for breakfast, I often watched my brothers from the upstairs bedroom working in our garden. They pulled weeds, put them in buckets and took them to the shed where we kept them for chicken feed.

One day, Alfred pushed our wheel barrel filled with urine-drenched straw from the goat's stall down the garden path and dumped it on a heap behind the back fence. A few days later, I saw Jürgen carry a pail filled with chicken manure in one hand, holding his nose with the other. Father used the straw and manure to fertilize the garden in the spring.

On warm afternoons, my brothers met their friends and went to the canal. I usually followed a few minutes later. My best friend Ilse couldn't go. Her mother didn't allow it. I always left before my mother could ask where I was going.

The boys had become a boisterous bunch and confident swimmers. I wanted to learn how to swim, too. They raced across the dock and dove into the water head first. I watched with envy as they swam to the middle of the canal.

At my dock, Dock 3, I undressed quickly and always stashed my clothes under the same dangling willow branches. To keep my underwear from slipping off my hips, I made a knot in the worn-out elastic. Slowly, I inched down the incline. The first piling under the dock seemed only an arm's length from shore. I put my feet in the cool water but didn't go in. Instead, I sat on my heels and pondered how to do the dogpaddle. When I finally gathered the courage I pushed away from the embankment. I kept my chin above water and my lips closed. When I felt no support under my feet, I flailed my arms and kicked my legs. Water splashed into my face. It stung a little and I closed my eyes. Then I couldn't see the piling anymore. Anxiously I used my hands as if they were paddles and pushed the water out of my way. I kicked my feet as hard as I could and felt my body glide forward until my fingers slammed into the moss-covered piling. I grabbed onto it but slipped off its slimy surface. I swung my arms and legs around the pillar and clung to it like a spider. Breathless, but feeling triumphant, I looked back to shore. I'd done it. When my heartbeat slowed, my legs tired and I started sliding down. Knowing that I couldn't hold on much longer, I pushed off and struggled back.

With enthusiasm, I practiced the dogpaddle to the piling closest to me and back. Eventually I learned to do it without splashing water on my face. Then I ventured out to the second piling, and rested only for a minute before paddling back to shore. I repeated it over and over until my arms and legs felt exhausted. I was still in the water, when I heard the boys' voices above and ducked under to hide from them. When I couldn't hold my breath any longer, I came up for air. They were gone. I climbed out of the water and collapsed on the ground next to the willow tree. When my drenched body dried, I dressed.

My brother Jürgen had become a good swimmer and ventured out into the canal with the older boys. He no longer flailed his arms.

I wanted to learn how to do that, too, and looked for a place on the shore of the canal to swim. It had to be a spot far enough away from the guys so they couldn't see me. To my surprise, there were no docks to protect me. I walked to where the embankment curved a little and was delighted to see a suitable little willow for hiding my clothes. This became my very own, new swimming spot.

The first time I dipped into the open canal, I went in quickly and dogpaddled out a stretch. On my return, the current had pushed me downstream from my little tree.

One day, when I sat at the shore of my new swimming spot, I noticed a barge under the bridge. Across the mouth of the bay from where the boys played, a man dove into the water and swam toward the middle of the canal. When the vessel came near him, he disappeared under water. He stayed below for a long time. It made me nervous. The barge floated noiselessly closer. The man's head popped up like a bouncing ball. To my surprise he swam toward the barge. When he reached the side of the ship, his body heaved out of the water and gripped the rim of the hull. The barge pulled him along like a weightless little speck. Then he hoisted himself up onto the deck and ran across to the other side. He stopped for a moment, looked around then he dove off. I had forgotten to breathe and gulped air.

The boys were also watching and started yelling and pointing to the stranger. I stood up expecting the angry captain of the ship to appear. But he didn't. When the barge passed, I searched for the man in the canal. He surfaced near the opposite shore.

"There he is!" the boys shouted jumping to their feet.

The daring stranger rolled on his back and watched the ship glide away. With strong strokes he swam back to the spot where he had started.

At home, my brothers boasted they could do what the stranger in the canal had done, too. "How hard could it be to climb onto a moving ship?"

"Ja, but don't get caught in the propeller," Alfred said gesturing a cut across his throat with his hand.

One afternoon while I practiced the breast stroke, I saw a barge leaving the coal harbor turning west. Up away, the boys pointed to it. One by one they went in waist-high and waited. When the boat came closer, they swam toward the middle without splashing or making a noise. When they were next to the barge, they grabbed its side, climbed on, ran across to the opposite side and jumped into the water yelling. Only Ömmes Bach didn't jump. He stood frozen.

A man, wearing a navy blue cap, burst through the door of the little house at the bow, flailing a broom through the air. He shouted, "Ihr Bande! Get off my boat. I'm going to report you to the police."

Ömmes stirred and jumped. I hid behind the willow. My heart pounding, I searched for the boys. The barge, only a dark outline against the setting sun, floated toward the Rhine River. The boys' heads bobbed up in the wake. They yelled in triumph and splashed water at each other.

When they climbed back to shore, I was so excited, I ran to them, and shouted, "You did it! You did it!"

They looked at me beaming and collapsed on the grass. They boasted about their adventure and patted Ömmes on the back. I squatted behind them, squinting into the sun, happy that they didn't shoo me away.

They ignored me and I went back to my spot to practice the breast stroke. I swam a little further every time.

Tired but feeling happy, I went home. Over dinner, Mother talked about having to mend our school clothes and darn our socks before summer vacation came to an end.

I felt anxious because I wanted to swim as well as the boys did before the end of the summer. So I went to the canal to practice even when they didn't go.

One day I felt confident enough to venture to the middle of the canal and back. To my surprise, that wasn't so hard and I repeated it several times. I climbed shivering onto the shore and fell onto a patch of grass near my favorite tree. The sun warmed me. Powder-puff clouds drifted overhead.

Then I spotted a barge laying low in the water. This was my chance. There was no one to stop me. When it floated under the bridge, I slithered down the incline. At the right moment, I went into the water. It squished through holes in my threadbare underwear. I swam out toward the middle of the canal, watching the steering house at the bow. A shadow moved behind the window. Quickly, I ducked under and swam below the surface toward the boat with strong and even strokes. Algae floated in the murky canal.

Under water, the ship groaned and creaked. For a split second, I wanted to turn back. I didn't. When I couldn't hold my breath any longer, I popped my head up and gulped for air. The vessel loomed above me. I heaved high out of the water, reaching for the ledge. When I felt its rough surface, I grabbed it. My body slammed against the iron hull. My legs and feet flapped against the rough shell of the ship. I struggled to hold on. My arms and shoulders ached. I panicked about being sucked into the rotating blades of the propeller at the rear, and realized that I didn't have the strength to hoist myself onto the deck.

How was I going to get away from this iron monster? I tried to pull my feet up. It was too hard. I wanted to put them against the hull so I could push away from it, but the drift was too strong. I had to try harder. With all my strength I pulled my knees under my chin, stuck my feet against the iron wall and pushed. Kicking and swinging my arms frantically, my body seemed to pull away from the tow of the vessel and away from the propeller. I slashed and kicked, barely coming up for air. When the wake of the barge waned and I couldn't feel the pull of the ship anymore, I dared to glance over my shoulder. The barge glided away toward the Rhine River. I turned on my back and watched its silhouette grow faint. Jubilant, I swam to shore.

With buckling knees I crawled up the embankment and sank on to the ground under the willow tree. The sun, at the horizon, had little warmth left. Shivering, I got up and pulled my dress over my wet hair. My socks resisted sliding over my damp feet.

Exhausted but exuberant, like I never felt before, I strolled home savoring my triumph. When I entered the kitchen, my family was eating the evening meal. Mother looked up. "Next time you go to the canal, I want you to come home with the boys."

I nodded but didn't say anything. Alfred and Jürgen looked at me questioningly. I ignored them and sat down. The fried potatoes and goat's milk tasted good. After dinner, Mother mended socks, Father went out to milk the goat and I went to bed.

A few days later, another policeman came to our street and talked with parents. Father had another chat with us.

"A boy had slipped off a barge into the canal. He was sucked into the propeller. The blades slashed his legs. His injuries were so severe that he bled to death."

I gasped.

"Captains are going to put black tar on the sides of their barges to keep children off."

Mother looked from the boys to me and said, "I never want to see tar on your clothes or bodies."

My hands trembled.

Giving Thanks, 1947

Chapter 49

There was a chill in the air and Mother insisted I wear long stockings and a warm undershirt to school. I looked forward to starting second grade, but not to the three kilometer walk to the Hausberge School in the cold rain. The first leaves on the poplar trees turned yellow and black smoke rose from the chimneys over the rooftops. I felt sad that the warm summer days were gone.

While chewing his bread Alfred asked, "Why wasn't our school rebuilt during our summer vacation? It's only ten minutes from here."

Father looked up from his newspaper. "The building material shortage has not improved. There aren't enough bricks, wood or roof tiles to repair buildings or glass to replace windows or pipes for fixing the plumbing and sewer."

We all looked up when we heard a loud knock on the front door. Before Mother got up, the door handle clicked and Sister Maria from our parish burst in. "Guten Morgen! Guten Morgen!" she chirped like a songbird. "Hope you all slept well."

"Danke, danke," Mother said. "Come in! Would you like a cup of ersatz coffee?"

"No! No! Danke schön—I had mine before dawn," she said rubbing her knotty fingers.

Sister Maria, dressed in a long black robe and a white starched deaconess' cap, joined us at the table. The shadow of a mustache and beard on her chin fascinated me. One curly hair on her chin bobbed up and down when she spoke.

"Autumn has arrived," she chimed. "Time to harvest vegetables—isn't it? Pastor Schwalbe is holding a Thanksgiving sermon on the lawn next to the church Sunday after next. He's asking members who have a garden to bring vegetables they can spare. We'll display them outside on a table next to the pulpit. After the sermon, we'll distribute them and any clothes or blankets you can spare to families in need."

Mother nodded. "I thank God for what we have, Sister Maria. We'll bring what we can."

The Sister jumped up. "Toodly-doo then," she sang. "Must go! Lots more people to see." She danced out of the room. "God bless! God bless!"

The front door slammed behind her.

No one moved until Father took a bite from his bread. Then he looked at my brothers and said, "Next week, I want you boys to do your homework right after school and help me harvest vegetables."

Father didn't ask me, but I felt I was old enough to work. My classes let out one hour before the boys. On Monday I hurried home from school, changed quickly into my play apron and rushed to the garden. I saw my parents bent over pulling beets near the back gate. I skipped toward them. In the middle of the path lay white and red cabbages.

"Can I help pick vegetables for the poor?"

Mother straightened. Her colorful headscarf had slipped and wisps of hair dangled over her cheek. She looked tired.

"You can put the cabbages into this crate. But don't drop them. They'll bruise."

Overjoyed, I skipped back. The cabbages were heavy. I used both hands to pick them up and put them into the wooden box.

When my brothers raced down the garden path, Father pointed to the crate and said, "Take these to the cellar. Put them in the back room against the wall under the window."

My grandparents also had been visited by Sister Maria and were pulling carrots and kohlrabi out of the ground in their vegetable patch.

Mother had left earlier to prepare the evening meal. We continued to pull turnips, kohlrabies and carrots and picked beans and peas until dusk. When we were done, we washed up with the rainwater in a tub near the empty rabbit hutch.

Father carried two full buckets, the boys a loaded crate between them and I, a basket of peas, to the house.

"Mother will can some for us for the winter and will put some aside to take to church for Thanksgiving" Father said. "Next week, we'll dig potatoes."

Exhausted, but smiling, we sat down around the table while Mother filled our bowls with milk-soup with flour Klunker in it. I liked Klunker—they tasted like noodles.

The following week, we harvested potatoes. Father dug them out of the ground with a pitch fork. Jürgen and I picked them up and removed clumps of dank soil with our bare hands. We made two piles, one for the big ones and one for the small ones. Alfred filled the aluminum pail with big potatoes and carried them to the house. When we were done, the boys raked the dried potato vines into a heap and Father held a lit match under the wrinkled leaves. He blew on them until they caught fire.

The first stars appeared in the unusually clear autumn sky. We sat cross-legged around the fire, stuck tiny potatoes on the tips of bare birch branches and held them over the bonfire. When the skin closest to the flames browned and cracked, we rotated the sticks so our precious treats wouldn't burn.

Father's potato had a brown crust. He blew on it and then took a little bite. "Not done yet," he said and returned it to the fire. "I have fond memories of growing up on the farm in Bavaria," he said. "In the Fall, Tante Kathel and I also roasted potatoes over an open fire. We, of course, had a big field to harvest and worked late into the night."

The orange flames leaping up to the twilight sky warmed the front of my body, but the cold evening breeze chilled my back. Listening to Father and sitting around the fire filled me with joy. But when I thought of my friends at school whose dads were killed in the war, I felt a pang of sadness.

Alfred broke the quiet moment. "My spud looks done." He blew on all sides and then bit into it. "Mmmm—it's good."

Mine looked done. I took a bite. The hot peel burned my lips. Immediately, I jerked back and ripped off a chunk of skin that had stuck to the sizzling crust. I dropped the potato and ran home crying.

"You're bleeding!" Mother said. "Let me look at you." She took my hand, guided me to the kitchen sink and lifted my chin. "This looks bad. I have to clean the charred potato skin off your lips."

"No!" I yelled. "Don't touch it. It hurts too much."

"Ulla, you'll get an infection if we don't clean it. You know that the doctors have no medicine for us."

Mother pushed a chair next to the wash basin. "Hold on to its back."

When she touched my lip with a wet cloth, I shoved her away, jumped back and howled. My face throbbed with pain. The taste of blood made me gag. My lower lip swelled like a sausage.

Mother gripped my shoulder firmly and pushed me against the wash basin. "Stand still. I must clean the wound."

Salty tears stung the open sore. When Mother finished, the men came home. Whimpering, I held my chin and cowered on the sofa. They ate left-over milk soup but I couldn't. The slightest touch of the spoon on my lip shot pain into my head.

The next day, Father cut my brothers hair in the kitchen. The boys chatted the entire time. Alfred said, "I heard that the farmer behind Lüschershof Street has a pair of rabbits and has young for sale."

I sat on the sofa, not able to close my swollen lips, watching Mother iron a blue satin ribbon for my hair. She stopped for a moment and looked thoughtfully up to the ceiling, "It would be nice to have meat again in my pot."

"Ja, it would be," Father answered. "I better visit farmer Braun. For a bucket of coal, I might be able to barter for a rabbit."

One afternoon, Father came home with two little rabbits jumping inside an old sack. "Unfortunately, the farmer had no full-grown rabbit we could roast. These are a pair. I hope they'll breed, multiply and grow fast. Mother, then you'll have meat for your pot," he said smiling.

The boys cheered. Even though my lip still hurt, my mouth watered thinking of roasted meat.

On Saturday, my brothers polished everyone's shoes while Mother heated water in a big kettle on the coal stove for our bath. Father brought the oval aluminum tub up from the cellar and placed it on the floor in the middle of the kitchen. Because I was the smallest, I bathed first, then Mother, then the boys.

Father always soaked his hands in warm, soapy water and brushed his fingers before taking his bath. Coal dust and garden dirt made the groves and cracks in his hands black. He liked clean fingernails when going to church.

My brothers and I couldn't go outside until our hair had dried. "You'll catch your death," Mother warned.

In the evening Mother laid out our Sunday clothes before we went to bed.

The next morning, Father looked handsome in his dark suit, white shirt and a tie. Mother brushed my hair and tied the blue satin bows in my braids. She looked nice in the black dress with the row of cloth-covered buttons down the front and a white lace collar. She had worn this dress on her wedding day. My brothers had combed their bowl-cut hair slick. When we were ready, Father carried our shopping net filled with green, red and orange vegetables on our way to church.

When we arrived, Sister Maria danced toward us and took the net from father. She added our carrots to the heap already on the table, the cabbages to others, and put the potatoes in a bucket standing on the grass.

On the lawn, adjacent to the roofless church were rows of chairs facing the Thanksgiving table. A white cloth with an embroidered cross covered the narrow, temporary pulpit. Father tipped his hat to friends and neighbors, while Mother waved and smiled.

We sat down and waited. More people arrived. Some put vegetables and apples on the table, others sat quietly on the chairs behind us. Some donated clothes and blankets were laid out on another table. Soon all the chairs were taken. People I didn't know arrived dressed in rags, looking haggard and sad. Latecomers had to stand. Father asked my brothers to give up their seat for an elderly couple, and Mother pulled me onto her lap to free another chair.

Pastor Schwalbe walked across the lawn in a black, floor-length robe carrying his leather-bound Bible. He stopped behind the pulpit and looked at all the faces in the audience nodding in friendly acknowledgement.

"It is nice to see such a big gathering," he started. "We would not all fit into the confirmation room. I'm also grateful that it's not raining this morning."

People laughed and shuffled in their seats.

"Let us pray."

We folded our hands for prayer and rose.

"Dear Lord, we give thanks on this day for this bounty so we may share it with those who have not enough to eat and no clothes to keep warm."

I didn't understand everything Pastor Schwalbe preached except when he talked about the Thanksgiving bounty. A few rows ahead of us, my friend Ilse turned around and waved. Her mother whispered into her ear, and Ilse turned to the front. Standing to my left, were my brothers with a group of boys who had given up their seats. They watched the birds overhead, flying south, while the minister spoke and the congregation sang.

After the last hymn, my parents visited with friends and then we headed home. I turned around and saw Sister Maria drop vegetables into people's open sacks. I felt proud that I had helped with the harvest.

Good Cigar, 1947

Chapter 50

Mother had canned peas, carrots and green beans, and the potatoes were stored in the cellar. It seemed we were ready for winter. But Mother looked worried.

In bed, before falling asleep, I heard her whisper to Father. "I didn't have enough vegetables for canning to last until spring. The young chickens are laying fewer eggs in this cold weather and the old hen has stopped laying altogether."

"I know," Father answered with a sleepy voice. "With luck, the rabbits will mate and have young. Then we'll have meat."

Our family spent the long winter evenings in the kitchen because it was the only warm room in the house. After dinner, Mother usually sat on the chair next to the stove mending clothes or darning socks. There was always one more patch she needed to sew on my brothers pants or a hem to let down on my dresses.

My brothers' played board games, did homework or read. Father fixed things. Shoes needed soles and knives had to be sharpened. My favorite time was when he told stories about growing up on the farm in Bavaria. I would snuggle up next to him. Everyone listened.

But not all was back to normal after the war.

One Sunday, after our midday meal, Father stretched his legs under the table and leaned back in his chair. "It's been a long time since I had a good cigar," he said.

Mother looked up. "I know what you mean. We're running out of everything. I just brewed the last pot of ersatz coffee and I don't know where to buy more."

Our big soup kettle was leaking. At the bottom of the aluminum pot was a ragged-edged gap the size of my little finger. The hardware store had nothing to fix it with. The salesman told Father about a customer who had repaired his pot with chewed-up bread and dried it at the back of the coal stove.

Father scratched his head. "I can't imagine it working, but I don't know what else to do."

Alfred volunteered, "Let me do it. I watched Ewald's dad fix their pan."

"Go ahead," Father said.

Alfred cut a chunk of bread and chewed it for a long time. Then he spit it into the palms of his hands and rolled it into a little sausage. He stuffed it into the crack in the pot and smoothed it out like putty with his thumbs and fingers. Looking satisfied, he positioned the empty pot at the back of the stove.

"Don't touch it," he warned. "I'll keep checking it and will know when it's ready."

Mother frowned. "This is the only soup kettle I have," she said.

Days later, I was surprised to see her cooking cabbage soup in the pot. I went to the stove. No broth leaked out. The chewed-up bread had crusted over the hole in the pot and plugged the leak.

We had just finished eating when Oma walked in. She glanced at the kettle and smiled. "Good work, Alfred. You can repair the leak in my pan next. Opa wants to see you. He's in the shed."

Alfred jumped from his seat. With giant leaps he left the house.

Oma joined us at the table and pulled a letter from her apron pocket. She handed it to Mother. "It's from your sister Änne. Read it."

Mother stopped clearing the soup bowls and wiped her hands on her apron. She unfolded the page and read aloud.

"My dear loved ones,

I have important news to share with you. I have just returned from visiting Kurt in an army hospital here in Germany. The sisters and Jan of-

fered to take care of little Manfred. Since the harvest is finished, they're not so busy on the farm. At five years, Manfred is a handful but they thought, together they could take care of him.

Kurt was happy to see me but heavily medicated and weak. He talked in between naps. Little by little I pieced his story together. In the last days of the war, his troop was defending Berlin when he was hit in both legs and captured by the Russians. They transferred him by train with thousands of other soldiers to a prison-of-war camp deep in Russia. They amputated one of his legs. Later, a severe infection in the other leg wouldn't heal. That is why they sent him home. The doctors here don't know if they can save it. Kurt refuses to have another amputation. I pray that he will respond to the treatment. As soon as I can, I will visit him again. You can't imagine how worried I am. I miss you all,
Eure Änne."

Mother wiped her damp cheek and Oma reached for her handkerchief.

Father said, "Two years in Russia. He's fortunate to be alive."

At that moment Alfred burst into the kitchen clutching a stack of huge, dried leaves in his hands. Opa followed grinning.

"What are those for?" I asked.

"They're tobacco leaves, Dummkopf. I'm going to make cigars. Opa will help."

Grandfather rubbed the shiny crown of his head and sat down. "Herr Stuhrhahn gave me some seeds in the spring. I grew the plants in an area behind our rhubarb."

The men broke into hearty laughter. Alfred filled a big bowl with warm water and laid a tobacco leaf flat on top. He waited until it sank to the bottom before putting the next one in. Everyone watched.

"They need to be completely flat. I hope they won't stick together," he said.

When all the leaves were submerged, he carried the bowl into the pantry.

Opa said, "If we had a little sweet plum juice and brandy, we could make a very good tasting product."

Everyone laughed.

A few days later, Opa came over again and Alfred brought the bowl with the tobacco leaves back into the kitchen. He spread an old sheet on the table and smoothed out all the folds. With thumbs and forefingers, he removed one delicate leaf from the brown water, dabbed it lightly on the cloth and held it up against the light to check for tears. Gently he laid the leaf flat on the same cutting board he had used for his taxidermy, mouse experiment. Sounding important, he explained each step like a teacher explaining a lesson. With the tip of Mother's potato peeling knife, he cut out the stem and carefully laid the halved leaves on the table.

When all were deveined, Opa cleared his throat and twirled his mustache. "Let me do the first one. Remember, not to roll them too tight or too loose or your Pappa won't be able to smoke them."

Opa rolled up the leaves, gently tapped the top with his finger tips. "I'm removing trapped air between the layers," he said.

When he was done, he picked up the roll and examined it from all sides.

"Not bad," he mused. "Hand me the scissors." He snipped off the ragged edges on both ends and looked at Father, "We'll cut these up for pipe tobacco later."

Then he laid the finished product in an empty cigar box and said, "Alfred, you do the rest."

Alfred eagerly repeated every step Opa had shown him. He was upset when he tore a leaf.

Opa said, "Put it in the pipe tobacco pile."

When Alfred was done, five dark cigars were in the box. "I'll let them dry on my dresser," he said and took them upstairs.

A few days later, when I walked by our outside drop-closet, blue smoke came out of the open window. It smelled like tobacco. Soon after, when I watched Mother peel onions in the kitchen, my brother Jürgen came in white-faced, clutching his stomach. His mouth contorted, he stumbled to the washbasin in the corner and threw up. Bent over, he dragged himself upstairs to his bedroom. He didn't eat supper with us.

After our Sunday dinner Alfred looked at Father. "I have a surprise for you."

He raced upstairs and returned quickly with the old cigar box and gave it to Father. "Now you have a good cigar," he said.

"Danke, Alfred. I will enjoy one right now." Father took a cigar from the box and held it to his nose. "Mmm, it smells good!"

My brother beamed and fetched the matches. Father rolled one end of the cigar in his mouth to dampen the tip to make it pliable. Then he struck a match and puffed. No smoke came out. Alfred squirmed.

"It's a little tight. Mother, give me one of your hairpins." He poked the pin through the middle of the cigar then he struck another match. This time, after a few puffs, the end of the cigar glowed and father blew smoke into the air.

"It's a very good cigar."

Alfred grinned.

Christmas Night, 1947

Chapter 51

A horrible stench wafted up from the kitchen. I got out of bed and went downstairs to see what smelled so awful. The stairwell was freezing cold and when I opened the kitchen door, the stench was worse. Smoke rose from the big iron frying pan Mother scraped back and forth over the stove top.

"What are you doing?" I shouted while pinching my nose.

"I'm toasting barley for ersatz coffee."

"It stinks."

"I'm hoping it'll taste better than it smells," she said. "But people say the flavor is similar to ersatz coffee."

"You're making coffee with barley?"

"Yes, I am. The grocer has none to sell and the holidays are almost here. At least I'll be able to brew a pot when we have Christmas cookies during Advent."

When Mother was done, she opened the kitchen window and doors. An icy draft passed through my flannel nightgown.

"I'm freezing," I complained

"I'm freezing, too, but I have to clear the air. I can't stand the stench either," Mother said. "Go back to bed."

I looked forward to the holiday season, especially the Advent Sundays before Christmas when my grandparents and neighbors came over to sing Christmas carols with us.

On the fourth Advent Sunday, our neighbor, Ida Borchard, joined us. After the last song, Mother served a plate of cookies and ersatz coffee. But the brew made with the toasted barley tasted as bad as it had smelled. After the refreshments, the adults chatted and I enjoyed listening.

Ida talked about the increase in crime in the city. Thieves had become more aggressive and were stealing not only coal and food but also coats and shoes directly off of peoples' feet and backs. They lurked behind corners, trees and in doorways waiting for unsuspecting passers-by.

Ida said, "A lady from my prayer group walked home after work last week and took a shortcut through the field behind the houses across the street. She heard footsteps behind her and a man's voice said, 'Don't turn around and don't scream. Take your coat off'."

Oma said, "That's frightening."

Ida nodded in agreement. "The woman was petrified and stripped the coat from her shoulders. The thief grabbed it and ran away."

"Times are more desperate than ever. Strangers have been spotted lurking in the back alley across the street," Opa said slurping his barley brew laced with goat's milk.

"It's best not to take short cuts through the fields in the dark," Mother said.

"It happens in bright daylight, too," Ida replied. "Women should pair up when they go anywhere."

Father said, "I heard that men are targets too. The thieves are also pairing up. It'll get even worse this winter. The situation in our city is horrendous. Every day I hear reports of people freezing to death and starving."

This talk was scary but I felt safe—no one would hurt a kid.

During Christmas vacation I often played at Ilse's house in the afternoon. Since it got dark so early, her father walked me home sometimes. My mother wanted me to come home before dark, but I always had so much fun playing with Ilse, I kept forgetting to leave on time.

One afternoon when I knocked on Ilse's door, her mother appeared. Before she let me in, she said, "Ulla, you're always welcome to play here, but you have to leave before it turns dark from now on. Ilse's dad can't walk you home anymore."

"I'll try, Frau Herzinger. I always have so much fun at your house."

She stroked my hair and said, "Come in."

☙

That year, I didn't wish for a gift for Christmas because I didn't get the beautiful doll I had wished for the year before or the bicycle before that.

On Christmas Eve, when it was time for our gifts, Mother pulled the table cloth off the covered surprises. I pretended not to care if I received anything and even refused to look at my plate.

Finally Mother said, "Ulla, look at your new gloves and shawl. They have embroidered flowers on them."

I felt crushed and only picked them up to please Mother. Even if I didn't want to admit it, deep down I had hoped I might get the beautiful doll with the light blue dress.

The next afternoon, after our Christmas day meal, I went to Ilse's house feeling gloomy. Mother handed me my new gloves and shawl before I left.

Ilse's family of seven now had two bedrooms. Because it was a special day, Ilse and I were allowed to play in her parents' bedroom. Her sisters played in the kid's bedroom and her brothers in the kitchen. Ilse proudly showed me her new doll clothes she got for her old doll. The tiny navy blue coat was made from the same material as Ilse's pleated skirt her mother had made for the beginning of school. The doll dresses were from the same fabric as Ilse's blouses.

Ilse said, "My mother made these while we were in school so we would have a surprise on Christmas Eve."

"Oh!" I said hiding a pang of envy with a smile.

"You can help me dress my doll. Look, she has new underwear, too."

After we played for a while, Frau Herzinger called us to the table. It was decorated with an embroidered tablecloth and fresh fir branches. She served sweetened, herb tea and offered everyone a

268

cookie. Then we sang a Christmas song and went back to playing in the bedroom. I loved Ilse's family. Their kitchen was always a little warmer than ours. That day, even the bedroom was heated.

I was surprised when Frau Herzinger poked her head in the door. She reminded me it was time to go home.

"We'll just finish putting this dress on the doll," I said.

It seemed like no time had passed when she pushed the bedroom door open again. This time, she looked stern. "Ulla, it's getting dark. Here are your coat and gloves. Go home right now."

I looked at the window. It was dark outside. "I'm not scared," I said defiantly, put my coat on and left.

The frozen ground crunched beneath my shoes. I took the shortcut through the garden path to our street. When I reached the back alley, I detected movement from the corner of my eye. My skin began to tingle and foreboding overcame me. I slowed and glanced over my shoulder. Out of the shadow from Herr Stuhrhan's shed, a dark silhouette wearing a hat and big overcoat moved briskly toward me.

Terrified, I raced out of the alley. The footsteps behind me sounded closer and I ran into our street knowing I couldn't outrun the man all the way to my house. I crossed over to the other side and dashed into the courtyard where the Witkes lived. Clambering up the stone steps, I burst through the front door and into their kitchen. I stopped in the middle of the room, trembling, grateful their doors weren't locked.

Everyone at the festive Christmas dinner table looked at me surprised.

Herr Witke stood up and said, "Ulla! What is it?"

Struck by fear, my mouth clamped shut. The urge to jump out of my skin frightened me.

"Did something happen to you?"

My lips wouldn't move. My arms and legs became rigid.

"Did someone chase you?"

I nodded.

"You better take her home," I heard Frau Witke say.

Several men pushed their chairs back. "Komm, Ulla, we'll take you home."

Petrified to go outside, I couldn't move except to shake my head.

"Look, four men are going with you. We won't let anyone harm you."

Herr Witke took my hand and guided me to the door. I resisted going down the outside stone steps. Someone else took my other hand and squeezed it. Together we went into the dark. My knees banged together as we walked hand in hand under the poplar trees. My breathing became rapid. The shadows from the glow of the street lights on the sidewalk and the brick walls frightened me.

Herr Witke said, "You two. Look around. See if you can find anyone."

Two men crossed the street. I watched them look around corners and into every courtyard. When we arrived at my house, Herr Witke knocked on our front door. The key turned in the lock and my father's looming figure appeared. He looked astonished. I knew I was in big trouble.

"Someone chased her, Herr Fischer, but she hasn't been able to talk. We don't know what happened."

Father took my hand and said, "I'm grateful to you for bringing her home."

"It was no trouble. We wish you a gute Nacht."

Father closed the door and guided me to a chair. "Now Ulla, tell us what happened."

My eyes burned, and my throat was dry but I could not speak.

Mother handed me a cup. "Drink this."

My trembling hands spilled the hot liquid into my lap. Mother held the cup to my lips. The tea soothed my throat.

"Now take a deep breath," Father urged.

When I realized he wasn't going to spank me for disobeying Mother, the tightness in my chest eased. After a few sips of tea, my breathing became easier.

Mother kneeled in front of me and put her hands on my shoulders. "Don't ever stay out so late again. You knew that bad men might lurk around any corner in our neighborhood."

I felt awful.

Later, when my brothers went to bed, I refused to go upstairs. Fear paralyzed me. My parents let me stay up until they went to bed. Usually I slept on the groove between them. But that night, I snuggled up to my father.

He put his strong arms around me and said, "You're safe now."

Piglet, 1948

Chapter 52

The fear from Christmas night stayed with me. The man who had chased me appeared in my dreams over and over and I was grateful that my father allowed me to sleep beside him. At breakfast, I was usually still tired and didn't feel like talking.

But when it became warmer outside, Father told me that it was time I slept on the groove between him and Mother again. The following nights, when I tried cuddling up to him, he pushed me toward the middle.

Slowly I became less fearful and started playing at Ilse's house again. But I always left in daylight.

One day, when Father came home from a doctor's visit, he looked sad. He took Mother's arm, guided her into the living room and pulled the curtain in the doorway closed. My brothers and I never entered when the curtain was drawn. I put my ear against the doorjamb to listen but couldn't understand their whispering.

At dinner that evening Father cleared his throat. "I have something to tell you," he said. "I won't be able to work underground in the mine anymore."

My brothers and I straightened and looked from his face to Mother's. Her eyes were red and damp.

"The doctor told me that I have silicosis. The dust generated from separating the coal from rock with a sledgehammer has settled in my lungs."

We stared at him.

"What will happen to us?" Jürgen asked.

"Life will change a little for us from now on. The doctor had to report my condition to the mining office. Fortunately a job had opened in the kitchen of the single-miners' home. I can start working there on Monday. But my pay will be less and my rationing cards will be smaller."

We sat quietly for a while. Then Alfred whispered, "I suspected it. I've heard you wheezing when you go upstairs."

Father nodded. "My lungs don't get enough oxygen and I tire quickly."

That evening Father sat on the sofa with his hands folded in his lap, my brothers didn't go out to play and Mother darned socks keeping her head bowed most of the time. We were quiet.

After Father began working in the single-miners'-kitchen, things returned to normal in our household, except that Mother and my brothers helped care for the animals and tended the garden more than before.

A few weeks later Father looked at me one morning and said, "Ulla, let's go for a little walk today."

"Where are we going?"

"I might be able to buy a young pig."

I remembered the last pig we had. It was three years ago, before the end of the war, when father butchered our little pig over the drain in the courtyard because we couldn't take it with us on the trek.

"What are you going to feed the pig?" I asked.

"The kitchen manager promised me the scraps from the miners' dinner plates."

"Where are we going to keep it?"

"Outside in the stall next to Lore. Get dressed now or we'll be late."

Father waited for me in the front yard holding a bulging sack. He stretched out his hand and took mine. I skipped next to him toward Harbor Strasse.

"What are you carrying in the sack, Pappa?"

"Coal. The farmer will take it as payment for a pig."

"Don't you have any money?"

"Yes I do. But the farmer needs the coal more. It's difficult for him to buy any because he doesn't work in the mine."

We walked past the soccer stadium and eventually turned into an inner courtyard through a big iron gate. In the right corner, away from the view of pedestrians passing by on the street, I saw a red-faced man with his blue work pants stuffed into his knee-high rubber boots. He talked to another man who leaned on a wooden crate. As we got closer, I heard young pigs grunt.

Father tipped his cap. The farmer waved for us to come. He bent over the rim of the bin and pulled up a squealing little pig with floppy pink ears. It wiggled in his hands. The farmer put the pig head first into the stranger's sack. He swung it over his shoulder and hurried out the gate.

"I see you have one left," Father said.

"Ja, he's the runt, five weeks old, but he'll grow. In winter, he'll be big enough to butcher."

While I watched the short–legged animal scramble from corner to corner in the wooden box, Father and the farmer talked. After they shook hands, Father gave him the coal and the man put the struggling creature into an empty potato sack.

Father tucked it under his arm and said, "Aufwiedersehn."

"Keep him quiet," the farmer warned as he tipped his cap.

Walking home, the little bundle wiggled and fought against Father's stronghold. Climbing the gentle slope of the Harbor Strasse hill, Father wheezed heavily. Once we reached the top, he stopped to catch his breath. I was glad that piglet had settled down.

When we arrived home, we let him loose in the pen. With his curly tail turned up, he scurried squealing along the walls of his new home. Father quickly gave him a scoop of slop and the runt calmed down.

Mother hurried in followed by my brothers. "I hear you were lucky," she said.

Alfred bent over the partition and stroked the tiny back. "It's really small."

"He only had the runt left."

Father put his hand on Alfred's shoulder. "Tomorrow after school, I want you to bring our two-wheeled cart to the back door of the kitchen where I work and pick up the swill for the pig. The gate will be unlocked."

"Can I go with you? I'm nine now."

Alfred didn't look happy. "Ja, why not. You can help me bring the slop home."

The next day, when my brother rang the bell at the back door of the kitchen, we had to wait for a while before the doorknob turned. Father came out wearing rubber boots and a long burlap apron.

His eyes sparkled when he saw us. "Alfred, come and help me put this barrel on the cart. Ulla, you hold the handle so the cart won't tip."

When they put the rusty container on the cart, the handle slipped out of my hands and hit my chin. Blood streamed from my mouth. Father and Alfred yelled and grabbed the barrel before it tipped over. I cried.

"Ach, look what happened." Father pulled a handkerchief from his pocket and pressed it against my lip. "Bite on it and put your weight on the handle so we can put the barrel back on the cart."

I bit on the handkerchief and resisted gagging. I noticed a stranger coming through the gate carrying a bucket. Father noticed him, too, went back into the building and returned with a tub full of potato peels. He filled the thin man's pail. The men shook hands and the stranger left.

"Why did you give him the potato peels? We need them for our pig," I said.

Father put a finger on his lips. Quietly he said, "The man's family is hungry. They'll cook them for dinner tonight."

"People eat potato peels?" I asked.

While walking back to the barrel, he said. "Many people don't even have that much to eat."

He and Alfred balanced the barrel in the middle of the cart and I leaned on the handle straining to keep it steady. This time I didn't let go. Then Alfred took the handle from me and pushed the cart out of the yard.

Father came with us to the gate. While he locked it, he said, "Put some into the pig's trough. It'll keep him quiet."

He turned around and went back to work. With the handkerchief hanging from my mouth, I glanced at Alfred. He looked embarrassed and gazed at his shoes when someone came toward us on the sidewalk. I cupped the bloody cloth with my hand and kept my head high.

At home, Mother and Alfred carried the barrel into the stall. Turning to me she asked, "What happened to you?"

"Oh! It's nothing." The bleeding started again when I removed the cloth to show her. She grimaced. My lip was sore but didn't hurt as much as when the hot potato crust had stuck to it last fall.

In the stall, my brother took a dented pot from a nail on the wall and scooped slop from the barrel into the trough. Piglet gulped it down.

Father didn't want the pig's trough to go empty. "When it has something to eat, it won't grunt and hungry people passing by won't hear it."

At night we kept the stall door locked so no one could steal our animals.

When the rabbits had young, Father sold some to neighbors. "Since I earn less now, I have to raise money in other ways," he said.

I burst with pride. My father was so smart.

A Pastor is Moving in, 1948

Chapter 53

Our church was still in ruins. However, attendance at Sunday service had increased and pastor Schwalbe started teaching Sunday school for the first time since the end of the war. Children met after the grown-up's sermon.

I didn't really like the late meetings, because I was hungry by the time the lesson ended. But my interest peaked when the pastor announced, "Anyone who'll memorize the twenty third Psalm and is willing to recite it in front of the class in three weeks, will win a Bible."

That day, as I hurried home from Sunday school, I didn't feel hungry. In the afternoon, while my parents took their Sunday nap, I retreated into our living room and searched for the Psalms at the end of the Old Testament. I found the twenty third titled A Psalm of David. I read, "The Lord is my shepherd, I shall not want." They were soothing words but some of them were difficult to remember. I stayed home from Sunday school for the next two weeks in order to practice the six verses aloud when no one was in the house. I wanted to avoid my brothers teasing.

Mother looked puzzled when I told her why I didn't go to church. She said, "I wonder where the pastor will get a Bible."

I shrugged.

By the third Sunday, I knew every word by heart and recited them on the way to church. When I arrived, the lesson had already started and I quietly sat down in a row in the middle of the confirmation room. I was nervous and barely heard what the pastor said. Anxiously I awaited the moment when he would ask us to recite the Psalm.

After the last song faded away, the Pastor closed his hymnal and said, "See you all next week."

"What?" I shouted raising my hand. He didn't hear me over the noise from chairs scooting over the floor. "Pastor Schwalbe, I memorized the Psalm," I yelled.

He looked at me, waved and left through the side door. I rushed after him pushing others out of the way, but the door slammed shut before I reached it. In disbelief, I slumped on a chair. How could he forget? Didn't anyone else memorize the twenty third Psalm? Devastated, I remained in the confirmation room wishing I could disappear into a hole in the ground. My heart raced. How was I going to explain this to Mother?

"It's time to go," a voice said behind me. "I have to lock up now."

Slowly I rose and walked home staring at the ground. My feet felt heavy and I swore never to attend Sunday school again. At our festive Sunday table, I couldn't say a word and hoped Mother wouldn't ask who won the Bible. I agonized for days over what might have happened but was too embarrassed to ask anyone.

Weeks later I heard that the pastor had been transferred, and a new one would take his place. I was elated, serves him right. Sister Maria told us that a prefabricated house was being built for the new pastor on Harbor Strasse hill. Because our congregation had grown, an assistant pastor would also start as soon as a place for him to live could be found.

One day a church elder came to our house. He talked with my parents in the living room behind the drawn curtain. With my ear to the doorjamb I heard Father say, "The extra income will be welcome. If you can help us with building materials, we can have the room ready in two weeks."

Soon after the elder's visit, I heard thunderous noise coming from the little room we used as storage half way up the stairwell.

When I peeked through the door, I saw Father and Opa slam long handled sledge hammers into the brick wall to the adjacent hayloft.

"What are you doing?" I yelled.

They looked like bandits with their noses and mouths covered with blue checkered cloths. With a tremendous bang, the wall broke open and bricks tumbled to the floor shrouding the men in dust.

Father lowered the hammer. "We're enlarging the room so the assistant pastor can move in."

"The pastor is going to live above our drop-closet and the pig sty?"

"There's no other place for him."

When I left, I felt uneasy thinking about living with a minister. He might see me in my underwear. Alfred passed me on the stairs carrying a shovel and bucket into the little room. Every day, after school, I went into the room to see how the construction was progressing. Soon the men whitewashed the walls and stenciled a border of green leaves around the top.

After they finished Mother hung white lace curtains on the window. The doors of the old wardrobe, where I had found the pink mice years ago, were polished. Under the window were two chairs and a round table covered with an embroidered cloth. A bouquet of fresh-cut peonies from our garden stood in the middle.

"This is nice," I said.

"Let's start a fire in the cast iron stove and see if the chimney is working," Mother said. "The young pastor will arrive tomorrow." She turned to me, "I want you to be polite and not fight with your brothers."

The next day, a stranger on a bicycle rode into our courtyard with a rucksack on his back—a suitcase tied to the rack, and a briefcase dangling from one hand. He stopped at our gate planting his long legs on the ground while still seated on his saddle.

He tossed his blond locks from his forehead and said, "You must be Ulla."

Behind me, Mother chimed, "Ach! Guten Tag Herr Pastor Hübner, please come in."

He dismounted gracefully, untied the suitcase and came into the house. Mother brought a cake to the table and filled the kettle with water for brewing ersatz coffee.

He took a little bag from his rucksack and gave it to Mother. "These are real coffee beans. My mother wanted you to have them."

"How kind of her," Mother said. "I haven't smelled real coffee for years."

"Ulla, get Pappa from the garden."

I hurried down the garden path. When I saw Father I yelled, "Pastor Hübner is here. He's really tall."

While my parents and the pastor had coffee and cake in the living room with the curtain drawn, there was a knock on the front door. I opened it and a stranger said, "I'm Pastor Beckmann. Is your mother home?"

Father appeared behind me, "Doctor Beckmann! Please, come in."

The adults talked for a long time. Then the young pastor took his suitcase to the little room. The door to the wardrobe creaked and he hummed a hymn.

Mother served the pastor's dinner in the living room. Then one day he requested to eat with the family in the kitchen. He and Father discussed the needs of the congregation. Sometimes he talked about his family and his first assignment after seminary school in Ida Oberstein, where the finest diamonds, emeralds and rubies were cut into gems. I liked him and enjoyed his stories. Every morning Mother took a bowl with warm water, soap and a clean towel into his room for his morning routine.

Because Mother had more work now, she asked my brothers to wash the dishes. One evening they disappeared before the water was hot. When they didn't return, Mother asked me to clean them.

"I'm too little," I complained.

"Kneel on the chair."

"I don't want to," I grumbled.

Mother's face turned red. Pastor Hübner pushed the curtain aside from the living room and came into the kitchen smoking a cigarette. "Ulla, let's do the dishes together, I'll wash and you dry."

Mother looked upset. "No, Herr Pastor Hübner, she has to learn to behave."

He smiled and got the water kettle from the stove. With his cigarette hanging from his mouth, his blond locks dangling into his eyes, he poured soap and water on the plates. Then he swooshed the washcloth over a dish and gave it to me to dry. When he scrubbed the cast iron frying pan, his cigarette ashes dropped into the water. He mixed them in until they disappeared.

He was lucky Mother didn't see him.

When we were done, he said, "That wasn't so bad. Was it? But now, I have to prepare Sunday's lesson." He went upstairs to his room and closed the door.

Sometimes he visited the sick and housebound after dinner. One evening he returned early obviously upset. "Frau Fischer," he said. "I just visited a family with small children who have nothing to eat tonight. The father looks sickly and the mother gave birth to a child this afternoon that might not make it. Do you have some food you can spare?"

Mother looked worried. She went into the cellar and returned with a few eggs and a chunk of bread. "I have a little goat's milk here in this jar. And some peppermint leaves for tea."

The pastor put the food into his knapsack and left in the dark on his bicycle.

The next day, when I returned from school, Mother put her finger over her lips when I entered the kitchen, then she pointed to the drawn curtain. I heard pastor Hübner's voice.

"Shush! He's holding an emergency baptism."

"Why?"

"The baby might not live."

Before I removed my school satchel, the curtain opened and a thin, sad man came into the kitchen cradling a baby in his arms. Two whimpering children clung to his pant legs. Mother offered them some bread. They took it and left.

Pastor Hübner also looked sad. "The mother is very weak."

Summer of Change, 1948

Chapter 54

We didn't see Pastor Hübner much. He left early in the morning on his bicycle to attend the needs of the people in our congregation and he returned at dusk. Mother packed sandwiches for his lunch and kept his dinner warm in the oven at night. While eating, he often read the Bible to prepare his Sunday school lesson. Sometimes he joked and wrestled with Alfred and Jürgen as if he were an older brother. I liked him, too, since the day he had helped me wash the dishes and was disappointed that he wasn't around more.

After the pastor had moved in, Mother was busier having to cook, wash and clean for an extra person. She asked me to help and go shopping for her sometimes.

Early one morning, she handed me her shopping bag and said, "Ulla, I want you to go to the bakery and buy bread. Because today is the coal miners' payday people will arrive long before the shop opens. Don't let anyone push you out of line."

She gave me her wallet and rationing cards. "You ask for three loaves and one for the pastor."

I hurried along Klein Strasse, past the City Harbor School and toward Vogelheimer Strasse. In the distance I saw the line of people on the sidewalk in front of the bakery. I started to run. Out of breath, I lined up behind a toothless old woman. Immediately people folded in behind me.

They talked about money not being worth anything. The old woman next to me said, "On payday, the price for a loaf of bread always goes up later in the day."

A grandpa turned around and said, "I hope it doesn't turn into hyper-inflation as it did after the first war. Remember?"

The woman nodded.

When I heard the shutters of the bakery being rolled up, the line began to move and people behind me pushed me toward the door. At the entrance, a man yelled, "Stop pushing, I'm only letting a few people in at a time. When they're done, more can go in."

My stomach rumbled when I smelled the aroma of freshly baked bread. The line in front of me eventually became shorter. Finally, I stood at the door next to the man who guarded the entrance.

"What's your name?" he asked.

"Ulla Fischer."

"You're Anton Fischer's girl?"

"Ja!"

"I hear Pastor Hübner lives with you now."

"He does. I have his rationing card and need extra bread."

When it was my turn to go in, the door guard came in, too, and pushed me toward the baker with the white apron standing behind the glass case. The man whispered something to the baker who looked at me and shook his head while putting bread into a boy's shopping net.

Then he took my bag. "I can only give you three loaves today. I don't have enough for everyone in line. Come back in a few days."

I rushed home and handed Mother the shopping bag, rationing cards and the change.

She took a deep breath. "That smells good." She peeked inside the bag. "Only three loaves?"

"The baker didn't have enough bread. He'll have more in a few days."

She put the change in my hand and said, "You can keep it."

Excited, I put the coins into my shiny steel piggybank. People had been giving me coins in the past few weeks for no reason at all and my piggybank was getting heavy.

One balmy June morning, I meandered to the corner of Oma's house to see what was going on in our street. But I only saw miners rushing to work carrying lunch boxes and people hastening to the bus stop on Harbor Strasse.

Mother often talked about how lively our street used to be and I wondered when Herr Tennagel with his horse drawn buggy would start selling vegetables again.

A young man with a bounce in his step hurried along the sidewalk. He stopped in front of me. "Open your hands," he said while pulling a handful of coins from his pocket. "They're for you."

Thinking of my half-empty piggybank, I said, "I can't accept these." But I didn't really mean it.

"It's alright, your mother won't mind. Open both hands."

I cupped my hands. He filled them with coins, laughed and went down the street, whistling.

I hurried into the house yelling, "Mutter! Mutter where are you?"

"What happened?" she shouted racing down the steps.

"Look, a stranger gave me this money. Now I can fill my piggybank. We can take it to the bank and deposit it in my account."

Mother sank onto a step and pulled me toward her. "Ulla, the money isn't worth anything anymore. The bank won't accept it."

"Why not?" I asked clutching the coins to my stomach.

"Tomorrow is June 21, a historic day, when the Reichsmark will be replaced with new money called Deutschmark."

"But why?"

"It's complicated. You'll understand it someday when you're older."

I was disappointed. Mother patted my head and went back upstairs to making the beds. I refused to believe her, put the coins into my piggybank and hugged it.

❧

During the summer vacation I didn't swim in the canal. The harbor police patrolled the area to discourage youngsters from climbing onto the barges. My brothers didn't go much, either. Instead they explored new places with their friends.

One day, they came home excited. Alfred said, "Construction has started at the City Harbor School. We watched truck loads of building material arrive at the schoolyard."

Jürgen said, "Maybe we'll start the fall semester here and won't have to walk three kilometers to school anymore."

The gate to the schoolyard had been locked since 1942 when the buildings were destroyed by bombs. The gymnasium was gutted. Five years later, the roofless walls streaked from soot and rain looked like eerie sentinels from the war. I always walked faster when I passed the school going shopping for Mother.

I was also curious to see how the construction progressed and went to the school to watch one morning. To my surprise several adults and children had gathered in front of the gate already. Near the two-story school building, two workers shoveled the sand from a big pile into a smaller one and made a depression in the middle. Another man poured water from a bucket into the hole. Others mixed the water with the dry material with shovels.

"They're making cement," someone said behind me.

The workers filled wheelbarrows with the mixture and pushed them toward the building. Two men on the roof picked up broken tiles and threw them to the ground. The broken glass in the window frames had turned black over the years. As the sunshine warmed the air, more onlookers joined the crowd.

The man next to me said, "I heard they only have enough material to finish classrooms on the second floor. God knows if they'll ever rebuild the gymnasium."

"Did you know the school was an advanced design and supposed to be a model for the future? This school was the first of its kind in our area," someone said.

I watched a while longer and then left. When I turned into our courtyard, Mother came back from the garden with a basket full of lettuce, green onions and carrots.

"Where have you been?"

"I was at the school watching workers fix the roof."

She cocked her head and smiled. "It's been a summer of change."

City Harbor School, 1948

Chapter 55

Mother sent me back to the baker to buy the extra bread he had promised. Even though I arrived early at the store, the line was already long. People worried that the baker would sell out before lunch time and close the door. While I waited, I listened to the adults talk about the new currency, the Deutschmark.

One woman said, "Prices are rising every day. The exchange rate of one new Mark for every ten old isn't much to live on."

Everyone nodded in agreement. An old man in front of me took money from his wallet and together with the women around him, looked at the design on the new bills. I glanced at the money Mother had given me and realized that I had never looked at the old bills and couldn't tell the difference.

The old man said. "Did you know that the Soviets are rejecting our new currency? They're going to mint different money for the Russian sector."

One shopper turned around. "I read about that. It's scary how the Soviet military has put a Blockade around the eastern zone allowing no traffic from the west to enter. No food can get into West Berlin by truck or train. Thank God the Americans are airlifting supplies to the city."

I wondered if Tante Emmy, who lived in East Berlin, had bread to eat. She was so nice when Mother, Jürgen and I stayed at her apartment on our way to East Prussia during the war.

After I purchased my bread, I rushed home but stopped at the construction site at the school. Through the mesh-fence I watched workers install gutters under the eaves. Others attached downspouts and put in wooden window frames. The hammering inside the upstairs classrooms never stopped. Trucks laden with sand, bricks and wood drove through the open gate, unloaded in the schoolyard and rumbled away empty. Miners stopped on their way to work and women carrying shopping nets lingered to watch.

One man said, "I think much of the restoration will be completed by the end of summer."

My heart beat faster at the thought of starting the fall semester at this school. That night, at the dinner table, I talked about everything I had seen at the school with my family.

Alfred said, "I wonder if the auditorium will be finished."

"What's an auditorium?" I asked.

"It's a big hall. Before the school was bombed, the choir held the holiday program in there and we performed skits for our parents."

"That sounds like fun," I said.

Opa visited Father after dinner sometimes. I usually was nearby reading or drawing and heard their conversations. Lately both looked concerned. They talked about the spread of communism in the Soviet occupied zone in East Germany. My brothers talked about the upcoming soccer game.

One evening the family was still at the table when Oma brought another letter from Tante Änne. She gave it to Mother who read aloud.

"My dear family,

I hope you receive this note in good health. I wanted to let you know how we are getting along since Kurt has been released from the hospital.

The housing authority has finally allotted another room in the farmhouse to us. It's nice to have a bedroom where little Manfred can nap undisturbed. We use the other room as a combination cooking and sitting area.

Kurt enjoys getting to know his son and Manfred isn't so shy with him anymore. But Kurt is experiencing severe nerve pain that shoots down where his leg used to be. He cries out in his sleep and reaches for the limb that is no longer there. After his stump heels, he'll be measured for a wooden prosthesis. It may take a while before he will get it because the clinic can't get the materials needed to craft one. As soon as Kurt has mastered walking with his crutches, and his raw and swollen underarms heal from practicing so much, we'll come for a visit. I miss you all.

Viele Grüsse, Eure Änne"

ॐ

I looked forward to seeing Tante Änne. Last time, she brought real butter from the farm.

During the few weeks of warm weather, our chickens laid more eggs. One evening, Mother announced, "Everyone will get a whole egg for dinner. Father will have two."

My brothers jumped from their chairs and shouted, "Prima!"

Mother served sunny-side up eggs on top of potatoes fried with onions. I savored every delicious bite. Alfred poked his yoke with the fork and let it run over the potatoes. Jürgen finished his portion first and licked his plate. Mother pretended not to notice.

Fall started with raging storms and rain. Our roof leaked and Mother put aluminum pails on the floor in both bedrooms to catch the water. The constant drip into the buckets disturbed my sleep. Father climbed into the attic but didn't have enough material to repair all the leaks. After days of rain the soaked ceiling in the boys' bedroom drooped so low that the pressed boards split apart at the seam. A torrent of water gushed to the floor.

Father looked worried. Pushing his curly hair from his face he said, "I hope the waterlogged ceiling won't crash to the floor. I don't know what to replace it with."

After the rain stopped, the ceiling dried in the sagged position leaving a gaping hole through which I could look into the attic and see the sky through the damaged roof.

We were all glad the raining stopped. Mother accompanied me to the City Harbor School on opening day. I skipped next to her and squinted at the sun breaking through the grey cloud cover. When we arrived at the schoolyard, I was surprised to see so many students and parents and wondered why no one went inside. Then I noticed a man lining up chairs in rows on the gravel in front of the steps leading to the wooden entrance.

I looked around for my friend Ilse and saw her in the distance with her mother, brothers and sisters talking with neighbors. I waved. She waved back.

Finally the big door opened. Men and women descended the double sided staircase and walked toward the chairs. When all seats were taken, the others stood in the back. One man dressed in a pin-striped suit stepped forward and motioned for people to come closer.

"My name is Schnabel. I'm the principal. I welcome you and would like to introduce the teachers."

I only knew Fräulein Meirich, my first and second grade teacher and recognized Mother's old teacher with the wooden arm sitting in the first row.

Herr Schnabel continued, "We are finally able to provide a full day of instruction for the students. You have probably noticed that only classrooms on the second floor have been completed. When the lower levels are finished, additional children will be admitted. I'm happy to announce that the auditorium has been restored. From now on, every Monday morning, the students will gather in there for a short blessing. We will alternate between the protestant pastor and the catholic priest. I invite you now to the auditorium where we will start the opening ceremony of the school with a prayer."

The kids cheered and the crowd climbed the steps and streamed into the building. Once inside the entrance hall, I noticed the broad stairwell to my left leading to the second floor. Students packed into the auditorium while parents stayed in the hall and listened through the open, double door.

After the short ceremony and prayer, we said good-bye to our parents. My teacher, Fräulein Meirich, took the third graders up the stairs to the second floor. Our classroom was at the end of the hallway. It had tall windows from wall to wall. I liked the spacious, sunlit room. When I glanced outside, I noticed how much bigger the schoolyard was compared to the one at the old school. I looked down on the canopy of the trees growing in the grass-covered field to the south. They looked like a little forest from the second floor window.

It started snowing early that year. I was happy that the school was so close to our home because I never arrived with wet feet or frozen toes. Our neighborhood appeared peaceful and sparkling clean after it had snowed all night. When I arrived at school, the boys were already having snowball fights. I loved watching them. I shaped a few snowballs and threw them at the boys. I stopped after my gloves were soaked.

When I ran toward the bathrooms, I heard someone call my name and turned around. I saw a snowball flying through the air. It hit my eye. Screaming, I clutched my eye and bent over in pain.

Within minutes a teacher was by my side. "Let me see," she said.

"It hurts!" I cried.

She took my hand from the eye and touched my cheek. "Oh my goodness, this looks bad. You have to see a doctor. I'll ask someone to take you home."

My eye hurt so much that I thought the impact had pushed it into my head. Suddenly we were surrounded by several students. They made room for the principal.

Herr Schnabel said, "Who did this?

"I don't know," I whimpered.

"They will be punished for throwing the snowball at you. Someone will take you home so your mother can take you to a doctor."

"I can take her," Ilse said. "I know where she lives."

"Here, take my handkerchief to protect your eye," Herr Schnabel said. "I'll talk with your mother later."

I pressed the folded cloth against my eyelid just enough to stop my eye from moving. It eased the pain. Ilse carried my backpack. She took my hand and guided me toward my street. When we arrived at my house, I smelled the soap laden air and knew Mother was in the cellar doing the wash. Ilse called down the stairwell, "Frau Fischer, Ulla is hurt."

Mother clambered upstairs and rushed toward me. When she took my hand from my eye, the pain shot into my forehead and cheekbones.

"It scratches inside," I wailed.

She thanked Ilse and said, "I'll change my clothes and then we'll go to the doctor."

We left the house together with Ilse. She went back to school and Mother and I continued toward the Vogelheimer Strasse. It seemed we walked forever.

"Where is this doctor's office?" I asked.

"It's near the swim hall. We still have a ways to go."

By the time the doctor could see me, my eye was swollen shut. He pointed for me to sit in a special chair. "Let me look at you," he said.

When he pulled my swollen eyelid up, I cried and pushed his hand away. He asked his assistant to stand behind me and put her arms over my shoulder and hold my hands.

"It's important you hold still so I can examine the damage. If you wiggle, it'll hurt more."

While the doctor rinsed my eye with warm water, the assistant held me firmly in place. The pain was excruciating.

"So," he said wiping my tears from my cheek. "I got most of it. You can relax. The snowball was filled with gravel. The cornea was scratched. Unfortunately I have no medicine to give you. At home rinse the eye with warm chamomile tea. It'll be soothing."

The nurse covered my eye with gauze, put a strip of white fabric over it and tied it behind my head. On our way home, Mother held my hand. I sobbed the entire time. People looked at me with curiosity. Some smiled.

When we arrived home, mother prepared a bed for me with pillows and blankets on the sofa in the kitchen. "I'll heat some milk with a little honey that Tante Kathel sent from Bavaria. It'll make you feel better."

Then she changed into her work clothes and went back into the cellar to finish the wash.

I didn't go to school for a few days but soon got bored at home. On my first day back, my eye was still red and swollen and I had to wear the gauze for protection. When I arrived at the schoolyard, several students came to me and asked to see my eye. When I lifted the gauze, I could see they were impressed.

An older boy jogged across the yard and stopped in front of me. "You're Alfred's little sister aren't you?"

"Ja?"

You should have seen your brothers beat up that kid who threw the snowball at you."

They all accompanied me to my classroom and I felt much better.

Sliding into a New Year, 1948

Chapter 56

The winter wasn't as cold as the two previous ones but it snowed on and off. Even though Father had stuffed the gaps in the roof with rags, a little snow trickled into the attic. In my brothers' bedroom, along the edge of the damaged ceiling board, I noticed tiny ice crystals sparkle in the glow of the electric light bulb. The room was cold and damp. I was grateful Mother put extra blankets over the feather comforters to keep us warm.

Overnight, the bucket of pig slop froze in the stall. Alfred had to break the ice with a pick before he could scoop some into a pot. He heated it on the kitchen stove before feeding it to the pig. "Piglet is growing," he said.

My brothers heard from their friends that the pond in the forest behind the slagheap had frozen over. Alfred and Jürgen raced into the cellar and returned with the rusted clamp-on skates. From my seat on the sofa, I watched Jürgen sitting across at the kitchen table scraping off the rust with a piece of sandpaper. Alfred oiled the screws and clamps and sharpened the blades. He strained to turn the screw, but it didn't budge.

"Scheisse!" He yelled. "It won't turn."

"Don't let Mother hear you swear," I warned.

Alfred ignored me and fetched Father's pliers. Then he tried over and over to turn the screw.

"It's frozen!" He said looking disgusted and tossed the pliers on the table. "We might as well throw the skates away."

The boys dropped the skates in the corner near the cellar door, bundled up in warm clothes and left the house. I knew they were heading for the pond in the forest. After a while, I too bundled up and followed them.

When I climbed the snow-covered path over the slagheap that led into the forest, I heard children in the distance and ran toward them. The snow crunched under my soles as I rushed along under leafless trees. To my right, a small patch of fir trees dressed in white looked festive and peaceful.

At the pond, some kids skated, leaving trails on the snow covered ice. Others, who had no skates, had cleared a long, narrow path of snow. It shone like a mirror. Boys formed a line at one end of the mirror a few steps away from the start. The first one in line ran as fast as he could and slithered along the glossy path with one foot in front of the other. He struggled to stay upright by balancing with his arms stretched out like wings. The older boys slid all the way to the end. Then they ran back to the line to wait for their turns again. At the far end of the pond, kids skidded down a small hill on sleds. Their laughter traveled across the frozen surface.

I wanted to slide across the shiny ice and lined up behind a boy. When it was my turn, I ran and put one foot ahead on the ice but immediately lost my balance and fell.

"Get, up! Get up! I'm right behind you."

I didn't move fast enough. The boy tripped over my shoes and fell on top of me. I looked away embarrassed, but he helped me up, and we ran back to take another turn. After falling several times, I learned how to slide standing. With every try, I went a little further. When I finally made it to the end, the boy who had helped me up cheered. We played until the sky turned dark.

From the edge of the pond Alfred called, "Ulla, it's time to go."

My brothers and I walked home together. I noticed how cold my feet were. My shoes were soaked and my gloves wet from falling in the snow. When we reached the top of the slagheap, I saw the lights on in every house of our street and looked forward to warming up next to our stove.

When we opened the door, the kitchen smelled so good that all three of us yelled, "What's for dinner?"

Mother stood at the stove and turned around. "I'm making Pfannekuchen. Wash your hands and come to the table."

She put a plate with a tower of pancakes in the middle. "I'll have to keep a few for Pastor Hübner, you can have the rest."

We rolled up the pancakes on our plates and cut them into bite-sized pieces. "Mmm, they're good," I said.

Mother looked at me. "I used up our last eggs. In this cold weather, the chickens are hardly laying."

After the holidays, food was in short supply again, especially meat and fat. In February, Opa came over to talk with Father. They went into the living room, closed the drapes and spoke quietly. I could only hear a few words but understood enough to know that they were going to slaughter the pig.

"If we do it ourselves instead of calling the butcher, we can't have the pork tested for trichinae, but the meat allotment on our rationing cards won't be cut," Father said.

Opa said, "Let's do it."

The next morning at dawn, I heard voices outside. The door to the animal stall scraped over the cement tiles. After a while, I heard a muffled squeal and knew what the noise meant. Before I went to school, Father came in carrying a bucket filled with blood and took it into the cellar. When he returned to the kitchen, he sat on the sofa and Mother served him a slice of rye with jam and a mug of ersatz coffee.

"Did you butcher the pig?" I asked.

"Yes, Ulla. Although it was very small, I had to. We need the meat. But I don't want you to talk about it. Your friends at school may have none."

"Why didn't you bring it inside?"

"It has to hang to cool for a few days and age before we can cut it up. Mutter will prepare a roast for Sunday's dinner."

Days later, when it was dark, Father and Alfred each slung a side of pork over their shoulder and carried it into the cellar. That evening, Mother fried fresh liver and onions for dinner.

"Eat. You need the iron," she said.

She also served boiled potatoes and sweet and sour red cabbage. Pastor Hübner came home early and joined us for dinner at the kitchen table. When he finished eating, he rubbed his stomach.

The next day, Father salted slabs of bacon and chunks of meat and put them into earthenware tubs. "I wish I had a smoke chamber instead of having to use the salt to preserve the meat," he said.

Mother closed all the windows and pulled the drapes. Then she boiled sausages and baked buckwheat pudding with scraps. I watched her dice strips of belly fat and fry it for lard.

When the air got stuffy in the kitchen I said, "Why don't you open the top window?"

"Hungry people passing buy would suffer smelling sausages being boiled. The pig was so small, you children are so thin, and your father works very hard, I need to make it last."

Our School, 1949

Chapter 57

O nce my brothers and I started classes at the City Harbor School, we had lessons until late afternoon during the week and until noon on Saturdays. In the old, crowded school, I only had two hours of instruction five days a week. Our teacher said we now had a lot of catching up to do.

We enjoyed the new school and were delighted that during the winter the classrooms were heated from radiators under the window sills—an improvement over the little cast iron stove in the old school where students in the back rows shivered and kept their coats on.

Parts of the new school were mysterious. The old caretaker and his wife lived in an apartment in the attic with white lace curtains on the windows. I hardly saw his wife. He roamed through the hallways noiselessly, carrying buckets, shovels or a broom. I never heard him speak except when he chased the boys away from the construction site in the schoolyard. My brother Alfred told me that the caretaker worked at the school before it was bombed. I was scared of him.

On Saturdays even the teachers rushed out of the classrooms. One such Saturday, I copied notes from the blackboard and was the last student to leave. The hallway was quiet. I wondered if the rooms for the higher grades looked different and opened the door to the eighth grade classroom. It was similar to ours.

Once downstairs, I peeked around the corner into the stairwell to the basement. The door was open a crack. I looked around to make sure no one saw me and went down the steps. Gently I pushed against the door with my shoe. Without making a sound, it swung open a bit more, but I couldn't see inside. Another nudge and it opened enough for me to slip through.

Cautiously, I stepped into a long corridor. After a few paces, I stopped, listened. Even though I heard nothing, I was spooked. If the caretaker found me down here, I would be in big trouble. If he locked the door, I would have to spend the weekend in the basement and be in trouble with my parents. I had the urge to leave but was too curious.

At a snail's pace, I looked right and left. On both sides were classroom-sized areas open to the hallway. I had expected a gloomy, dreary cellar and was surprised how light it was. Daylight streamed in through windows under the ceiling and threw shadows across the hallway.

In one area was a pile of sand, on the opposite side, stacks of bricks. I walked on and saw roof tiles and metal pipes of different lengths. This must be building material for the unfinished classrooms. Crackling sounds interrupted my thoughts. I stopped. The sound came from down the corridor. As I inched toward the noise, it became louder. Behind a wall to my right, loomed a gigantic iron furnace with a big door and a lever in front. The flames inside its belly crackled and swooshed. Behind me, across the corridor, were piles of black coal.

Then I heard voices through the open door. My mind raced. Where could I hide? Keeping my eye on the door, I backed into the area next to the furnace and crouched behind a stack of bricks. The voices came closer. Boys! I recognized my brothers' friends' prattle and peeked around the corner. They are exploring just like me. I stayed out of sight but looked around the wall occasionally. They stopped at every interesting place, pointed, talked and laughed. As they got closer, I retreated back to my hiding place and jumped when someone kicked a metal pipe.

When their chatter became excited, I knew they had discovered the furnace. "That's a monster," a boy said and all of them talked at once. If they didn't tone it down, the caretaker might hear them.

I worried they'd chase me away if they found me. Someone bumped against a shovel. It crashed to the floor. They shut up only for a minute.

Finally, they strolled past my spot and down the hallway. One boy said, "Let's play hide and seek. There are great places to hide down here."

"You're it!"

"Eins, zwei, drei...," Footsteps scurried over the cement floor. "Vier, fünf sechs...."

I started when someone jumped behind my bricks and squatted next to me. My brother Alfred's mouth dropped open when he saw me.

"What are you doing here?" he croaked.

With a finger over my lips, I whispered, "I wanted to see what was down here."

"If Mutter finds out, you'll be in trouble."

"You, too," I hissed.

"Go home!"

"No! I want to play too."

A boy peered around the corner and shouted, "You're it!" His eyes widened when he looked into my face. "What are you doing here?"

"The same as you."

The three of us left the hiding place and stepped into the hallway. The others showed up one by one.

Before they could say anything, I said, "I want to play, too."

"What?" they shouted together.

Alfred looked from face to face and said. "We better let her. Then she won't tell."

"All right, you're it."

I covered my face with the crook of my arm, leaned against the wall and counted to ten. The boys scuttled away. "Ready or not, here I come."

I rushed down the hallway and searched for the boys behind bricks and tarp-covered stacks. Someone yelled, "I'm free!" Soon another shouted the same.

Then I saw a crown of chestnut hair behind a barrel. I lunged forward, tapped the head and shouted, "You're it!"

My brother Jürgen looked at me with big brown eyes. "Shucks!" he said.

We played for a long time. Suddenly, the hinges of a door squeaked at the far end of the corridor and the silhouette of a man appeared.

"Run! It's Wohlgemoot!"

I looked over my shoulder, recognized the caretaker, and bolted toward the door where we had entered. The boys were faster and passed me. I chased after them but the school satchel on my back slowed me down.

"Come on!" Alfred yelled holding the door open. He slammed it shut behind me.

We raced up the stairwell through the entrance hall and out the heavy wooden door.

"Keep running!"

We raced across the schoolyard, out the gate and hid behind bushes on the other side of the fence. I gasped for air. The caretaker rushed out the door but stopped on the top stone step.

"I better not catch you again, ihr Bande." he shouted shaking his fist. After scanning the surroundings for a while, he went back inside. The key clicked in the lock and the door handle twitched.

We all took a deep breath and laughed nervously. One by one, we went home, everyone in a different direction. My brothers and their friends crossed the street. I stayed on the other side.

Over the weekend, the boys boasted about their adventure in the school's basement but never mentioned my name.

On Monday morning, on my way to school, I worried that the custodian had reported us to the principal. Anxiously, I entered the schoolyard hoping not to run into Herr Wohlgemoot on the way to my classroom. When I sat down at my desk, I folded my hands to stop them from shaking.

The door opened and my teacher came in followed by the principal and a man I didn't know. My stomach cramped. I had the urge to go to the bathroom.

Fräulein Meirich said, "Guten Morgen, Kinder. Herr Schnabel would like to introduce someone to you."

My teeth chattered.

The principal smiled.

"This is Herr Petschalk, our new teacher. He will talk to you for a while this morning. We don't know yet which grade he'll be teaching. Fräulein Meirich and I will leave. Please welcome the new teacher."

"Guten Morgen, Herr Petschalk," the class sang like a chorus.

I couldn't believe what I just heard. The principal wasn't going to reprimand me? I closed my eyes. Tears of relief welled up. I wiped them away with my sleeve, took a deep breath and looked at the blackboard.

Herr Petschalk stepped in front of the desk and said, "I was a sailor on a U-boat during the war and want to tell you a little about it. Did you know that U-boats can dive deep down under water in the ocean?"

"No," we chimed.

"The submarine I was assigned to patrolled the Mediterranean Sea at the end of the war."

He went to the world map on the wall and pointed to a blue area. "This is where we were and this narrow spot is the Strait of Gibraltar. But we were not alone. British and American submarines and warships were also in the area. We dove to the bottom of the sea and stayed below for a long time so our boat wouldn't be detected. Eventually our food supply ran low and oxygen was running out. That's when the captain decided we must make a run for it and try to exit through the Straits."

A boy raised his hand. "Were you scared?"

"A little. We knew we had lost the war before it was over. I just wanted to go home to my wife and two boys. But our captain issued so many orders that we didn't have time to be frightened. We surfaced once, slowly at night, to observe the situation through the periscope. We were surrounded by Allied war ships and dove again. When we ran out of oxygen and food, the captain gave orders to move through the narrow passage in the middle of the night."

Awestruck, we listened to his fascinating story.

"What happened then?" Walter asked.

"The motion of our U-boat was detected and we were forced to surface. Undernourished and hungry we were glad to breathe fresh air again. The crew was taken to an American war prison in the south of France. Most of the sailors were sick. Many had lost their teeth. But I wasn't so bad off."

"Why not?" I asked.

"I'll tell you. We had little food left except for lemons we had purchased in a harbor in the Mediterranean Sea. But no one wanted them. I cut a lemon into wedges every day and sucked on it. Did you know that citrus fruit is loaded with vitamin C?"

"No," we chimed.

"When we were captured, I was thin, but not sick."

The classroom door opened. Our teacher and the principal returned. Herr Petschalk said, "Auf Wiedersehen. I must visit another class now."

I looked after him spellbound. The image of the U-boat under the sea whirled through my mind. Later we learned that Herr Petschalk was going to teach fourth grade next semester. I might be in his class.

New students joined our school from time to time. Refugees from the Russian occupied zones in East Germany continued to flee to the west looking for shelter and work.

In the spring, Fräulein Meirich introduced Sigrid, a student who had moved to our area recently and didn't know anyone. The teacher asked us to make friends with her.

Ilse and I played with the new student during recess; after class, she walked home with us. On the corner of Förder Strasse, Sigrid suddenly stopped. Ilse and I stopped, too, and looked at her.

"I better turn back and go home or my mother will worry," she said fussing with her long, blond braids, gazing at us with her sad, sky-blue eyes.

"You have to turn around?" Ilse asked. "Where do you live?"

"On the farm behind the dredge-hole."

"You're walking in the wrong direction," I said.

"I know. There's no one to play with. The farm is too far away from everyone."

I remembered seeing the little farmhouse once when I followed my brothers to the dredge-hole where they wanted to catch the little Stieglitz fish. A few trees shaded the farm house. It seemed deserted, standing alone, surrounded by freshly plowed fields. Then I remembered my father had purchased the rabbits from the farmer.

"You're so tall," Ilse said.

"I'm twelve. The principal put me in your class because I have a lot of catching up to do."

"I'm ten," I said.

"Do you want to meet in the field to play this afternoon?" Sigrid asked.

"I have to ask my mother," Ilse said.

"I'll wait for you over there." Sigrid pointed across the street to the field covered with yellow flowering mustard plants. She turned around and walked in the opposite direction.

Ilse rushed down Förder Strasse to her home and I skipped along the sidewalk toward my street.

When I opened the kitchen door, my brothers were sitting at the table eating. On the back of the stove, the big kettle was keeping the soup warm. It smelled delicious. My stomach growled. I threw my satchel on the sofa and filled a bowl with bean soup. It tasted good. While we ate, Mother came in from the cellar carrying a basket full of washed sheets and shirts to be hung on the clothesline behind our garden.

"Finish your homework before you do anything else," she said looking over her shoulder.

After lunch, the three of us cleared the table and did homework. The boys talked about Herr Petschalk who taught history to the upper grades until the end of the school year.

"How do you like the new teacher?" I asked.

Jürgen looked up and grinned. "I like him. But he hasn't started history lessons yet. He only talks about his seafaring days on the U-boot. That's more interesting anyway."

The boys chuckled.

When I finished my homework, I put my play apron on and hurried to the field where our new friend wanted to meet. From a distance, I saw two heads over the yellow mustard blossoms and rushed toward them. Ilse and Sigrid sat crossed legged on the ground with tiny, white daisies in their lap.

"What are you doing with the Gänseblühmchen?" I asked.

"She's going to show us how to make a wreath for our hair," Ilse said. "Look, they grow over there."

Sigrid held up a string of daisies. Her sky-blue eyes still looked sad. I sat next to the girls and watched how Sigrid made a daisy chain. Her face fascinated me. When she looked up, I turned away. Finally I realized that I had never seen a person with thick, blond eyelashes before. When the daisy chain was long enough, she tied the ends and put the wreath on Ilse's auburn hair. We laughed.

"Now, you make one," she said.

After I got the hang of joining one daisy to the next, I asked, "Where did you live before you moved here?"

"In a little village in Silesia, that's in East Germany now."

"Why did you leave?"

"It was too dangerous. Russian soldiers occupied the town. They raped my older sisters."

"Do your sisters go to our school?"

"No. They're in a special hospital in a town nearby."

"Are they sick?"

"My mother told me that they were raped so many times, their insides were raw. They can't ever have children."

I didn't know what rape meant but was too uncomfortable to ask. Instead I said, "Did the soldiers hurt you?"

"No. I hid in a closet under the stairwell when they came near our house. We could always hear them talking loud and stumbling up the steps because they were drunk. Sometimes the soldiers didn't allow my sisters to come home for days and my mother went to fetch them. Then she didn't come home sometimes, either."

The conversation made me nervous. Ilse looked sick.

"Are you scared of the farmer?" I asked.

"No. He's alright. He likes my mother's cooking."

We strung daisies in silence for a while. Then Sigrid asked, "Have you ever looked down there. You know, at your plum?"

"No! Never! " I said embarrassed.

"Sometimes I put a pencil inside and move it in and out."

"Why would you do that?" Ilse asked.

"It feels really good."

I got up and said, "I have to go now." I never talked to anyone about that conversation.

That night, I couldn't sleep wondering how the soldiers raped Sigrid's sisters and made them so sick that they had to be in a special hospital. I was still awake when Mother came to bed.

I snuggled up to her.

Miserable Spring Days, 1949

Chapter 58

Spring was wet and stormy. The wind, howling around corners and eaves, disturbed my sleep. But one morning, it wasn't the wind that woke me — it was the sound of Mother's retching downstairs in the kitchen. I was worried. Her migraines must be getting worse.

I gathered the courage to go downstairs. Through the barely open kitchen door, I saw Mother on the floor, clutching the rim of our aluminum bucket, throwing up. My mother, who always took care of us, was lying sick on the floor. When the heaving stopped, saliva dripped from her mouth. With the corner of her apron, she wiped her face.

The cold from the floor tiles penetrated to my bones. I shivered. Oh, dear God, please don't let her die, I pleaded. Shaken, I rushed back upstairs and slipped under the featherbed. After a while, the retching stopped, but I couldn't go back to sleep. My brothers whispered in the front bedroom — they couldn't sleep either.

Then Mother called, "Kinder! It's time to get up."

She sounded like she always did, as if nothing had happened. I waited until Alfred and Jürgen dressed, then I got ready and clambered down the wooden steps. When I opened the kitchen door, I was relieved to see Mother sitting at the table spreading rhubarb jam on slices of rye bread. Three cups of steaming ersatz coffee on the table were ready for us. Through the kitchen window I saw the elderberry bush whip back and forth — another dreary April morning.

"We're out of milk. Here, put goat's milk in your coffee." Mother handed a pitcher to Alfred.

He wrinkled his nose. "Bah! Goats milk again."

"Stop complaining. Your bodies need fat."

My brothers grimaced and poured only a few drops into their drinks.

Mother's deep-set eyes had dark shadows underneath. They were half closed when she put the jam sandwiches into our metal-lined, leather lunch boxes. She didn't notice I hadn't added milk to my drink. Her usually well groomed hair looked uncombed. The braided bun at the nape had unraveled and dangled down her back.

On the way to school I teamed up with Ilse at the corner of Förder Strasse. Her face was damp from the rain.

With a heavy heart I told Ilse what happened at home that morning. "I think my mother might be dying," I said.

"Ulla, your mother isn't dying," Ilse giggled. "She's expecting a baby. Alfred told my brother Paul yesterday when they walked to school together."

Bewildered, I stopped and gazed at my friend. "That can't be. We have no room for a baby. I'm sleeping between my parents in their bed." I turned my head to hide my fear. "Maybe they'll throw me out."

Ilse put her arm around my shoulder. "Your parents will never do that. Maybe Herr Pastor Hübner will move out."

"They need the income from his room and board. Where could he move to? I can't sleep with my brothers either. They're sharing a bed."

I felt miserable.

That day I had trouble concentrating in class. When the teacher asked me a question, I couldn't answer. After school, I didn't even want to go home. When I turned into our courtyard, Father came around the corner carrying a pail filled with greens for the chickens. He looked at me with a big smile and lifted eyebrows.

I didn't want to talk to anyone, looked away and hurried towards the steps.

"Ulla!" he said. "Wait, I have something to tell you."

I didn't stop.

He reached for my arm.

I slowed and looked at my shoes.

"You're going to have a little brother or sister before Christmas."

"Oh!" I mumbled, shook his hand off and climbed the steps to our entrance hall. So it's true, I thought. They're going to have a baby even though we have no room for one. Maybe they'll change their mind.

After dinner that night, Mother told us to use the chamber pots only when absolutely necessary during the night. "From now on, you boys will have to take turns emptying the pots every morning."

My brothers giggled, pointed fingers at each other and shouted, "You first!"

"I'm afraid to go outside in the dark to the drop-closet," I complained.

"Don't drink so much in the evenings," Mother said.

I felt my life falling apart. There was no room for me in our home. No one wanted me anymore. The overcast sky and constant rain didn't help. It was too wet to play in the field or explore at the canal. Often I just sat on the wooden boards in the drop-closet even though it was damp and cold.

One day, while I sat on the hole in the drop-closet reading the funnies from the newspaper we used as toilet paper, the sun came out. I opened the window a bit and continued reading the comic strip *Kumpel Anton*. Anton was a coal miner who always did something funny. I loved reading it.

Then I heard boys outside and stopped rustling the paper. They chatted excitedly and congregated near my window on the cement cover of the honey pit. I perked up and listened.

My brother Jürgen, who was usually quiet, talked loudly, "You guys will never guess where we went this afternoon."

"Where?" Several voices shouted.

"A bunch of us went to the old warehouse at the canal. You know? Where the barges used to deliver groceries for the city during the war?"

A boy said, "Ja, we know where that is. My dad told me that once the Tommy's left, the American GIs started patrolling the area."

"Well, we didn't think about the GIs—we just wanted to see if there were groceries stored in the warehouse."

"How did you get in?" a voice asked.

"The entire complex was surrounded by barbed wire. But we found a hole to climb through."

"Were you crazy?" shouted a manly sounding boy.

In my hiding place, I hardly breathed because I didn't want to miss any part of their story.

Alfred's breaking voice croaked, "We all stood in front of a window, looking through the grimy glass for food, when a voice at the end of the building boomed, 'What are you boys doing in here?'"

"Our knees turned to rubber, believe me."

"What happened then?"

"Three soldiers pointed their rifles at us," Jürgen said. "You should've heard little Päule's squeaky voice say, 'We're just looking.'"

They laughed.

Alfred said, "I almost wet my pants."

Boisterous laughter.

"'You better come inside' one soldier told us in broken German," Ewald said. "I thought they were taking us to a stockade."

I wanted to look at him but didn't for fear the boys might see me.

One boy said, "The soldiers came closer, pointing their rifles at us and demanded we follow them. One of them turned around and we fell in behind him. The other soldiers walked behind us. They took us to a room with long tables and benches. With their rifles they pointed for us to sit down."

"Weren't you scared?"

"Plenty! I could hear my own teeth chatter."

"The soldiers leaned against the window and checked us out. It seemed an eternity."

"'You boys hungry?' The older soldier asked. We looked at each other, and then nodded."

"Two of them went into the other room and returned with flats of eggs and a platter of sliced meat. 'Spam!' one GI said and put the meat in a frying pan. Another smeared butter on slices of soft, white bread and built a tower on a plate. Along with the scrambled eggs and fried Spam they served us tin cups filled with milk," one boy said.

"Cow's milk," Alfred shouted. "It was heaven. No one spoke while we gulped down every morsel."

My mouth watered as I listened to the boys from my cold hiding place.

Alfred said, "You won't believe this, they asked if we were still hungry. Of course, we all nodded. They scrambled more eggs and buttered more bread. After we devoured the second batch, the soldiers sent us home through the front gate."

I perked up when I heard bicycle brakes squeal outside in the courtyard.

The boys shouted, "Guten Tag, Pastor Hübner."

"Tag, Jungs!" the pastor answered.

"See you tomorrow!" a chorus of high and low boys' voices rang through the air and footsteps scurried away.

My stomach growled, and I wished I could taste a slice of fried Spam. I waited inside the drop-closet until our front door closed and I heard no more talking. Then I opened the door and went into our house.

Innocence of Childhood, 1949

Chapter 59

Father's wheezing had became louder over time. One morning I watched him from the upstairs window taking our goat, Lore, on a leash, down the garden path to graze in the field behind the back fence. Lore pulled him along. He stopped ever so often and leaned against the fence. His silicosis was getting worse. After he pushed the stake into the ground he returned and stopped in front of every raised vegetable bed, alternately pulling weeds and resting. It frightened me to see him like that.

But when I saw Ewald, who was two years older than I, weeding his family's vegetable patch, my heart grew lighter. I loved the way he pushed his head back tossing his blond waves away from his forehead. When he called on my brothers, I watched him from our living room window through the lace curtains. His blue eyes were bluer when the sun shone on his face. I looked for him in the schoolyard, but he only played with boys.

In early summer, Herr Tennagel, the vegetable man, returned to our street with his horse-drawn wagon. When he clanked his brass bell for the first time after so many years, women, children and old men rushed to the street to greet him. When he had the first local vegetables for sale he announced them, as he used to, by singing their names.

Mother's stomach had become huge. Her skirt was much shorter in the front that people could see her knees. Lately, she pressed her fist into her arched lower back and pulled her shoulders back to balance herself. When she walked, she waddled as if her stomach was too much for her to carry. It looked odd. Why wasn't she seeing a doctor? She asked me to carry the net filled with vegetables she had purchased from Herr Tennagel into the house.

As I hurried home with my load, I heard him say, "Ach, Frau Fischer, you've got one in the Backofen? How are you feeling?"

He often talked in strange ways.

On warm days during summer vacation, the boys went to the canal. They had found a new swimming hole on the north shore to the right of the bridge. Mother's warning, not to swim in the canal, was forgotten.

I thought it would be fun to dip my body into the cool water again, practice the breast stroke and learn to dive from the dock like the boys did.

Before the school year ended, some of the older girls chatted about swimsuits. Some had gotten hand-me-downs from older sisters, others talked about the colors of their new ones. I had never seen a girl's swimsuit and asked my mother if she would buy one for me.

"Ulla, you have to wait until I've saved enough money. I know that the swim hall has been rebuilt. When you start fourth grade in the fall, your class will take lessons there."

"How do you know?"

"Your teacher, Fräulein Meirich, told me."

I huffed out of the kitchen and went upstairs to the window hoping to see Ewald weeding in his garden. But he wasn't there.

A few days later my brothers and their friends congregated in our courtyard and I overheard them talking about meeting at the corner of Harbor Strasse.

"Bring a towel," one boy said.

They were going swimming in the canal. I got excited. Unfortunately Ilse and Sigrid wouldn't go. Their mothers didn't allow it. I never told mine.

Grownups talked about the increased barge traffic. They said it was a sign that times were getting better.

When Mother laid down to rest, I tip-toed out of the house, closed the front door so flies wouldn't get in and strolled toward Harbor Strasse. This would be the last summer I had to swim in my briefs. I skipped along in the middle of the street. It was hot, and the air smelled of tar. The sun melted the asphalt and my shoes squished into the blacktop.

I welcomed the sight of the bridge and hastened along. Long ago a ferry used to pull people across to the other side with a wire that wound around a wheel. When I arrived on the bridge, I stopped half way across to watch the approaching barges. A woman hanging laundry on a clothesline talked to a toddler playing at her feet, and a barking dog ran along the planks. Were families living on barges now?

I hollered, "Hello!" and waved.

The woman turned around, squinted into the sun and waved back. The child squealed and flapped its arms. I watched and waved until they disappeared under the bridge. Then I scanned the north shore for the boys. To my surprise it was covered with patches of overgrown reeds and bush. There were no docks and the boys were nowhere to be seen.

Disappointed, but determined, I walked to the north side, strolled along the dirt-path on the embankment and listened for the boys. Where could they be? After a long walk I gave up and turned around. I felt uneasy being so far away from the bridge and disappointed I didn't find their new swimming hole. Determined to swim, I looked for a suitable place with access to the water. When I saw a narrow opening through the cattails and a willow tree nearby, I stopped and named it my swim spot. I went to the tree and removed my apron, dress and shoes and hid them under the branches behind the trunk, so no one could see them from above.

I squatted on broken reeds that lay flat on the ground, hidden from sight and realized that I was all alone. In previous summers, the boys were always nearby. Feeling a bit nervous, I waited for a while. Eventually I scooted down the embankment. My legs brushed against broken reed stalks that poked across the path. They scratched my skin. I ignored the scratches even though I felt blood trickle down. It would rinse off in the water.

The canal flowed by in silvery ripples. Wearing only my panties, I inched toward the water's edge and dipped my toes in. The sun's shimmering reflection blinded me. It took a while for my vision to clear and I noticed ships floating by with a crewman sweeping the planks and heard the noise from cranes loading coal onto barges across in the harbor.

Suddenly I realized that I stood exposed where boys swimming by, crews on barges and people crossing the bridge could see me. Quickly I crossed my arms over my chest and stepped back into the reeds. I scrambled back up the embankment and hoped the boys wouldn't come. Shaken, I dressed, buttoned up, slipped into my shoes and crawled back up to the dirt-path.

There I took a deep breath and looked around. The barges had passed and the cranes on the other side continued working as if I had never been at the shore. The boys were nowhere.

Feeling sad, knowing I would probably never swim in the canal again, I strolled home. Quietly I opened the front door and went into the kitchen. When I heard my parents talking in the living room, I stopped.

"No one has lived more than seven years after a diagnosis of one hundred percent silicosis," Father said.

Mother sobbed softly.

"If only I could see this child start school," he said.

Without disturbing them, I went back outside.

Big Surprise, 1949

Chapter 60

One day Father asked Alfred to take our two-wheeled cart to the train station in Bergeborbeck and pick up a box that had arrived from Tante Kathel in Bavaria. He returned with a big wooden trunk. My brothers carried it inside and opened it. Father unpacked old clothes and put them on the floor. Then I smelled the smoked sausage. He laid a ring of Mettwurst on the table, a little sack filled with dried, wild mushrooms and a round loaf of farmer's bread. The boys unpacked books and stacked them on the table. Alfred leafed through some of them.

"Books?" I said disappointed.

Father straightened his back. "The Nazi government burned books it didn't want citizens to read. But I didn't want these to be destroyed. So I put them into this trunk and sent them to Tante Kathel. She stored them in her attic all these years until it was safe to return them."

Later that summer, Mother stopped retching in the mornings. Her tummy had swollen so big that her whole body looked lopsided. When she climbed the steps, she moaned and leaned against the wall to rest a few times. When something dropped to the floor, she asked one of us kids to pick it up. Oma helped her on wash days and my brothers carried the laundry baskets to the clotheslines. Her legs were swollen but she never complained.

Father, too, had less energy and gasped for air as if his lungs didn't get enough. He went to work every day while still tending to

315

the garden at times and feeding the goat, pig, chickens and rabbits. My brothers helped with heavier chores.

With both parents sick every day, I felt insecure and unsettled.

After dinner, the boys often cared for the animals so Father could rest. After a short nap, he usually started reading his books. He even subscribed to a monthly magazine with articles about faraway lands. I loved to look over his shoulder at photos of pyramids and elephants.

When autumn set in and the evenings became longer, he had eventually read all his books and Pastor Hübner lent him some of his. Father had started collecting the change from the grocery money and stored it in a cup. When he had saved enough for a new book, he gave Alfred bus fare, money for a book and a slip of paper with the title on it and sent him downtown to the book store.

After he started *Gone with the Wind*, he never dozed off while reading. He often asked Mother to join him, with her darning, in the living room. He told her the passages he had just read of the civil war in America, Scarlet O'Hara and the life on Tara. I lingered nearby, spellbound by the story.

A week before the fall semester started, Mother handed me a package wrapped in brown paper. "Open it!"

Inside was a moss-green bathing suit.

"It's new. Try it on."

I went into the living room and changed behind the closed drapes. The rough material made my skin itch.

I stepped through the drapes and said, "It scratches. Where did you get it?"

"Ida Borchard bought it in Altenessen. It was the only kind they had. When you're in the water, it'll stop irritating your skin," she said.

I knew complaining would be fruitless and hushed up.

A few weeks after I started fourth grade, our teacher announced that one Friday a month our class would go to the rebuilt indoor swim hall for swimming lessons. "You must have a swimsuit to participate," she said.

Then I was glad that I had one. It was true, once I jumped into the water, the swimsuit didn't irritate my skin anymore, but I never liked it.

One morning I woke with my brother Alfred shaking me, "Ulla, get up! It's late! Get ready for school." He woke up Jürgen and raced downstairs making enough noise that I jumped out of bed and dressed quickly. Something was wrong. Alfred had never woken me before.

When I entered the kitchen, I saw Mother leaning against the living room doorjamb, squeezing her eyes together and holding her stomach. She looked at Alfred. "Take Father's bike—tell the doctor it's time."

He grabbed his jacket, hurried out the door and yelled over his shoulder, "You two! Make sandwiches and go to school."

Jürgen scooted behind the table onto the sofa. Seeing him look so serious made me nervous. He reached for a slice of rye and spread lard on it. I couldn't eat. What was going to happen? I was afraid to ask.

"You'd better go to school," Mother whispered.

As we left, she moaned. I glanced at her. She bit her lip. Her face looked flushed.

At school I couldn't concentrate. Sitting still was impossible. Instead of taking notes from our lessons, I doodled on my paper. During recess, I walked back and forth in the schoolyard avoiding my friends.

After the break, an older student burst into the classroom before the teacher could say 'come in'. He rushed to Fräulein Meirich and whispered into her ear. Then they both looked at me and the teacher came to my desk. I squirmed in my seat.

She bent down and said, "Ursula, you have twin sisters."

My body went numb. I looked at her in disbelief. "How could that be?"

She smiled, her eyes even sparkled. "They were born this morning."

I looked around the classroom. Everyone stared at me.

"You're excused for the rest of the day. Walter and Egon will take you home."

The boys carried my satchel but walked silently next to me. My stomach didn't feel good. Now, where was I going to sleep? There wasn't enough room for five people in my parents' bed.

When I entered, the kitchen was still. I closed the door gently and peeked into the living room. Mother lay asleep on the couch covered with a feather comforter. She looked so peaceful. Where were the babies? The door opened and Jürgen came in. He stopped next to me. We stood quietly looking at her calm face. Her eyes flattered then opened.

"They're in the crib in the corner."

Mother sounded weak. I looked toward the crib. Jürgen went to it and put his hands on the rail. I followed. Two tiny bundled up babies lay side by side wrapped in one blanket. Little knitted caps were pulled over their foreheads. Their faces were smaller than Tante Hildegard's Schildkröten doll. Their tiny fingers twitched ever so lightly. I had never seen a newborn baby before and couldn't take my eyes off them.

I was relieved that they had their own bed.

Baptism, 1949

Chapter 61

That afternoon, when the twins were just a few hours old, they sounded like little kittens when they cried. When they made the faintest whimper, Father rushed into the living room and gently picked up the fussy one. He cradled her in his cupped hands, took her to the sofa and tenderly put her into Mother's outstretched arms.

She looked at him. "I'm worried, Anton. They only have enough energy to suckle once or twice then they fall asleep exhausted. How am I going to keep them alive?"

I peeked into the room from behind the doorjamb feeling like an intruder. Then the other baby moaned.

"Bring her to me, too," Mother said. "Lay her on my stomach. She'll feel my warmth while I nurse this one. Let me keep them both for a while. I can feed them alternately as they wake."

When Father came back into the kitchen, I followed him to the sofa and sat next to him. "Why are the babies too weak to eat?"

"Because they were born seven weeks early. The firstborn weighed only three pounds and the other one two. If I remember correctly, you weighed about six pounds."

We sat close but didn't talk. Then I asked, "What did you name them?"

"We only had one name picked out. We didn't know we were going to have twins. For now, I'll call them *die Kleinen* because they are so small."

A knock on the door and Pastor Hübner rushed in. He came to the table and said, "I'm so sorry Herr Fischer. I came as soon as I heard. The doctor gave me the sad news. The midwife told him that the children didn't make it."

"Herr Pastor, the children are alive. Come into the living room and see. "They are small, but they're breathing." Father rose. The men went into the room where Mother and the babies rested. They talked for a long time.

I stayed on the sofa and felt forlorn. My brothers had come home from school, too, but they went out. I was glad when our neighbor, Frau Kersting with her knitting basket on her arm, came in.

"I'm relieved the pastor is here," she said. "I saw his bicycle in the front yard." She tip-toed to the chair next to the warm stove and rubbed her hands together before sitting down. She picked up her knitting needles and untangled the yarn. "The autumn sun is fading—it's getting cold."

A little later, Oma joined us. "What a surprise," she sighed and settled onto the chair at the other side of the stove. The women talked quietly.

Oma said, "I'm sorry I wasn't home this morning to help."

Frau Kersting rested the knitting in her lap. "Who could've known the babies would arrive today. I came over just as the midwife said, 'Aufwiedersehn'. Can you imagine she left the firstborn in an empty cigar box here on the sofa? The midwife thought the child was dead. She told Gertrud that the umbilical cord was wrapped between the babies legs and half of her body had already turned purple."

Oma gasped and cupped her hands over her mouth.

"But Gertrud asked me to bring her the child," Frau Kersting said. "Her tiny body was ice cold. Gertrud put her on her stomach and stroked her."

Oma wiped away a tear.

"After a while, we heard a faint whimper—the baby's tiny fingers twitched and then she cried. Gertrud's eyes filled with tears."

Oma folded her hands in prayer and lifted her gaze toward the ceiling. "Dear heavenly Father help them."

Our neighbor smiled. "We certainly need His help."

The men came back to the kitchen. "I'll conduct an emergency baptism tomorrow," Pastor Hübner said.

Father nodded. He looked sad.

I remembered one emergency baptism in our house soon after Pastor Hübner had moved in. That baby was sick and didn't survive.

The Pastor said, "I'll come tomorrow as soon as I can get away from my other commitments."

That evening, Frau Kersting brought dinner and Father washed the dishes. It felt strange eating without Mother at the table. No one spoke.

Then Father said, "Ulla, you don't have to sleep on the crack between Mother's and my bed. You have her bed all to yourself for a while. She'll sleep on the couch in the living room to be near *die Kleinen*."

I was relieved that the twins had their own crib for now and my parents wouldn't throw me out of the house yet.

The next day, Father didn't go to work and my brothers and I didn't have to go to school. Everyone got dressed in Sunday clothes to be ready for the baptism when the pastor arrived.

Oma brought a delicious smelling apple cake and put it in the pantry. After lunch, our neighbor brought real coffee beans and ground them. She and Oma draped an embroidered linen cloth over the table and set up our blue and white china. Father brought a bouquet of dark-red dahlias from the garden.

When the pastor arrived in the afternoon, he quickly draped his shawl with gold embroidered crosses on each end over his shoulders and invited everyone to join him in the living room. Because there was so little time and the godparents lived too far away, Oma and Frau Kersting stood in for them, each holding a baby in their arms. Mother remained on the couch, propped up on several pillows. Father folded his hands behind his back and joined my brothers and me in front of the window. The adults looked somber. The church service in our house made me feel uncomfortable. During the sermon I gazed at the silver bowl on the table filled with the christening water.

When I heard Pastor Hübner say, "I baptize you Edelgard and you Margarete in the name of the Father, the Son and the Holy Spirit," I choked up hearing their names spoken for the first time. I looked at Father. A tear rolled down his cheek.

Afterwards, Frau Kersting brewed the coffee and Oma cut the cake. Herr Kersting had come home from work and joined us along with Opa. The pastor only sipped a little coffee and lit a cigarette before leaving on his bicycle for other pressing commitments in the parish. Frau Kersting took a slice of cake to Mother who was nursing the babies. Father invited everyone to sit.

"Now we have five children," he said. "I've always wanted five little Fischerlein."

New Dawn, 1949

Chapter 62

The doctor never visited our house to check on Mother or the babies. When the twins were ten days old, Mother got out of bed and started performing light household chores. She continued to sleep downstairs on the living room couch to be near the little ones.

I was glad to have her bed upstairs to myself a little longer. Every morning before getting up, I lingered under the covers, stretching my arms and legs wondering where the babies would sleep once the crib became too small for them.

For a while Oma cooked for us and Frau Kersting washed the diapers. Father kept the kitchen stove going all night to keep the living room warm. Mother still nursed around the clock.

"If I don't feed them whenever they wake," she said, "they won't make it."

Mother ate with us at the table again. One day after she sat down and started eating her soup, a baby stirred. Mother's shoulders slumped.

"I'm too tired to get up—Alfred would you check which one is fussing?"

From the living room, he whispered, "It's the one in the back."

"That's Margarete. Bring her to me and the towel from the cabinet."

She laid the baby in her arm, draped the towel over her shoulder and the little one and nursed at the table. While she burped little Margarete, Edelgard cried. Alfred got up without being asked and picked up the baby. Mother ate her soup between feedings.

Sometimes she fell asleep while eating still holding her spoon. Her head would sink lower and lower until her chin touched her chest. She always looked exhausted. Our family life had changed.

Father only picked up a baby when Alfred wasn't around. He always looked uncomfortable when he had to help. He said once, "They're so tiny they fit into my cupped hands."

Only Mother could tell the babies apart. Finally Frau Kersting brought a pink and blue ribbon and put them on the baby's wrists. It didn't help. We would say, "The pink one is awake or blue one is fussing."

Father continued to call them die Kleinen.

One day I watched die Kleinen being bathed in our brown enamel bowl on the kitchen table. Mother locked the door to protect the babies from cold drafts. I was surprised how crumpled and pink their bodies were. Loose folds of skin on their legs and stomachs made them look like wrinkled old people. Without clothes, they were even tinier. Their toes were the size of small peas. After the bath Mother laid the baby on the cloth-covered metal tray of our kitchen scale and wrote her weight on a piece of paper.

"She's gained a little," she said.

❧

One sunny fall afternoon when my friends and I jumped rope, a stranger with a camera in his hand stopped in the courtyard and smiled at us.

"Which one of you is Helga?" He asked.

Helga raised her hand as if she were in a classroom.

"Your mother wants me to take your photo. Stand over there."

Helga followed his instructions but looked uncomfortable.

"I just have to set my light meter," the photographer said.

After he adjusted the lens on his camera he said, "Look right into the camera and smile."

Then he turned to me. "Let me take your photo, too."

"I have to ask my mother," I said while watching Helga and Irmgard disappear around the corner.

"If you ask her, she'll say 'I can't afford it'! Believe me, once she sees the beautiful picture of you, she'll love it and buy it."

I knew he was right. "But I have to comb my hair first," I said.

"No! No! You look great just the way you are. Stand over there."

I moved to the spot where Helga had stood.

"Now give me a big smile. I bet you're the prettiest girl in your class."

I flashed a big smile and his camera clicked.

"Now, I just need your name. Which house do you live in?"

With a pang of guilt, I said, "Ulla Fischer. I live in 33a."

"Don't worry. Your mom will love it."

Weeks later, Mother showed me the photo. "I know it's been years since you had your picture taken but you should've asked me first," she scolded.

But I knew she didn't really mean it.

Mother was always busy taking care of the little ones, or cooking, washing, ironing, scrubbing the floors or cleaning our soot-stained windows. During the cold and gloomy winter days, when die Kleinen fussed and Mother was busy with housework, she put them into a baby carriage and asked me to rock it back and forth in the kitchen until they fell asleep. Sometimes, it took forever.

Alone in the house, with no one to talk to, I felt trapped. Mechanically pushing the handle up and down, making the carriage bounce slightly, I tried reading a book, but the bouncing motion made the pages move and I couldn't follow the lines. As long as I rocked, the babies were quiet. If I stopped before they had fallen asleep, they cried, and I would have to start again. My friend Ilse didn't come over anymore because I had little time to play.

Once, when it took especially long for them to fall asleep, I wandered outside to play. I walked through the field behind our garden to the duck pond and watched the pair of wild ducks that stayed there all winter. When I finally returned home, Mother had a screaming baby in each arm and was pacing back and forth in the kitchen.

"Why didn't you stay with die Kleinen when no one else was in the house? They screamed so hard when I returned—I can't calm them down. They're too small to exert so much energy. I'm trying so hard to keep them alive, and you leave them alone?"

"You didn't tell me that I had to stay when they're asleep."

I felt guilty and miserable. I thought of running away.

~

When Pastor Hübner was around, my spirits always lifted. One day he came home early in the afternoon—about the same time Father came home from work. While they washed up, Mother made coffee, sliced the pound cake Frau Kersting had baked and set the table. I moved my homework to make room. The babies were sleeping in the living room.

After the adults joined me at the table, the pastor said, "Herr und Frau Fischer, I'm grateful for the warm hospitality you've offered me in your home. But you are very crowded now that you have a family of seven. I know that you will need the extra bedroom soon."

"Ja, Herr Pfarrer Hübner, we've enjoyed having you stay with us," Father said. "I know the congregation is looking for another family to take you in."

While scooping three teaspoons of sugar into his cup, the pastor said, "The Reineke's have agreed to fix up a room they haven't been able to use since the war. They'll rent it to me. It may take a while before they can get the material and start the repairs."

"There is no hurry," Mother said. "The twins will be fine in the crib down here for several months. Besides, it's too cold in the unheated bedroom upstairs. I just hope they won't wake you at night."

"Their cries are so faint, I barely hear them."

The pastor spent more evenings at home. He and Father talked at the kitchen table after our evening meals. My brothers and I stayed after finishing the dishes. Sometimes Opa and Oma came over and joined us. I loved the company and listening to the adults.

One evening the conversation was especially interesting.

Pastor Hübner said, "I'm sad that our country is divided into East and West Deutschland. The year 1949 will be remembered for many positive but also disturbing developments. But I'm glad that in the West, we have adopted a new law based on democratic principles."

"And," Opa said, "We've held our first post-war elections." He got his leather tobacco pouch out, filled his pipe and lit a match.

Father said, "It's a shame Berlin is split into East and West. It is an island in the middle of the Russian zone."

Opa puffed on his pipe and Oma said. "The farm in East Prussia where I grew up now belongs to Poland. Will I ever see it again?"

"I pray that the separation of our country will not be permanent," the pastor said.

"Now that we've elected Konrad Adenauer, I wonder what he can accomplish," Father responded.

Mother served the coffee. The aroma of real coffee beans, a gift from the pastor's mother, drifted over to me. My brothers and I got sweetened peppermint tea.

Then Father got up and went into the pantry. He returned with a bottle and three shot glasses. "My sister Kathel gave me this schnapps when Alfred and I went to Bavaria in the spring. I've been keeping it for special occasions."

He poured the clear liquid into the little glasses. The men lifted them and said, "Prost!" They downed the schnapps with one swallow.

"That's very good." Opa put his glass back on the table.

The pastor did the same. "Have you noticed, the good things happening in our congregation? Many families, who lost their homes during the war and were evacuated to other parts of the country, are returning.

Father said, "The attendance at Sunday services is increasing." He filled the glasses again.

෨

I, too, noticed that more children were coming to Sunday school. One Sunday, after our Bible lesson, Pastor Hübner announced that he had a surprise for us. "Children from a congregation in Sweden have sent a little gift for every child in our parish."

I clutched my wrapped package to my chest and watched other children open theirs. I was hoping for chocolate, like we had received in the CARE packages from America, but saw none. I was disappointed. The pastor encouraged me to open mine. Inside was a washcloth, a toothbrush, toothpaste and bar of Lux soap. It smelled good. When I got home, I gave it to Mother.

Mother had no time to go shopping. She looked forward to hearing news from neighbors on Friday mornings when the fishmonger came to our street. The women waited in line for their turn to buy fresh fish or salt herring, shared news about items they had seen on shelves in this store or that. She was delighted when Helga Lamm, a family friend, told her that the yarn shop in Altenessen near the swim hall had white wool for sale. She offered to go shopping for Mother and to knit little dresses for the babies. Mother was delighted. Helga suggested a seashell pattern with a crocheted pink border along the scalloped hem. They turned out beautiful and would fit the babies in the spring. When Mother sent me shopping I heard the women talking about how the times were slowly changing for the better.

In school, too, our lessons changed. We learned not only reading, writing and arithmetic but also history and geography of faraway places.

My heart always beat faster when the teacher talked about the huge North American continent. I could picture the snowcapped Rocky Mountains, higher than the Alps in southern Germany and the beautiful National Parks where elk and prehistoric-looking buffalo roamed freely.

Then I'd sit very still and wonder—would I ever see them?

❧

Coal mine where Father worked

Shepherd with flock — Coke Furnaces in background

Shopping for Food 1946

Entrance to the Potato-Cellar-Church

About the Author

Ursula Anna Fischer Smith was born in Essen, Germany nine months before World War II began. The impact of six years of war and the struggle that followed left indelible memories. At the age of eighteen, speaking no English, the author sought a fresh start with a one-way ticket to Canada. Six years later, she moved to California. In 1986, Ursula graduated from San Jose State University having earned a Baccalaureate degree in Economics with an emphasis on Finance. She worked for Lockheed Martin Missile and Space Company until she retired. Now she tells her story of growing up under wartime conditions and the struggle of her family to regain a normal life after the war. Ursula lives with her husband, Edward, in the San Francisco Bay Area. Their five grown children live in four different states.